THE NEW AMERICAN SERVITUDE

ANTHROPOLOGIES OF AMERICAN MEDICINE:
CULTURE, POWER, AND PRACTICE
General Editors: Paul Brodwin, Michele Rivkin-Fish, and Susan Shaw

The New American Servitude

Political Belonging among African Immigrant Home Care Workers

Cati Coe

NEW YORK UNIVERSITY PRESS

New York

NEW YORK UNIVERSITY PRESS
New York
www.nyupress.org

References to Internet websites (URLs) were accurate at the time of writing. Neither the author nor New York University Press is responsible for URLs that may have expired or changed since the manuscript was prepared.

Parts of chapter 2 and interlude 3 were previously published as "Longing for a House in Ghana: Ghanaians' Responses to the Dignity Threats of Elder Care Work in the United States," *Ethos* 44, no. 3 (September 2016): 352–74. Copyright American Anthropological Association, 2016. Reused with permission.

Library of Congress Cataloging-in-Publication Data
Names: Coe, Cati, author.
Title: The new American servitude : political belonging among African immigrant home care workers / Cati Coe.
Description: New York : New York University Press, 2019. | Series: Anthropologies of American medicine | Includes bibliographical references and index.
Identifiers: LCCN 2018026982| ISBN 9781479831012 (cl : alk. paper) | ISBN 9781479808830 (pb : alk. paper)
Subjects: LCSH: Home care services. | Caregivers—United States. | Foreign workers, African—United States.
Classification: LCC RA645.35 .C62 2019 | DDC 362.14—dc23
LC record available at https://lccn.loc.gov/2018026982

New York University Press books are printed on acid-free paper, and their binding materials are chosen for strength and durability. We strive to use environmentally responsible suppliers and materials to the greatest extent possible in publishing our books.

Manufactured in the United States of America

10 9 8 7 6 5 4 3 2 1

Also available as an ebook

CONTENTS

Introduction

Marie, a widow in her nineties, lived in a cozy house near Washington, DC. Four years earlier, after Marie suffered a heart attack, a wealthy daughter of a friend generously paid for a home care worker for eight or nine months, until the friend's daughter herself died.[1] After initially receiving care twenty-four hours a day, Marie slowly reduced the hours to twelve and then to eight hours a day because of the cost and as she slowly recovered her strength. When I met her in January 2016, a care worker came five hours a day, five days a week. Marie paid the agency $25 an hour, costing her $32,500 a year. Marie no longer drove, struggled for breath, and tired easily. She could not stand for long periods of time. Her current care worker, Fatu, a middle-aged woman from Sierra Leone, drove her to the grocery store, the hairdresser, and medical appointments and helped with cooking and light cleaning. They walked very slowly together around Marie's cul-de-sac. Precise and exacting, Marie cared that Fatu followed her directions about maintaining the household; she did not want a friend. Marie had known a series of care workers over the years, from Haiti, Sierra Leone, and Ghana, about whom she had definite opinions. Given her extensive experience, Marie thought that, despite Fatu's faults, they could manage.

Marie's arrangement with Fatu is common among frail seniors in the metropolitan area of Washington, DC. Home health workers provide hands-on care with basic "activities of daily living" (ADLs, as they are called in the industry), such as bathing, dressing, toileting, eating, and transferring or lifting, as well as driving, meal preparation, housecleaning, and medication management. Migrants are a growing segment of care providers for seniors, constituting 28 percent of home health workers in the United States in 2014 (PHI 2016), with greater concentrations in two dozen metropolitan areas (Martin et al. 2009).[2] From the perspective of healthcare experts in the United States, migrants make up for the potential shortfall in elder-care workers that is anticipated with the rapid increase in the infirm and senior populations in the United States (Harmuth 2002; Institute of Medicine 2008; Leutz 2007; US DHHS 2003). The first of the baby boomers—or the postwar generation born between 1946 and 1965—turned sixty-five years old in 2011. Studies estimate that those requiring long-term care will rise to 27 million people by 2050, double the number in 2000. At the same time, the number of women aged twenty-five to fifty-four—the major population pool from which most care workers are drawn—will remain relatively stable (US DHHS 2003).[3] Many of those older adults will be helped at home rather than in institutions, and many by unpaid caregivers, such as family members, friends, or neighbors. However, some will also receive care from home health workers, often at a ratio of one patient to one worker, unlike in a nursing home, where one worker cares for eight to fifteen residents.[4] Given the demographics of an aging population, the Bureau of Labor Statistics expects the number of home health workers to increase rapidly to 1.3 million in 2018 and 1.7 million by 2020 (Lockard and Wolf 2012). Already, 60 percent of states in 2008 reported shortages of home health workers (Martin et al. 2009), as did home health agencies in northern New Jersey in 2014 (Gomstyn 2014; also see Graham 2017).

That migrants are such important employees—particularly in specific metropolitan regions—speaks to the poor conditions of the work and its association with domestic service and women's labor. Those conditions are shaped by the fragmented and market-based healthcare system in the United States, in which commercial, profit-driven providers play an important role in the provision of health care, including in state-funded services. Wealth also increasingly determines the quality of care that people receive. Home health care provided by private agencies, the focus of this book, is used by wealthy and upper-middle-class seniors, who can afford to pay tens or hundreds of thousands of dollars a year. Home care offers a window into what is working well and what is not working well in the American healthcare system. This book illustrates the dysfunctional system of elder care in the United States from the perspective of those who provide care and those they care for.

I talked to Fatu about her life in Sierra Leone and the United States and how she had entered elder-care work in the United States. In addition to helping Marie twenty-five hours a week, Fatu worked full-time in a continuing care community, which offers residents relatively easy transitions within the same facility, from living independently in a separate apartment to round-the-clock care in a nursing facility. After working with Marie from nine o'clock in the morning until two in the afternoon, five days a week, Fatu cared for eleven bedridden residents in the continuing care community from three in the afternoon until eleven at night. She also substituted there on the weekends. At the nursing home, she was "busy, busy," she said. After an accident while trying to help a resident, her knee gave her trouble, so she was always in pain, particularly when she walked. She had been told she needed surgery but delayed doing so. She said she would "keep going for now and see how it goes." Between her two jobs, she had very little time. She slept four to five hours a night and lacked the time to cook every day as she would like, so she froze enormous batches of food when she prepared meals. Aged forty-one, she lived in the United States with her husband and two of her children, with two other children in Sierra Leone. She worked so many hours in order to raise the money needed to bring these children to the United States. To save money, she had not visited Sierra Leone in ten years, since she first came to the United States, following her husband who came several years before her. Once her children had been reunited, she anticipated leaving home care and using the extra time to go back to school, perhaps to study food preparation, her first love. She planned ultimately to retire to Sierra Leone (interview, January 15, 2016, Maryland).

I was surprised when, seven months later, Marie told me that she had asked the agency to send a different care worker. I called Fatu after hearing this news. Fatu was unhappy, commenting that she had worked with Marie for a year. She recounted how much she had done, going above and beyond the job description by cleaning the windows and tidying outside Marie's house, as well as inside it. She talked about how she had worked on holidays when she would rather have been home with her family. She was upset that Marie had failed to appreciate her, and she thought that Marie would regret her decision to fire her. She grew increasingly angry as we spoke. Fatu raged against the agency for not asking her about the incident that had caused Marie to ask for someone new—an incident caused, in my opinion, by Fatu juggling too many responsibilities at once. Fatu told me that she felt respected when I asked her what had happened, in contrast to the agency. From this experience and others like it, she concluded, "We Africans are treated like nothing" (field notes from phone conversation, July 8, 2016).

As illustrated by Fatu's summation, African migrants generalize from their work in care about their position and status. In Fatu's response, she abstracted from her experience to a "we," naming a collectivity to which she felt she belonged or in which she was positioned as "African." Furthermore, her statement strongly articulated an injustice, in which Africans were "treated like nothing," implying that they were not treated as they should be, as somebodies or human beings. Although Fatu's indictment arose from her work, interactions with the agency, and Marie's rejection, the implications also encompassed the United States, the place where she was seen as or became "African." Fatu's statement illustrates how care workers evaluate their belonging in the United States: work relationships are taken as a sign of whether America is fair to them and willing to incorporate them as full and equal members. Work conditions and interactions are interpreted by African care workers as indicative of the society at large.

Feeling unwelcome, less than human, or like "nothing" for being black or African is not an unusual experience for care workers in their employment. To do their work well, they have to manage distancing and even aggressive tactics from the people receiving their care. They are treated like servants and not as social equals. Low pay, few benefits, and disrespect from agency staff indicate a lack of appreciation and cause emotional pain, as Fatu's experience indicates, but also have material consequences for their well-being. It shows that their efforts of caring for others does not elicit a reciprocal response: care workers might not be cared for during their own periods of frailty and vulnerability, which all human beings experience at some point in their lives. This realization makes them seek other resources to provide for their future care. For example, they invest in their own and their children's education, but they also rely on kin resources in their birth countries and plan to retire there, aware that their low-wage work cannot pay for their own elder care in the United States. Their care work keeps them "perpetually foreign," to echo Rhacel Salazar Parreñas's elegant title for a paper on Filipina domestic workers in Italy (2008). Their perpetual foreignness explains their placement at the bottom of a stratified labor hierarchy

(Showers 2013, 257) and makes them "much more vulnerable" to the racial structures of the United States (Pierre 2004, 159).

At the same time, caring also leads to deep connections in some cases, particularly when a care worker has helped a patient for many years. Some care workers and their children are temporarily adopted by patients, and vice versa, with invitations to key ritual occasions—birthday parties, funerals, Grandparents Day at school—at which they want their close relationship to be recognized by others. Many care workers mourn a beloved patient who passed away years before. Some wealthy patients act as patrons of care workers, who often struggled financially, by giving them small presents as well as major, one-time gifts of tuition assistance, cars, and housing, worth thousands of dollars. These gifts function as a quasi-inheritance when the patient dies, acknowledging the kin relationships that temporarily developed between care workers and their patients.

Popular concerns about migrants often highlight their failure to adopt national norms and values, symbolically marked by dress or fluency in English. The concern about these performative aspects of identity masks the ways that migrants' belonging is shaped by their employment. Although this is not the only site that affects their belonging, it is an important one given how many hours of their day they often spend working. Home health care, like other employment sectors, affords particular social hierarchies, language use, collegial networks, and employment conditions that impact migrants' interactions, networks, and economic mobility in the United States. In the case of home care, the structural weakness of care workers as a labor force contributes to African care workers' sense of vulnerability and mistreatment in the United States. For long hours and low wages, they care for someone who can hire or fire them on a whim, on whose fragile health their continued employment depends, and on whose satisfaction the agency, their nominal employer, relies. The emotional and material exchanges forged in care work affect care workers' sense of belonging. The ability to create and solidify interpersonal bonds accounts for the pleasure in care work, but humiliation and denial of connection cause tremendous hurt.

This book highlights a more complex process of racialization and incorporation than is commonly posited in the literature on migration.

The classic work of John Ogbu (Gibson and Ogbu 1991; Ogbu 1978) contrasts the worldviews of migrants with those of caste-like or subordinate minorities in the United States. Migrants see economic opportunity in the United States, Ogbu argues, and dismiss the racism and humiliations that they encounter as a temporary phenomenon, which their children will overcome by becoming Americans. Caste-like minorities, on the other hand, with a longer history of discrimination in the United States, tend to embrace an oppositional narrative that economic mobility might not be possible for them, given structural racism. Further studies of migration from sociology have shown that the first generation of black migrants from the Caribbean proved Ogbu's theory: they had a positive view of America that dismissed structural inequalities. However, some of the second generation assumed the viewpoint of caste-like minorities as a result of their experiences with the police and other public figures (Waters 1999).[5] The African migrant care workers I encountered, however, did not conform to this model. Instead, like the West African nurses discussed by Fumilayo Showers (2015b), they had a sense that the United States was unfair to them because they were African or black.[6] Their care work led them to an oppositional view, in which they felt that they did not belong or were treated unfairly, like the interpretation of Fatu above. After a decade or more of care work, they felt less like newcomers and attended more to the conditions of work and their social position in the United States. This is similar to what Michael Piore (1979) and Héctor Delgado (1993) suggest, through their research with different migrant groups, is part of the transition from being temporary migrants to permanent settlers. However, the response to such injustice does confirm Ogbu's theory, in that the African care workers I interviewed tended to respond by "exit"—by investing in their home countries—rather than "voice"—by speaking out, becoming politically active, or participating in unions in the United States (Hirschman 1970). They realized through their care work that the United States was a place where a good life and a respected personhood were not possible for them. Their emotional response was one of bitterness, in which they were angry about the lack of gratitude for their output of energy, through which they lost their strength and health. However, they felt that there was no course of action to pursue in the United States. I argue that this interpretation had implications for their political belonging in the United States.

Political Belonging through Care Work

By "political belonging," I mean the affective ways in which people identify with political orders and political forms of membership, or feel excluded from them, through perceptions and performances of commonality, mutuality, and material and immaterial attachments. This definition includes but surpasses the narrow meaning of formal citizenship, participation in social or political movements, or voting in national, state, or local political elections. I treat political belonging as one kind of belonging, as understood in anthropology. Joanna Pfaff-Czarnecka (2011, 201) usefully defines belonging as containing three aspects: perceptions and performances of commonality; a sense of mutuality and modalities of common allegiance; and material and immaterial attachments that often result in a sense of entitlement (see also Crowley 1999; Feldman-Savelsberg 2016; Geddes and Favell 1999; Soysal 1994; Yuval-Davis 2011). Furthermore, anthropological studies have argued that belonging is not given and determined by birth but constructed processually through nurture and care, such as eating together and giving gifts, which develop feelings of mutuality, commonality, and attachment (Carsten 1997; Weismantel 1995). As a subset of belonging, political belonging entails these elements of mutuality, commonality, and attachment—made and unmade by everyday interactions and exchanges, in relation to a political unit—whether the nation-state, local government, unions, ethnic groups, or broader collective memberships, such as humanity. These political units are "means, like the nation-state, by which rights and access to resources are claimed" (Thelen and Coe 2017, 5).[7]

There are several reasons why this definition of political belonging is more productive than a more limited one focused exclusively on voting rights or active political participation in the nation-state. First, globalization has weakened attachments to the political order of the nation (Holston and Appadurai 1999). Social and economic forms of inequality fracture the sense of commonality among fellow citizens and disengage workers and the owners of capital alike from national projects. As a result, the nation-state is currently failing to "produce convincing fantasies of the commensurability of its citizens" (16). Political identifications are becoming untethered from formal processes of citizenship and, instead, are emerging in "proliferating sites," not all of which are connected to the nation-state as a political order (Soysal 2002, 139). Furthermore, such political identifications are no longer primarily constituted through territory and culture, which were used to imagine the nation and control population movements in Europe in the nineteenth century and in post-colonial states in the twentieth century (Balibar 1991; Coe 2005; Handler 1988; Herzfeld 1997). Urban social movements in India, where squatters claim land rights "outside the normative and institutional definitions of the state and its legal codes," are one indication that political membership—as a basis for claims to resources and rights—is finding "new social bases" (Holston and Appadurai 1999, 11, 12). Another indication is the rise of right-wing movements in the United States and Europe and their articulation of race-based forms of belonging, which attempt to shore up affective ties to the nation by moving the signifier of national belonging from democratic citizenship to whiteness. Given the waning emotional pull of the nation, political belonging is claimed and denied in multiple contexts that do not, at first glance, appear political.

I argue here that work is one site where political belonging is negotiated in everyday life. Workplaces are hierarchically organized and distribute resources accordingly, with those on the bottom receiving lower pay, fewer benefits, less respect and autonomy, and greater scrutiny and surveillance. Work gives people social identity and status, within both the workplace and the wider political community, especially in occupationally differentiated societies in which work is linked to prestige and pay. Workplaces are often ethnicized. New migrants are frequently clustered in particular economic niches, such as taxi driving, dry cleaning, or meat packing, and work under the management of more established residents (D'Alisera 2004; Lamphere, Stepick, and Grenier 1994; Waldinger and Lichter 2003). The micropolitics of elder care has placed African migrant care workers into particular gendered and racial hierarchies with extensive histories in the United States. Furthermore, the workplace, rather than the state, has become a major vehicle for providing a social safety net in the United States, functioning as mini–welfare states through the provision of retirement benefits, health insurance, and sick leave (Hacker 2006). Thus, workplaces become sites outside state institutions for making claims and establishing rights to wages and benefits. In these ways, the belonging established and denied through work becomes indicative, to care workers and patients alike, of care workers' political belonging in the United States, above and beyond more formal measures of political incorporation, such as citizenship or political participation. As we saw with Fatu, she interpreted her interactions with nonstate actors—Marie and agency staff—as a denial of her political belonging as an equal member of society due to her othering: "We Africans are treated like nothing." She took her treatment at work as indicative of her treatment as a member of a political collectivity, above and beyond the workplace.

The second reason to consider political belonging more broadly, including its affective dimensions, is that research has revealed the limits of formal citizenship in generating "inclusion, voice, and rights" and the ways that citizenship is not coextensive with political belonging (Krause and Schramm 2011, 119). Latino scholars in the United States have analyzed the distinction between formal citizenship status and belonging (termed "cultural citizenship"), where Latino citizens may feel excluded on the basis of their racial classification (Rosaldo 1994). One example is being lumped with noncitizens, as when they are stopped by police while driving. Another sign of the separation of formal citizenship from affective belonging is that many unauthorized residents of the United States consider it to be home, despite their lack of citizenship (Boehm 2012). Because of their feeling of affective political belonging, people who migrated to the United States as children have been active politically, making claims to the rights of citizens as Dreamers. The everyday recognition of rights by state authorities as well as nonstate actors may be as important as the formal rights that citizens are accorded. Similarly, Blair Rutherford argues that we need to "avoid assuming that legal categories and social identities actually operate on the ground as they do on paper, or presuming that some actions are caused by improper consciousness on the part of some social actors. Rather, through this heuristic tool one can attend to the varied forms of dependencies and interdependencies and their associated cultural styles, through which power operates in specific localities during particular political economic conjunctures." I follow Rutherford's lead by exploring the ways that power operates through a local "cultural politics of recognition," in this case, in care relationships (Rutherford 2008, 95). Relationships of dependence and interdependence between migrants and more established residents, constructed through care practices and workplace hierarchies, generate political belonging on the basis of local cultural politics of acknowledgment and disparagement.

This point leads to the significance of recognition, a key and controversial concept in political philosophy. The philosopher Axel Honneth has forcefully articulated the importance of recognition in liberal political systems (Fraser and Honneth 2003). Honneth argues that recognition is a way to achieve egalitarian self-realization and to correct injustices in liberal societies, in which all individuals have an equal claim to political power. He bases this political ideal on human development, in which, from very early on, human beings desire to recognize and be recognized by others, through making eye contact, responding to smiles, and imitating one another (Honneth and Whitebook 2016). The political version of recognition derives from a psychological model of emotional health in which others are recognized qua others—located outside of and distinct from the self—and as having similar rights to respect and integrity as the self.

African care workers evaluate both the "thick" relations formed through paid care work and the "thin" relations of being fellow members of a political and social community according to recognition. While I appreciate Honneth's consideration of the political salience of recognition, I take a more poststructuralist approach that sees recognition as not only positive or necessarily mutual between two people. Instead, as Fatu said, one can be recognized as "nothing."[8] All acts of recognition create personhood, but depending on the kind of recognition, they create certain sorts of personhood. As Judith Butler argues, "One 'exists' not only by virtue of being recognized, but, in a prior sense, by being *recognizable*" through a particular discourse (1997, 5). Paddy McQueen similarly argues that "recognition functions to produce and regulate particular forms of identity" (2015, 43). Acts of recognition both enable and constrain a person. Constituted dialogically, for example, "African" or "black" are designations that do not have much salience in the countries from which Africans come and that gain most of their emotional and political charge from African migrants' experiences in the United States. In her brilliant study of African migration to Portugal, Kesha Fikes (2009) provides an example of this social phenomenon of recognition, although she does not call it that. She argues that daily interactions in a fish market in Lisbon teach migrants how to be migrants and Portuguese citizens how to be citizens. Although recognition may seem less significant in institutional mechanisms of power and domination, such as redlining by insurance agencies (McNay 2008), I would argue that these processes rely on a construction and representation of certain people even if those being recognized are not aware of them.

Care work requires recognition. Lisa Stevenson (2014) defines care as the way in which people come to matter in a particular way. Or, said otherwise, "An act of caring requires a differentiated other to focus particularist attention upon" (Hamington 2015, 94). Care is the product of a moral imagination situating people within a moral universe (Livingston, 2005); some people become deserving of care—as kin members or fellow citizens, for example—within this moral community, and others are excluded from care (Thelen and Coe 2017). Furthermore, care is oriented around shared constructions of need, such as "activities of daily living" or companionship (Thelen 2015). Exploring his own experience of caring for his grandfather, Joel Reynolds (2016) notes that care entails treating the person as an object momentarily, which he terms leveling; he argues that temporary dehumanization is necessary for the work of care to actually be done. Care therefore requires fluctuating kinds of recognition, in which different aspects of the person and context need attention at various moments. Mutuality and interdependence also do not result in equality, as paid care work strongly illustrates. In paid care work, both care worker and patient have a mutual, interconnected dependency, but their dependency is not the same: the care worker needs income and appreciation, and the patient needs help with certain activities or medical care. The recognition of these dependencies is negotiated. Practices of attending to and coordinating action in care create intense feelings of recognition and belonging, or misrecognition and exclusion.

Care also has material consequences. It requires labor and an expenditure of energy and attention (Buch 2015a; Chen 2015; Held 2005). Whether paid or unpaid, care work in the United States is often devalued and associated with feminized labor. Key elements of recognition, I argue, are reciprocity and exchange: What is the economic and social value of care? From the care workers' perspective, does care work pay off in the ability to sustain themselves and those for whom they are responsible? Do they receive gratitude and respect, if not in the here and now, then at least in the future? From the perspective of patients, are they receiving the kind of care that they have paid for? The consideration of who is entitled to what and under what circumstances is fundamental to understanding not only the frustrations and disappointments of paid care work but also the political arguments for the right to care.

In the United States, African care workers often use material exchanges and reciprocity to evaluate their political belonging. These exchanges are not solely within the realm of interpersonal employer-employee relations but also concern claims to national belonging through state forms of care, such as affordable health insurance, Social Security, and retirement benefits. Although Western ideology separates care and money into different spheres of endeavor (Zelizer 2005), care often entails exchanges in which people share material resources with one another (Folbre 2001). One of the signs of kin in the United States is the willingness to share resources. Among the Korowai of West Papua, Rupert Stasch argues in his beautiful ethnography, "material actions are how people express and experience their emotional, moral involvement," and the main material action signifying kinship is giving and sharing resources (2009, 134).[9]

Honneth argues that struggles over the distribution of material and immaterial resources take place through a politics of recognition, whereas Nancy Fraser and many other political philosophers disagree, arguing that the politics of distribution should not be overtaken by concerns about recognition (see Fraser and Honneth 2003). My research tends to support Honneth in this philosophical debate: care workers speak about recognition as a key issue and aim for a particular kind of recognition. Interpreting injustice as humiliation and disrespect, they want to be treated as human beings. Their desire for recognition is simultaneously a claim for the distribution of material benefits.

Finally, the third reason to approach political belonging through this wider lens is that registers of belonging that are not overtly political are used to indicate political membership. Political belonging is discussed using nonpolitical registers signaling commonality and mutuality (Thelen and Coe 2017). For example, members of a nation may be represented symbolically as kin or brothers (Thelen, Coe, and Alber 2013). Political discourses in colonial Zanzibar used metaphors of race and kinship, in addition to that of national identity, as ways of categorizing and differentiating people (Glassman 2011). Racism supplements nationalism and is "indispensable to its constitution" but also exceeds the nation-state by positing longer histories and different categories of persons (Balibar 1991, 54). Race is a political category, not simply a social identity (Sheth 2009). Thus, discourses of race and kinship should be examined as fundamental to modern politics, in that they define membership in political orders in concert with competing discourses more overtly concerned with the nation.

The way that a person recognizes another is shaped by power, including both contemporary and historical relationships of power. Butler argues that "the terms that facilitate recognition are themselves convention, the effects and instruments of a social ritual that decide, often through exclusion and violence, the linguistic conditions of survivable subjects" (1997, 5). As noted above, it was through registers of belonging that the care workers and patients in this study became recognizable to one another. The registers that seemed close at hand in care relationships concerned racial identity, geographic origin, kinship, slave-master relationships, and human-animal distinctions. Care workers and their patients used multiple terms of belonging because none entirely accorded with their sense of reality. A surfeit of terms was articulated in conversations with me and in interactions with one another to try to get a handle on complex relationships created through care, to name the kind of emotions being generated, and to feel the proper emotions in response to the situation (Reddy 2001). These registers of belonging were used to define one another and articulate the terms of relationships.

These registers overlap in various ways, yet I discuss them in their specificity. For example, the difference between animals and humans has long been used by racist, hierarchical constructions of some kinds of peoples as more human than others (Balibar 1991, 57). Similar to kinship, registers of race, ethnicity, nationality, and humanity are invoked in multiple domains to distinguish insiders from outsiders and thus, I argue, are deeply political. Race, national origin, and humanity "evoke the ideology of a vast genealogical unity that is at once more restrictive and more abstract" than kinship (Faubion 2001, 14). These registers, particularly when used in conjunction, have histories that are mobilized in the present to interpret what is happening and to persuade others of the legitimacy of a particular action. The belonging enabled or constrained by these registers of recognition is deeply political because of their historical resonances and their reenactment in the present.

While all these registers—including kinship—signal hierarchy, they differ in that kinship expresses mutuality and commonality *despite* hierarchy and social difference, whereas race, geographic origin, servanthood, and animality express lack of mutuality *through* hierarchy and difference. For African care workers, narratives about insults or humiliations using registers of race, origin, servanthood, and animality become paradigmatic stories that encapsulate their experience in the United States, including challenging work conditions, poor remuneration, and lack of appreciation from patients and agencies. They use these stories to highlight their political exclusion within the United States. Modes of political belonging instead use the language of kinship and humanity, in which differences in race and geographic origin that mark other interactions are ignored or downplayed to foreground mutuality and attachment, at least partially or episodically. The political belonging of African migrant care workers is mediated by the conditions of home care work, which distributes material resources and social recognition in particular ways and rejuvenates many long-standing discourses of racialization and othering.

Home Care in the United States

Elder care in the United States is haphazard, fragmented, and improvised. Elder care relies on different streams of government funding whose rules and regulations vary from state to state and require extensive paperwork and management by individuals. Neoliberalism as a philosophy has dominated thinking about the role of the state since the 1980s, generating a complex brew of state, for-profit, and nonprofit elder-care services that can be reimbursed by state funding. This mix results in discontinuities in care as people transition between hospitals, nursing homes, and home care, all managed by different entities.

Neither medical practice nor state funding for care has adjusted to treating the older and infirm individuals who increasingly constitute the population of patients in medical facilities (Kaufman 2005, 2015). Medicare and Medicaid, the major forms of public financing for elder care, were developed over fifty years ago, and healthcare experts consider them to be too focused on acute care rather than the management of the chronic conditions and disabilities that beset older adults today (Institute of Medicine 2008). Medicaid, the major funding source for the medical care of the poor and the disabled, does pay for skilled nursing care (such as wound or catheter care) and personal care services (such as cooking or bathing) at home for those eligible. To qualify for Medicaid, seniors need to meet certain medical and financial requirements—including having few assets, such as a house or savings—making Medicaid a last resort for many older adults. Medicare, which funds medical care for seniors, pays only for hospitalizations, physicians' visits, and short-term rehabilitation following a three-night hospital stay.[10] The only home care it provides is skilled, intermittent care and occupational and physical therapy—not personal care, such as bathing, cooking, and companionship. As a result, a third of home care services are purchased directly by individuals, and elder care falls mainly to family caregivers (Buhler-Wilkinson 2001). Furthermore, Medicaid and Medicare have not kept pace with the development of various services that create care options beyond nursing care (Institute of Medicine 2008). As the advocate Ai-Jen Poo notes, "This [system of elder care] doesn't make any sense, it doesn't work for anyone, and many people are at the brink of their capacity to live in this upside-down world" (2015, 67).

Most older people would like to avoid nursing homes as long as possible, fearing neglect and loss of autonomy. By purchasing home care, the wealthy can delay living in institutional facilities or, if they have to reside there, can supplement the labor of the overworked nursing-home staff with a privately hired care worker. For example, Essenam, a short and cheerful Togolese woman in her fifties, provided home care for Sharon for four years and then accompanied her to a nearby nursing home for two years until Sharon's death. Essenam found the nursing home a little boring, as Sharon mainly slept during the day by the sunny window in her room. Essenam roused Sharon to feed her meals, a slow and laborious process, as Sharon closed her eyes sleepily, ignoring the spoon before her, or swatted Essenam away. Essenam always responded gently and patiently, where the nursing staff, who cared for multiple patients, might have tried to rush Sharon. If Sharon did not finish her tray of food, Essenam gave her a bottle of the protein drink Ensure, which she drank eagerly (summary of field notes from four visits, January 6–July

15, 2016, Maryland). Although wealthier seniors can handle the gaps in public forms of coverage through their own savings, low- and middle-income seniors cannot.

The patients featured in this book purchased home care services through long-term care insurance or private savings. Home care, like independent and assisted living, devours a frightening amount of money—tens or hundreds of thousands of dollars a year—making it affordable only to the upper-middle class and the wealthy and, even for them, for only a few years at the ends of their lives. For example, a retired professor spent $9,000 a month, out of retirement savings, for round-the-clock live-in care for his wife with a dementia, at a cost of $108,000 a year. Those with long-term care insurance paid thousands of dollars a year for decades before they started making insurance claims, and many still paid hundreds of dollars in premiums. They were also fortunate to come of age at a time when long-term care insurance plans were much more favorable to patients than they are today, now that insurance companies have learned the true costs of long-term care.[11]

In the Washington area, many of the patients I encountered were highly educated members of the upper-middle class, including retired academics, scientists, lawyers, and mid-to-high-level civil servants in the federal government. Mainly born in the 1920s and 1930s, they had entered adulthood during the postwar economic boom and the national project of making America into a middle-class society (Ortner 2003).[12] They lived in one of the wealthiest areas of the United States, benefitting from the federal government's proximity (Lerner 2017). Those over the age of sixty-five represented about 13 percent of the population, similar to the nation as a whole.[13] All of the patients I met were white, except for one African American woman, a retired nurse. One agency staff member commented that their patient population was the top 1 percent: "Very wealthy people, former senators, very accomplished people" (interview, January 5, 2016, Maryland). Another said about their clientele, "They are highly educated, intellectual, extremely independent. They are used to doing things for themselves. It is not easy for them to accept help" (interview, February 4, 2016, Maryland). My own sense is that they were in the top 10 percent, rather than the 1 percent, because they relied on savings from income derived from a lifetime of working. Many were Jewish, and three were themselves migrants from Europe who left in childhood or early adulthood during or after World War II. This clientele appreciated home care because it allowed them to stay in their own homes. Their homes were single houses, surrounded by lawns, azalea bushes, and flowering trees, in leafy suburban neighborhoods in or near Washington, DC, requiring a car to get around.[14] Receiving home care allowed them to maintain their independence and autonomy, of which they were fiercely protective. Some used home care to delay a move to an assisted-living facility or nursing care; others hoped to die at home. For those who lived independently in apartments in continuing care communities also located in these suburban neighborhoods, home care prevented the transition to less spacious residential arrangements, higher monthly fees, and more hospital-like environments in assisted-living or skilled nursing care units in the same continuing care community.

In the Washington area, there was a plethora of for-profit agencies offering home care. In the United States as a whole, in 2014, there were 12,400 home health agencies, 80 percent of which were for profit (CDC 2016b). There were 66 home care agencies serving Montgomery County, Maryland (Montgomery County 2016), where this research partially took place. I interviewed staff at a few agencies that offered services to Medicaid patients, but most of those whom I interviewed only accepted patients who paid privately. Some agencies were family-owned businesses, others franchises of chains, and still others large corporate agencies with a national or regional presence. Because of their involvement in health care, African migrants sometimes express interest in opening a home care agency, where more money can be made than as a care worker, and I met three agency owners who were migrants from Cameroon, Ghana, and Nigeria.[15] Some agencies operate as registries, in which the home health workers are independent contractors who manage their own taxes, Social Security contributions, and benefits.

The national median hourly wage for home care workers was $10.87 in May 2016 (BLS 2017a), reflecting Medicaid reimbursement rates (Graham 2017). Among my interlocutors, living in expensive areas of northern New Jersey and Washington, DC, hourly independent contractors earned $14–$18 an hour, and hourly employees earned $10–$13 an hour—about half of what their patients were charged by the agencies ($20–$25 an hour). However, in the end, both earned about the same, as independent contractors paid a fee to the agency: in some registries 20 percent of their salary, in others $2–$5 an hour. Live-in care workers in northern New Jersey and the Washington, DC, suburbs earned $100–$120 a day, resulting in a daily wage of about $75 after taxes. Live-in care was reckoned as ten hours of work, even though care workers are expected to be on call day and night, in case the patient needs to go to the bathroom or asks for a drink of water. Deborah, an intelligent young woman from Ghana, said about live-in work, "Of course you can't ignore them at night. Night is where everything happens" (interview, February 18, 2016, Maryland). Yaw, who provided live-in care in Pennsylvania, commented, "It is not enough. If you calculate it, it is not good money. If you earn $1,000 a week, for twenty-four hours a day, it is like $4 an hour [perhaps after taxes; my calculation, pretax, is $6 an hour]. If you sleep, they will call you. You can get up five times a night. You think it is not a big deal [but it is]" (interview, May 14, 2016, Pennsylvania). Both hourly and live-in care workers complained bitterly about the low rate of pay. One agency manager commented, "The care workers barely make a living wage. They work so hard" (interview, February 17, 2016, Maryland). Nationally, the average income of home health workers, both live-in and live-out, is $13,300 annually, with one in four living below the poverty line and over half relying on public assistance (PHI 2016). I did not encounter a widespread use of public benefits among African care workers; only a few said that they used food stamps (Supplemental Nutrition Assistance Program, or SNAP) to pay for infant formula after giving birth, when they took an unpaid parental leave, and the children of some used the government-funded Children's Health Insurance Program (CHIP), which is available only for minors.

Reports by healthcare experts note that low pay and few benefits contribute to the labor shortage of direct-care workers (Institute of Medicine 2008). Although the conditions of home care make it unattractive to many workers, many African migrants encourage those in their social networks to enter this field.

"The Only Job You Can Do Quick": African Migration and Home Care in the United States

African migrants in the United States have been aptly described as "invisible sojourners" (Arthur 2008). In the United States, the number of African migrants remains small in comparison to migrants from other countries. The 2008–12 American Community Survey estimated that there were only 1.6 million Africans living in the United States during that period, out of a total foreign-born population of 39.8 million people, of whom half were from Latin America and the Caribbean. Africans were therefore about 4 percent of the foreign-born population and less than 1 percent of the US resident population. Nigerians, Ethiopians, Egyptians, and Ghanaians were the largest single national groups among Africans in the United States, together constituting 41 percent of African migrants (Gambino, Trevelyan, and Fitzwater 2014), although a wider range of countries was beginning to be represented (Capps, McCabe, and Fix 2012). While census figures undercount the number of African migrants (D'Alisera 2004), they give some sense of where Africans are concentrated. My research took place in areas with some of the largest African-born populations: northern New Jersey, which is considered part of the New York City metropolitan area, and the Washington, DC, metropolitan area. Africans represent 13 percent of all migrants in the Washington metropolitan area (McCabe 2011). Montgomery County, Maryland, has the second-highest number of African migrants for any county in the United States, after Los Angeles, with approximately 50,000 African migrants, roughly 5 percent of Montgomery County's population of 1 million residents and roughly 10 percent of the nation's total African migrants. Of the African migrants in Montgomery County, the major countries of origin were Ethiopia (27 percent), Cameroon (12 percent), and Ghana (11 percent) (CountyStat 2016).

African migration to the United States increased sharply in the 1990s. The Immigration and Nationality Act of 1965 dismantled long-standing quotas that discriminated against residents of countries outside Europe. In an effort to atone for this previous discrimination and diversify migration streams, the Immigration Act of 1990 put in place lotteries to distribute green cards to citizens of countries with low rates of migration to the United States. African nationals have benefitted from this provision, receiving 41 percent of the fifty thousand green cards distributed worldwide through the lottery to those who meet certain educational or work experience requirements. Among African migrants who arrive through authorized means, the major routes are through family reunification and the diversity lottery and as refugees and asylum seekers (McCabe 2011). Three-quarters of African migrants have come after 1990, indicating that voluntary African migration is relatively recent and growing rapidly (Kent 2007).

At the historical moment at which this research was conducted, African migrants were becoming interested in settling permanently in the United States, resulting in a change of perspective in which they care about their political and social positions in the United States. In contrast to my earlier research in 2005–10 (Coe 2013), African migrants are slowly becoming more of a second-generation community, oriented toward the United States (Piore 1979). Because many African migrants arrived in the past ten to thirty years and are here in small numbers, they are much less politically and socially organized than migrant groups with larger communities and older migrations, such as Latinos. Thus far, African migrants have mainly organized houses of worship. Care workers do not have much cultural or symbolic capital in their migrant communities; they are often invisible because their long work hours prevent their attendance at community functions, and they do not become wealthy enough to serve as patrons of community projects (Donkor 2018). In response to my research presentation at a meeting of Montgomery County's African Affairs Advisory Group, a male participant commented that nursing assistants are important, but "their work is not appreciated" in his Sierra Leonean migrant community (field notes, December 2015, Maryland). Instead, the educated people with professional jobs assume leadership roles in churches and hometown associations, including on the advisory board for the county government, and distance themselves from more low-wage compatriots (Showers 2015a).[16]

Because the routes of entry favor the highly skilled, the average African migrant is more educated than the average American (Capps, McCabe, and Fix 2012). Forty-one percent of African migrants had a bachelor's degree or higher in 2008–12, compared to 28 percent of Americans aged twenty-five or older (Gambino, Trevelyan, and Fitzwater 2014), although there are certainly less educated and working-class African migrants in the United States (Manuh 2006). Despite the high average educational levels and very high labor participation rates for both African migrant women and men, they tend to earn less than Americans with comparable levels of education (Capps, McCabe, and Fix 2012). This suggests that the problems they face in the labor market are perhaps due to racial discrimination, the length of their stay in the United States (because earnings and career mobility correspond to length of employment), or the undervaluing of their African academic credentials and employment experience (Zeng and Xie 2004). A study of new green-card holders in the United States in 1996 found that 50 percent of those surveyed experienced occupational downgrading (Akresh 2006). Like other migrants, Africans are generally overqualified for the jobs they have (Capps, McCabe, and Fix 2012; D'Alisera 2004; Dodoo 1997; Kent 2007). They thus experienced what Boris Nieswand (2011) has called the "status paradox" and what Rhacel Salazar Parreñas (2001) has termed "contradictory class mobility": migrants who had a low-paying but high-status job in their home countries may find a higher-paying but low-status job abroad, which some may convert into high status at home.

Kwadwo was a teacher for over twenty years in Ghana and, after obtaining a college degree, rose to an administrative position in the local education office. He described his anticipation when he had received a green card through the diversity lottery four years earlier: "Somehow, when I was coming here, there was a miscalculation of benefits. When I was coming with the lottery visa, we thought [that] whenever you are coming, you would get your preferred job. They gave [presented] a list of job opportunities at the interview, so I was thinking, 'I'm going to have it so easy'" (phone interview, December 17, 2014). Instead, he was disappointed to be a live-in care worker in northern New Jersey, although he conceded that the pay was much better than what he would have received in Ghana as a teacher.

African migrants enter home health work because it is entry-level work that pays somewhat better than retail and fast-food services, particularly if one can work more than forty hours a week. Because of the high demand for care, the work promises continuing employment. Comfort, who came to the United States from Ghana in 1995, noted that "this nursing—nursing-assistance job was the only job you could do quick" (phone interview, January 18, 2016). Speed was important because many in the home country, sometimes including the migrant's children, were awaiting financial support.

Africans' concentration in the field of home health work is one sign that their previous credentials and experience have little value in the United States. Sixty-two percent of African migrant direct-care workers—including personal care assistants, home care workers, and nursing assistants—have some college education or a college degree. This is a much higher education rate than the direct-care workforce as a whole, 7 percent of whom have a college degree (Campbell 2018; Khatutsky, Weiner, and Anderson 2010; Leutz 2007; McCabe 2012). Some of the African migrants with high educational levels whom I encountered were working as home care workers temporarily, while they worked through the bureaucratic and examination processes required to practice their previous professions in the United States. Yet, many had given up their old professions or had chosen to go back to school in another field, mainly in health care and nursing. Some who had been middle-class professionals or white-collar workers in their birth country—as office secretaries, international bankers, teachers, or lawyers—initially looked for similar work in the United States. However, they were told by friends or relatives who had more experience in the United States that such dreams were impossible.

Africans constituted 11.7 percent of direct-care workers in the United States in 2003–9, with the numbers doubling from 2005 to 2015 (Campbell 2018; Martin et al. 2009). The countries best represented were Nigeria, Ghana, Liberia, Kenya, and Ethiopia. Thirty-nine percent of Africans working in health care were nursing, psychiatric, or home health aides (McCabe 2012). However, in some cities, such as Washington, DC, and New York City, the foreign-born share of care workers was much higher (Martin et al. 2009) and has increased since 2009. The agencies that I interviewed in the Washington metropolitan area and northern New Jersey in 2013–16 reported that their workforce was 60–80 percent African. In the expensive housing market of the Washington metropolitan area, African home care workers lived in cheaply built and shabby-looking rental apartment complexes, oriented around parking lots, in the far suburbs of Montgomery and Prince George's Counties. Some live-in workers, who stayed with their patient for weeks or months at a time, lived an hour or two away, in Frederick, Maryland; Smyrna, Delaware; or York, Pennsylvania. They had long commutes by car or bus through heavy and unpredictable traffic to their patients' residences in the more expensive and wooded neighborhoods close to or in Washington, DC.

Because of the agency requirement that workers have a nursing-assistance certificate regulated by the state, most home health workers are legal migrants. However, agencies do report that, once in a while, a potential employee presents the papers of another person as if they were her own, or the person who applied at the office has substituted a friend or relative (no doubt without proper work documents or a license) to work in the patient's house in her stead. Care workers employed directly by patients are more likely to lack work authorization and licensure than those hired or screened by agencies. All of my interlocutors had legal work authorization, although some had lacked authorization in the past, and they knew of others working without documents. Like other scholars of West African migration (Showers 2015b), I did not actively seek out unauthorized care workers and hesitated to ask about immigration status.

Africans' employment in home care affects not only their experiences of the United States but also patients' experiences of care, illustrating the ways that the global restructuring of capital affects both migrants and nonmigrants (Glick Schiller 2012). Both patients and migrant care workers are engaged in a social context that is new to them—having a paid care worker in the case of the patient, doing paid care work on the part of the care worker, for example—which is the result of the growth of a private market in home care in the United States. Through care work, migrants' belonging is shaped by their interactions and interdependencies with more established residents.

Understanding Africans' Experiences as Care Workers

I became interested in elder care during my previous study on Ghanaian transnational families (Coe 2013), when most of the migrants whom I interviewed about parenting worked with seniors, reflecting that it served as a niche employment for Ghanaians in the United States. In that study, I learned that their work experiences shaped their evaluations of life in the United States, including whether the United States was a good place to raise their children (Coe and Shani 2015). I decided that my next project would explore their experiences with elder care. These interests were also stimulated by observations concerning changes in elder care in Ghana (Coe 2017).

I began the research by taking a six-week certified nursing-assistance course in a school run by a Sierra Leonean couple in a Philadelphia suburb in September and October 2012, to learn about the training of home health workers. The other members of the class were four women in their twenties and thirties: an African American already working in health care; a second-generation Jamaican American, who was taking the course to retain welfare benefits; a first-generation migrant from Ghana, who had recently arrived in the United States; and a first-generation migrant from Sierra Leone, who had worked previously as a home health worker but whose licensure lapsed when she had a baby. I learned about my fellow students' dreams and histories as well as, more technically, how to take someone's blood pressure, lift someone without hurting myself or the patient, and wash my hands to prevent the spread of disease.

I toyed with the idea of working as a nursing assistant in a nursing home, as some ethnographers have done (Diamond 1992), but ultimately decided it was too ethically problematic, since I wanted residents and staff to be properly informed of my purpose. I then tried to obtain access to a long-term care facility as a volunteer/researcher, the route Nancy Foner (1994) used to study a nursing home. I spent several years attempting to negotiate access to a long-term care facility through my contacts in Philadelphia, southern New Jersey, and Maryland. My failure did not surprise my interlocutors; they thought that long-term care facilities had too much that they wanted to hide. My research participants, at least, felt forced by those facilities to cut corners because they were assigned too many residents. I am not as clear as my interlocutors were on the reasons for my lack of success: One facility, which was part of a corporate chain, worried about worker unionization and litigation of resident abuse, despite my reassurances. Another, a nonprofit continuing care community linked to a religious organization, was concerned that its nursing-home residents had dementias that would preclude their ability to give consent, despite my protocols to ask their relatives for permission.[17] In general, frontline care workers were much more excited about my research than the managers. Other studies (Diamond 1992; Rodriquez 2014) have noted the financial and regulatory pressures on long-term care facilities; my interpretation is that these pressures made nursing-home managers cautious in their operation of a complex institution, instead of curious about what an anthropologist might offer them.

Ultimately, because of my lack of success with long-term care facilities, I focused on home care, where individuals, and not institutions, could give consent. This switch meant I was studying the most unregulated sector of elder care. One home health agency in northern New Jersey was interested in my research because most of its live-in workers came from Ghana. I attended two daylong orientations that it gave to potential employees (on November 25 and December 18, 2014). The agency facilitated my contact with seven live-in Ghanaian home health workers but did not want me to interact with their patients. Our arrangement was that I could call the care workers every other week for six months (December 2014–May 2015), so long as I did not get in the way of the patients' care. Through these multiple thirty-to-forty-five-minute phone interviews, I saw situations change over time, both for patients and care workers. I have remained in contact with some of these care workers into the present, including visiting Monica in Ghana in January 2017, when she returned to stay with her teenage children; meeting Kwadwo and Ohemmea separately for lunch in Newark, New Jersey, near where they stayed when they were not working (in August 2015 and August 2016, respectively); and attending a church revival with Janet and her four children in northern Virginia in October 2015. In May 2016, I followed up with six care workers by phone to see how they were doing.

Talking to live-in care workers made me realize that it would be beneficial to hear patients' perspectives on the same issues and to talk to home health workers whom I did not encounter through an agency. I also decided to expand the study to Africans in general, rather than focusing on Ghanaians, because of how they were described in this labor market and also, to some extent, how they talked about themselves—as, for example, in Fatu's complaint in the incident above. In December 2015, I relocated to a suburb in Montgomery County, Maryland, near Washington, DC. I stayed in Maryland for seven months, until July 2016, and drew on several diverse networks to find care workers and their patients. One set of contacts came from my Ghanaian friends, whom I knew from doing research in Akropong, Akwapim, in the Eastern Region of Ghana, since 1997. My parents—my father in his early eighties and my mother in her late seventies—provided another source of contacts. Their social networks of friends, neighbors, and fellow congregation members included people receiving home care. The final resource in Maryland was an agency that agreed to link me to five pairs of patients and care workers. Ultimately, over the seven months, I interviewed forty-six African care workers, and three non-Africans—a Jamaican migrant, a US-born African American, and an Indonesian migrant—as a limited comparison. I also used my networks from previous research to connect with four additional Ghanaian home health workers in central New Jersey, Connecticut, and Minnesota, as well as one who had retired in Ghana.

Out of the sixty-two care workers interviewed overall—during my initial research in northern New Jersey, the more extensive period in metropolitan Washington, DC, and from other contacts elsewhere—fifty-nine were from Africa. There were nine men; the rest (fifty-three) were women.[18] Of the fifty-nine African participants, fifty-three were West African: thirty-four from Ghana, five from Togo, five from Nigeria, four from Sierra Leone, three from Guinea, and one each from Cameroon and Cote d'Ivoire. The remaining six were from Congo-Brazzaville (one), Ethiopia (one), Tanzania (two), Kenya (one), and Burundi (one). The age range was twenty-three to eighty-two years. The median age of those working (a range of twenty-three to sixty-six years old) was forty-eight years, similar to the median age of forty-five years for home health workers as a whole (PHI 2016), with the two oldest (aged seventy-three and eighty-two) retired in Ghana. None of those whom I interviewed were new migrants who had arrived in the United States in the past year. They had been working in elder care for one to thirty years, with most having worked for ten to twenty years, an average of twelve and a half years.

I relied on interviews more than I would have liked, although I saw that interviews respected the limited time available to care workers, given their multiple jobs and long work shifts. Much of their emotional lives were conducted through the phone, particularly for live-in workers. Interviews by phone delocalized the fieldwork, which seemed to accord with the ways that care workers experienced geographic space (on the use of interviews, see Ortner 2003). Where there was interest and willingness, I followed initial interviews with ongoing conversations and interactions. I attended a church picnic with one care worker and a baby shower for another. I visited Elizabeth in December 2016, after she retired to Ghana, where we sat under a mango tree and cooked together.

I retained contact with a few patients, calling occasionally and visiting them when I was in Maryland for a short visit in March 2017. I attended the funeral of one patient in May 2017, which was also attended by three of her care workers, and the funeral of another in July 2017. In general, however, I struggled to find ways to participate more meaningfully. Others, such as Elana Buch (2013, 2017), have been more successful in this regard. Instead, I worked to maintain relationships over time. Balancing out these more limited interactions were multiyear relationships with four care workers from Ghana, with whom I had regular discussions about health, house building, children, marriage, and the ups and downs of employment. These four women deepened my understanding of home care work and the family life of home care workers, particularly over time. I use their experiences to supplement and contextualize my interviews with a broader range of care workers who told me mainly about their work experiences.

I also interviewed twenty-five patient families, over thirty-one interviews in total. Sometimes, I just interviewed the patient or, if the patient had a dementia or had recently died, the patient's spouse or adult child; sometimes, I interviewed multiple members of the patient's family unit, such as a patient and two of her children (counted as one patient family). All lived in the Washington area, except for one in Ohio, whom I encountered by chance and interviewed by phone. Twelve of these patients were cared for by care workers whom I also interviewed, and three of these pairs allowed me to visit them between three and five times, for about an hour at a time, to observe their care interactions or accompany them on outings. For one pair, my mother also visited with me several times, and I went on two outings with them: to a noontime free concert popular with seniors on one occasion and for lunch and a walk around a lake on the other.

The twenty-five care recipients ranged in age from their sixties to one hundred years old, with a median age of eighty-five years. Ten were male; fifteen were female.[19] A dementia affected twelve of the patients.[20] In addition, Parkinson's afflicted four men in their seventies—relatively young in age within the larger population requiring care. Four patients used home care workers for driving, light housekeeping, and companionship; others needed lifting, more skilled nursing care, or supervision due to a dementia. Twelve of these patients were married, and their spouses provided a lot of care as well. I also interviewed sixteen staff members of fifteen nursing agencies and ten staff members of government agencies and advocacy organizations interested in African migrants, workforce issues, or elder care.

My own relationship to care work is complicated. Until the age of eleven, I grew up in Chile, Ghana, and India, the daughter of a diplomat. In these contexts, as was not unusual in middle-class households in these countries, I was cared for by servants and nannies: a middle-aged woman in Chile, an older woman in India, and two young women in Ghana. I remember them as warm but strict; I was often chastised by them. Some of my habits differ from those of my parents, which I attribute to my upbringing by these other mothers, who had higher standards of hygiene for self and household and stricter notions of appropriate demeanor than my liberal-minded parents. I regret losing contact with these other mothers and not being able to thank them or develop new memories about them today. But I also feel shame about these relationships: I remember at the age of six or seven being angry at my Indian ayah for her scolding and using my status position as her employer's daughter to say that she was "dirty" for her darker skin color. I knew at the time that I was wrong, and it was a serious insult to someone who valued cleanliness so much. I do not think word got back to my parents; at least, I was not punished for my racist remarks. I do not remember apologizing in words; I can only recall the feeling of shame. Speaking directly to the issue of power between children and their nannies in another context, Spyros Spyrou argues that racist ideologies allowed Greek Cypriot children to assert power in relation to domestic workers from Sri Lanka and the Philippines, maintaining racial modes of dominance while overturning age-based ones (2009, 167). I kept remembering my other mothers during my research on home health workers, where older American patients sometimes compensated for the vulnerabilities of being dependent and frail through representing themselves as white, educated, and wealthy, reproducing privilege and dominance as they could. From my childhood cruelty, I could understand this, and such understanding was itself horrifying; I cringed at this understanding and felt shame all over again.

Within the social hierarchies that pervaded care encounters, the patients and I had much in common. I was white, financially secure, and well educated, a professor at a university. I shared patients' class position and their class projects. My loyalties swung back and forth between patients and care workers in their sometimes-conflictual relationships. Those with whom I most identified were the children of patients, a decade or so older than me, who were often overwhelmed by the practical complexities and emotional distress of organizing care for their parents and whose questions (and sometimes answers) mirrored my own. For example: I asked Seth, a fifty-year-old son of a former diplomat, "How does watching the aging of your mother affect your thinking about your own aging?" He replied, "I had better die young" (interview, March 23, 2016, Maryland). His reply was my answer too, now that I better understood the costs of care. To compensate for this bias, I kept reaching out to care workers, keeping in touch by phone and visits, helping out when I could, and accompanying them on outings, where possible, to understand their perspectives.

Some care workers, including Millicent, talked to me because they considered me a potential source of new jobs, due to my social networks among local seniors. Millicent was caring for my mother's neighbor, whom my mother checked in on occasionally, when my mother realized that both Millicent and I would be in Ghana simultaneously in the summer of 2015. I met Millicent in Ghana and saw the house she was constructing in a suburb of the capital, Accra. After she returned to the United States, in October 2015, she brought over her daughter, who was in her twenties and had been living in Ghana, and it was a challenging transition for everyone. In my weekly calls to her, Millicent appreciated my willingness to listen to her troubles and seemed to treat our conversations somewhat therapeutically. Aged sixty-two when I first met her in 2015, she spoke with excitement about building a house in Ghana, at the same time as her house in the United States was going through foreclosure. I went with her to see a lawyer about the foreclosure and helped occasionally with transportation, since she did not drive. Millicent had a series of patients during the spring of 2016, both private duty and agency hired in an independent-living facility. Open, voluble, and self-effacing, Millicent was highly focused on work as a way to earn money. She knew that my mother was prominent in her neighborhood and therefore a potential source of new patients, and she called me when she needed more work. My mother did in fact help Millicent obtain one job.

For some care workers, my closeness to the patient side of the relationship made me untrustworthy. I tried to mitigate this perception by highlighting the sides of myself learned through living in Ghana. I spoke to care workers about staying with my parents, as a good daughter should, and they responded appropriately with appreciation, although in many ways my parents were supporting me by providing free housing and did not need much care beyond help with heavy chores. My "Ghanaianness" was also important to Elizabeth. Elizabeth, whose niece Deborah introduced us, commented when we first met that she thought Ghana must have affected me. She had not believed I was a white person because of the way I approached her on the phone. She told me she had called her niece after we hung up to ask, "Are you sure she is white?" which Deborah had affirmed. Thinking back to what I had said, I could only recall that I had been respectful by Ghanaian standards, calling her "Auntie."

Other care workers enjoyed having someone listen to their troubles, and they considered my proposed book important to their cause of being recognized for their labor. Fatu, for example, was willing to talk to me initially because she was glad that I was working on a project that "appreciated" African home care workers (field notes from introductory phone conversation, January 7, 2015). Binta was a forceful and commanding woman from Guinea who replaced Millicent in caring for my mother's neighbor. Binta enjoyed speaking with me and recommending her friends to me because she was so angry at the agencies. She said that someone needed to advocate on behalf of care workers; I would be their "arrow" in this effort (field notes from phone conversation, February 25, 2016). Care workers thus approached me with a variety of different agendas and purposes of their own. I hope this book addresses Binta's expectations, at least to some extent.

Conclusion

In the new kinship literature, care and nurture are often considered critical to the making and breaking of kin relationships. I argue, building on this scholarship, that care is central to processes of belonging in general, including political belonging. Elder care mobilizes feelings of belonging across different scales, from interpersonal interactions to larger polities, as Tatjana Thelen and I have argued elsewhere (Thelen and Coe 2017). Here, I focus on the intensities of recognition created by care. Care becomes a complicated site of dependency by which migrants can be included in kin networks and humanity as a whole while also being cruelly and unpleasantly denied mutual recognition, whether interpersonally by more powerfully positioned patients or by the more impersonalized conditions of employment.

Much of the scholarship on kinship has focused on the positive aspects of belonging—that is, on the ways that belonging is generated and nurtured, such as through adoption. The ways that belonging is broken or denied is less elaborated in this scholarship (Edwards and Strathern 2000; Lambek 2011). In the philosophical discussion of the ethics of care, as well as in much anthropological work on the subject, care is too often seen as positive, an assessment that ignores the kinds of hierarchies, humiliations, and power struggles that are generated through care. Care does not solely entail positive associations, sentimentality, or good intentions but rather involves tensions and frictions, including power asymmetries (Mol 2010; Stevenson 2014; Thelen and Coe 2017). Through this research, I hope to correct these emphases and focus on the ways that political inclusion and exclusion operate in tandem through care in care workers' lives.

It is especially important to understand the processes by which political belonging is generated in the current period of global aging and global migration, when both nation-states and kin work are being reconfigured (Dossa and Coe 2017; Sassen 2014). These reconfigurations affect how political identifications are made. For adult working migrants, political subjectivity seems to be shaped in part by the contexts of their work. The state constructs political identifications through its social-welfare provisions and labor laws but so too do more established residents and nonstate representatives in their complex interdependencies on and interactions with migrants.

In the following chapters, we will explore the racialization of the care labor force by care workers, patients and their kin, and agency staff; the processes of making servants out of care workers through racial insults and the exercise of power; and the ways in which care workers become the temporary kin of patients. Then we will turn to a discussion of the significance of reciprocity and redistribution for recognition and belonging, through both personal interactions with individual patients and the more standardized and depersonalized conditions of work, such as pay, health and retirement benefits, sick and vacation leave, and the contingency of employment. Between these chapters are short interludes that focus on particular topics around which belonging is negotiated: food, house building in Ghana, leisure activities, gifts at the end of life, and home foreclosure in the United States. Through these narratives, I illustrate the complex dynamics of political exclusion and inclusion for African care workers in the United States.

Interlude

Food

This book is about political belonging, and so it may seem surprising to start with a short interlude on food. Yet food creates and is a sign of the attachments, commonality, and mutuality that make up belonging. Bodies learn to yearn for certain kinds of foods as a result of bodily routines organized by familial cultures, clever marketing, and food availability. Eating is much more than the physical act; it has emotional and social components. Familiar foods stir certain memories and create a sense of continuity across the life course. Eating together makes community, whereas eating separately signals difference and distance. For African care workers and their patients, sharing food, setting rules about food, having food constructed as different, and cooking all become fraught symbols of inclusion and exclusion. The domain of the intimate is used to maintain distinctions between Africans and Americans, as well as to dissolve them temporarily.

In Ghana, as I have learned through my fieldwork there, food often indicates the quality of a relationship. One of a woman's primary attributes is her ability to feed others. Cooking is in the normative contract between spouses, in that a woman's refusal to cook for her husband is tantamount to divorcing him and communicates her unhappiness in the relationship. Street restaurants, or chop bars, in urban areas are often named "Don't Mind Your Wife" or something similar, attesting to the power that wives wield through their meal preparation, albeit a power undermined by the women who earn a living by selling prepared food to errant husbands.

A good mother also feeds her children, and it is for the purpose of feeding her children that she works (Clark 2001). Yet the love that children have for their mother is not dependent on the quality of the food she gives them. Instead, the food is tasty because it comes from someone beloved. There is a common Twi proverb that expresses this understanding. A friend of Irene's reflected on this proverb as we sat in Irene's large and beautiful house in Kumasi, Ghana, in August 2005. I met Irene in 2004, when she was in her forties, as part of my previous project on transnational families. Her three children—the youngest an infant, the oldest a teenager—lived with her parents in Kumasi. She worked primarily as a live-in home health worker all over the northeastern United States, from Massachusetts to New York to New Jersey. When she was not working, she lived with her husband in central New Jersey. We spoke regularly on the phone between 2004 and 2009, when we lost touch with each other. Articulate, forceful, and eager to complain to such a willing listener, she introduced me to the problems of care work. Irene visited her children for two months in August 2005, and I had the chance to join her for a few weeks, staying in her spacious house with six bedrooms in Kumasi.

There, her friend told me, "Wo nsa akyi bɛyɛ wo dɛ a enti sɛ wo nsa yam" (The food eaten from the back of the hand will not be as sweet to you as that from your palm). When I asked him to explain, he told me that it referred to the importance of a mother. He explained further, "Wo fie ne wo fie" (Your home is your home). Elucidating on this point, he said that no matter how much you travel—even if you go abroad, as Irene did, where life is good—you still come home because it is your home. Even if someone is cooking something very special, and your mother is making garden egg stew (considered a plain and ordinary meal), you would rather eat with her. Her food will be tastier to you than that prepared by a stranger. No doubt he was reflecting on Irene's happiness at being with her children, when she was normally far away in the United States (field notes, August 14, 2005, Kumasi). His impromptu disquisition on motherhood, food, and migration was insightful.

Children raised by an aunt or nonrelative, a common occurrence in Ghana, will talk about the quality of food to indicate the way they were treated in that household. If they received good care, they talk about eating the same food as the biological children of the female head of the household; if not, they talk about eating the leftovers or a different meal altogether, signaling their secondary status (Coe 2013). Furthermore, neighbors will talk about abandoned older people in terms of food: the sign of their lack of care is that they eat rice without stew, meat, or fish

(Coe 2018, 2019). Ghanaians are therefore highly sensitive to food as a visible sign of affection and social intimacy and use food to praise or critique relationships. Tasty food comes from a woman who loves you.

In America, food is instead taken primarily as a sign of ethnic and cultural difference. Americans are quite open to tasting, trying, and adapting the food of others who are constructed as different—what Roger Abrahams (1984) terms "equal-opportunity eating"—even when they are less open to other cultural activities by the same people. As a result, food bridges cultural differences, as in ethnic street festivals (Cadaval 1991). Ritual celebrations are occasions to use food to symbolically communicate about ethnic identity and family relationships (Theophano 1991). Sharing food and eating together is a sign of unity, as in the ritual of Holy Communion or at Thanksgiving, symbolizing a rapprochement between American Indians and settlers who were often at war. Finally, as a domestic duty, food preparation also signifies lower status in relation to consumers: female/male, domestic servant/employer, server/client. One of the major but hidden ways that domestic service has been revived in the United States as a result of women's paid labor is through the outsourcing of food preparation to grocery stores, restaurants, and delis (Ehrenreich and Hochschild 2002).

The multiple symbolic meanings of food generate frictions between care workers and patients, particularly when they live together for weeks or months without a break, as in the case of live-in care workers. Eating the same food or, at minimum, cooking and eating in the same home means adjusting bodily habits and tastes to accommodate one another. Unlike childcare providers, who often use food preparation to assert their power as a provider over their wards (Brown 2011), care workers make the adjustment in the case of elder care. As Elana Buch argues, "Home care workers subordinate their own bodily needs to those of their elderly clients" as a form of hidden labor that maintains the older person's independence and sense of autonomy (2017, 96). One way they do so is through food.

As in Dutch colonial encounters with servants in Indonesia (Stoler 2002), food was a sign of difference. Patients told me that African care workers did not cook food the way they liked it. For example, one complaint was that the workers could not make a simple grilled cheese sandwich, and this inability was taken as a sign of their cultural difference and, therefore, incompetence and lower value. The wives of male patients in particular lamented that African men did not know how to cook, and so the cooking fell to the patients' wives, a burden from which they wished to be relieved. One described how one day she was in the basement, wrapping Christmas presents and doing laundry, when the male care worker came down to say that her husband wanted a fried egg. The wife told the care worker that her husband could have one, but the care worker said he did not know how to make it. She told him, she said, "The two little boys across the street [the children of a neighbor, ages eight and ten] could make a fried egg." She made this humiliating comparison because she was irritated that she had to leave what she was doing to cook for her husband (interview, April 5, 2016, Maryland). The representations of African men as unable to cook that circulated among patients and their kin contributed to stereotypes about African gender relations as less progressive than American ones—although most American men of this generation also seemed unable or unwilling to cook. The wives of male patients who had male care workers had hoped the employment of a care worker would mitigate their domestic duties. As noted in other studies of domestic work in the United States, conflicts that might otherwise occur when middle-class women went to work were instead avoided by outsourcing household work, whether housecleaning services, food preparation, or nannies (Ehrenreich and Hochschild 2002). The wives of patients similarly displaced their frustration about household labor onto the male care worker for being sexist, rather than turning emotionally on their husbands for increasing the burden of care.

Agency staff noted that patients raised concerns about food, and like care workers, staff interpreted those comments as racist and demeaning. For example, one potential patient asked an agency staff member if the care workers could cook "American" food, to which the staff member responded that they were learning to do so. The patient replied that he did not eat elephant. The agency staff member said that was ridiculous because Africans do not eat elephant, although I am not sure whether she simply shared this sentiment with me or whether she had also said it to the potential patient. She told me, interestingly, "So they [the patients] make the caregivers feel 'less than,'" meaning that they make them feel inferior to the patients (interview, April 5, 2016, Maryland). In these interactions, food was used to construct ethnic difference and, with it, inferiority and the inability to care.

African care workers usually prefer their own food to American cuisine, highlighting spiciness as the key difference. Many African female care workers expressed to me that they liked to prepare food and were proud of their competence in cooking. But the food that they found pleasurable was not always welcome in a patient's home. Some patients complained about the smell of their care workers' food while it was being cooked. As a result, many live-in care workers avoided cooking their own food in the patient's residence and instead brought a three-week supply of meals, which can sometimes take up a lot of the space in the small under-the-counter refrigerators common in apartments in independent- and assisted-living facilities. Buying prepared food every day was too expensive on care workers' meager wages. Some, but not all, interpreted a ban on cooking in the patient's residence as disrespectful to the workers. Paulina, an experienced care worker who mainly performed live-in work in northern New Jersey, complained, "Clients don't allow us to cook. It is very hard." She concluded, "At times, they are so racist" (phone interview, January 15, 2015). Several workers also interpreted a patient's verbal concern about the care worker's eating as a sign of whether the patient cared about the worker. For example, Janet said, "It is not always good. They don't usually ask you about food or whether you have eaten. Or the family is good, they will ask, 'Did you eat?' Or they may say, 'Don't use this; don't cook.' Like with my current lady [patient], I don't cook over there. When the food [I have brought with me] is finished, I have to come home. I bring my cooked food and reheat it there. They complain about my cooking fish." From this, Janet concluded, "They treat you like you are not a human being" (phone interview, December 31, 2014). Using the same register of food to measure the character of the patient, Kwadwo, who also worked live-in, felt respected by a male patient who offered him his own food because he did not want Kwadwo to "go hungry"—despite the agency contract stating that the care worker was responsible for his own food (phone interview, July 28, 2015).

Kosher dietary restrictions in some Jewish households inadvertently make care workers feel that they are not welcome or respected.[1] Many West Africans had not met Jewish people before they came to the United

States; they had only known of them, rather abstractly but respectfully, through the Bible. Given that kosher rules regarding kitchen equipment and food preparation are obscure or even nonsensical to them, care workers interpret being given separate plates and utensils for their own meals as demeaning and distancing—like being a domestic servant in Ghana who cannot eat the same food as the other members of the household—or as an indication that they are considered dirty and impure. Several agencies discussed doing special in-service training for care workers on kashrut, or kosher dietary practice, to help the care workers understand and follow the rules. Through their work, care workers become more familiar with Jewish families. Elizabeth said, "If they are strictly kosher, it is better to eat their food, or they will be telling you all the time to kiss the wall, put the knife back, all kinds of stuff. It is ridiculous. They are most discriminatory." But she made distinctions among kinds of Jews: "The Conservatives are a little better, more flexible." She commented, "I have been around them [Jews] a lot" (interview, February 29, 2016, Maryland). I interviewed a couple from Ghana, in their sixties, both of whom had worked live-in for decades and were very wise, open, and gentle. In their kitchen in a small row house in a working-class city in Pennsylvania—as they both kept watch over the bubbling pots on the stove—the husband, Yaw, complained, "And in the Jewish houses, you can't eat the food you want! They are totally kosher. Meat goes with meat and milk with milk. So, you can't cook. You cannot afford going out to buy [food], so you eat what they eat. It is like obeying a slave master." His wife, Belinda, commented that in those kinds of houses, she leaves after one week of work (joint interview, May 14, 2016, Pennsylvania). Regina described an experience of caring for a paralyzed middle-aged woman and her family. Because the woman's household kept kosher, Regina said that she was considered "not clean," and she had to use her own dishes and refrigerator and could not do the dishwashing, which was fine because the husband did it. She said she was okay with Jews, because they were the first people chosen by God (field notes from visit, October 20, 2012, Connecticut). In an interview with me, one patient's daughter in Ohio commented that her live-in Ghanaian care worker, Sandra, brought her own utensils and bowl on the first day of work. The daughter thought it was "odd" and asked her why she brought them. Sandra responded diplomatically that she did not know what the patient would want her to do (phone interview, May 31, 2016). No doubt previous work experiences had taught Sandra, with whom I did not have a chance to talk, that patients might tell her not to use their kitchen equipment. Taking on a new case, she did not want to run the risk of being unable to eat.[2]

These experiences of distance around food make care workers particularly warm toward patients who taste or eat the care worker's own food. Sharing food becomes a sign of the overcoming of difference. Millicent exclaimed that her current patient "likes pepper [spicy food]! Like a Ghanaian!" (phone conversation, May 19, 2016). The adaptation went both ways: she was happy to help the husband of the same patient cook the Passover seder meal (phone conversation, May 17, 2016). Similarly, when my mother and I visited her friend from Quaker meeting, her friend's care worker, Beza, offered us tea made from fresh ginger and nut snacks brought from Ethiopia. Lively and outgoing, Beza said that she had converted her patient and the patient's husband to drinking ginger tea after dinner, rather than their usual decaffeinated coffee; she thought that ginger had more health benefits than coffee (field notes from visit, January 4, 2016, Maryland). On another day, I visited Priscilla, an emotionally warm care worker from Ghana in her late forties, and her patient, a frail African American woman sitting in a chair, rigid with pain. Priscilla distracted her patient by reminding her of food that the older woman liked to make when she was feeling better: apple muffins and lamb the previous Easter. Both enjoyed cooking. Priscilla also said she had cooked Ghanaian food for the patient, namely *jollof* rice, or rice cooked in a tomato stew with vegetables, and fried ripe plantain. The patient commented that she was willing to try new foods because she had traveled so frequently earlier in her life, when her husband was in the military (field notes from visit, February 26, 2016, Maryland). Thus, care workers introduced "their food" to their patients and were overjoyed when their food was accepted because it was a sign that *they* were accepted and that they were good at what they did. The American patients congratulated themselves on their relative openness to "foreign" foods, rather than directly expressing appreciation of the food to me, with the result that I was not entirely sure how much they had liked it. Although some patients tried the care workers' food, for the most part, it was usually the care workers who accommodated to patients. As a result,

Monica said, "Living in someone else's house is not fun" (phone interview, September 10, 2015). With strong opinions and a desire to manage her environment, particularly by keeping it very clean, Monica struggled to adjust to another person's routines.

Food—in its cooking and eating—serves to build connections and highlight difference through religion and geographic origin. Boundaries constructed around race, religion, and nationality are crossed but also reinforced through food. Sharing, offering, or asking about food is interpreted as a sign of a good relationship or is used to mitigate a tense one. Frictions over food make both patients and care workers feel disrespected. These themes will be apparent throughout the book, and so I briefly introduce them here through food: a material resource that our bodies require and that gives us sensory pleasure but that is also taken symbolically as meaningful in many more ways, including in terms of political belonging.

1

"Anyone Who Is Not African"

The Racialization of the Care Workforce

I was speaking to Margaret, a middle-aged white woman who worked for an agency, about her agency's experiences with African care workers. Margaret told me, "Just now we had a phone call" that illustrated her encounters with racism from patients. A patient was asking about home care services, and she informed him, as she tells all new patients, "Most of them [the care workers] are African." His response, as she reported it to me, was, "I have to think about it then." Her internal reaction, she told me, was "Really? You have to think about it, when your relative is desperately in need of care!" Margaret said to me, "I tell them, 'Caregiving is the portal to the American economy for immigrants'" (interview, May 4, 2016, Maryland).

Because many of the home care workers in northern New Jersey and suburban Washington, DC, were African, I found agency staff eager to talk about their mainly African workforce and the lessons they had learned from working with them. As Margaret's story attests, all had experienced patients' racism against African care workers. In fact, because the patients assumed that agency staff were white—not always the case—they were often more blunt and direct in conveying their displeasure about an African or black migrant workforce to agency staff than they were to the care worker.[1]

One of the major tasks of home care agency staff comprises recruiting new patients and maintaining their satisfaction with the service. Patients keep the business afloat and revenue flowing. New patients are constantly required as existing patients move into a nursing home or hospital, pass away, or improve after a health crisis, requiring less care over time, as Marie did. Like childcare placement agencies in Canada (Bakan and Stasiulis 1995), when making a match between employer and employee, agencies scrutinize care workers more closely than patients.

Usually, agency staff do not directly confront patients' stereotypes and prejudices, particularly at the point of initial contact or recruitment, nor do they deny patients service as a result of these reservations. They make comments only to themselves and fellow office members after these conversations, as Margaret did to me, to relieve their suppressed exasperation.[2] The responses by agency staff truncate the potential for social change and the education of the patient. Care workers' weak structural position is revealed by the ways that agency staff mediate between patients and care workers.

Agency staff play a brokering role, educating patients about the care market and trying to placate their prejudices, and cajoling care workers to overcome these prejudices through good care. In her education of the potential patient over the phone, Margaret was correct: home care work is a portal to the American economy for migrants, mainly for women but also for some men. However, home care mediates African migrants' belonging in particular ways. Home care as a labor market recognizes the workers in ways that stabilize particular subject positions. First, the home care market positions them as African, black, and migrant. Second, like other forms of domestic service, home care places African care workers in hierarchical, intimate relationships with patients whom they have to please and whose personhood they have to support. Finally, home care plays a role in the economic stasis of African migrants to the United States: Care work is considered an entry-level and unskilled job. No career pathway for care workers exists, neither further professional development nor occupational mobility nor rewards for seniority. Care workers with more experience do not earn more than neophytes. The only route to higher pay and higher status is *out* of home health care and into nursing, another healthcare licensure, or another field. Home care work is a portal to the American economy, but the door leads only to a dead end.

Margaret was also suggesting that work is the mode by which migrants are incorporated into American society and that the patient ought to give the migrant worker a chance. The idea that migrants are politically and socially incorporated through workforce participation has been significant in Europe even more than in the United States (Lutz 1993). In Europe, it is unemployed migrants who are considered a social and political problem, but those who work assimilate by contributing to the economy. This also means that migrants' experiences of their new society are shaped by their workplace, including their relationships with both more established and newly arrived coworkers and customers.

Previous studies of migrant labor in the United States have noted how workplaces offer different vistas onto American society. *Newcomers in the Workplace* (Lamphere, Stepick, and Grenier 1994) examines meatpacking plants in Kansas, restaurants and textile factories in Miami, and factory work and Korean stores in Philadelphia. Each niche has its own employment hierarchies, ways of speaking, social networks, and work conditions, which impact migrants' interactions and networks in the United States. These are "bad jobs" in terms of pay, conditions, and stigma. Published a decade later, *How the Other Half Works* (Waldinger and Lichter 2003) looks at six migrant-heavy industries in Los Angeles: printing, furniture manufacturing, hospitals, department stores, hotels, and restaurants. When migrants dominate an occupation, more established Americans consider it to be an "immigrant job" and do not seek work in these fields. It is hard to know whether the job becomes "bad" because migrants dominate that field, or whether migrants enter the field because the job does not provide much in the way of pay or status. No doubt both processes occur simultaneously. Ethnic social networks steer new migrants into certain jobs and create migrant occupational niches. Employer stereotyping also plays a role in why certain migrant groups dominate a particular field. Being a migrant from a particular country or region in certain labor markets serves as cultural capital, that is, cultural resources that can be converted to economic resources—in this case, into employment (Bourdieu 1991; Lamont and Lareau 1988). In this case, African migrants have cultural capital among home care agency staff but not among patients, and the variation in their social worth in the home care market makes their sense of belonging precarious. Contrary to scholarship on the racialization of Caribbean-born migrants (Vickerman 1999; Waters 1999), although foreignness trumped or mitigated blackness among agency staff, it did not among patients.

These studies further note that workplaces are hierarchical contexts in which ethnic segregation is common. Racial and ethnic segregation is visible in the differentiated roles of workers or in the hierarchical organization and lines of authority in workplaces. For example, young, white waitstaff serve customers in the front stage of restaurants, the dining room, while Mexicans work in the restaurant's back stage, the kitchen, where Spanish may be the lingua franca (Barrett 2006). Or, as at the Miami Beach Convention Center, there may be Anglo upper-level carpenters and Cuban midlevel carpenters, while Haitians and African Americans are concentrated among the laborers (Lamphere, Stepick, and Grenier 1994, 12). On a strawberry farm in Washington State, farm managers may be either white or Asian, foremen mainly second- or third-generation Latinos, and farm workers mainly indigenous and mestizo first-generation migrants from Mexico (Holmes 2013). These hierarchies influence work networks and relationships, keeping new Mexican migrants in a Spanish-speaking enclave at work and among other Mexicans, for example. These hierarchies, combined with ethnic stereotyping, can also impede workers' advancement to positions of more responsibility, status, and pay in the workplace. "The workplace is a crucial arena where new immigrants and established residents . . . can meet," but it is also a place where new migrants and established residents reinforce their stereotypes of one another and interact in ways influenced by workplace hierarchies (Lamphere, Stepick, and Grenier 1994, 4). When mediating institutions are hierarchically organized, such as in management-worker, owner-tenant, and teacher-student relations, then "established residents have de facto power over migrants by dint of the structure of the mediating institution itself" (Lamphere 1992, 4).

Margaret was also implying that care work is the route to migrant assimilation and upward mobility. However, the literature on migration suggests that economic opportunities for migrants have changed as American society has become more characterized by economic inequality since the 1980s and as manufacturing has been replaced by service work. Furthermore, the migrant profile has also changed: whereas in the early twentieth century, most migrants were unskilled, now both highly educated, skilled migrants and poorly educated, unskilled migrants enter the United States, a consequence of US immigration laws that provide routes for highly educated professionals as well as for those without very much education through family reunification (Haller, Portes, and Lynch 2011). Thus, the more common contemporary pattern for migrant mobility in the United States is segmented assimilation, sociologists argue (Haller, Portes, and Lynch 2011; Portes 1995). By this, they mean that the children of some migrants experience upward mobility, while others experience downward mobility to the underclass. The social-class position of parents, as well as the racial positioning and educational experiences of the children, affects where the children of migrants end up.

Here, I focus on the mobility of the first generation of migrants, not their children. Healthcare employment does promise economic security for individuals and communities. As Ariel Ducey notes, "The proliferation of health care jobs available to women, immigrants, and people of color constitutes the possibility of reversing, or at least slowing, the growing inequality that characterizes contemporary America" (2009, 2). However, my research, like hers, suggests that entry into the home care labor market impairs care workers' upward mobility. I am concerned with how African migrants understand their opportunities in the United States and their actions in response to those interpretations, not with what migrant incorporation and assimilation mean for the coherence of the host society (Glick Schiller 2012).

What becomes clear from talking to patients, care workers, and agency staff is that the home care market racializes care workers as African and migrant. It positions them as unskilled and in subordinate positions in relation to patients. Like other unskilled jobs, home care does not pay very well and has no career ladder. Leaving home care work for a better-paid and higher-status occupation requires a commitment to more education, which is expensive, debt producing, and time consuming. Thus, care work has the potential to produce political belonging—as the portal to the US economy for migrants—but it also excludes them. Instead, it positions African migrant care workers in racialized and subordinate positions and tends to do so permanently.

The Changing Portals for Migrants in the United States: Domestic Service, the Service Sector, and Home Care

At the height of migration in the late nineteenth and early twentieth centuries, the manufacturing and textile industries were the entry point into the American economy for migrants. Although the manufacturing and textile industries did not pay well, after many decades of struggle and strikes in the course of the twentieth century, they became central to migrants' middle-class mobility (Lopez 2004; Milkman 2006). Domestic service in northern cities was another field where migrants, particularly Irish and German migrant women, dominated: in 1900, 26 percent of private household workers were foreign born, and an additional 18 percent were the children of migrants (Duffy 2011, 23). Migrants particularly formed the servant workforce in northern cities, where 15–30 percent of all households employed live-in servants (Dudden 1983; Katzman 1978). In the nineteenth century, household service was the most common occupation of working women, and the demand for servants rose, prompted by the elaboration of middle-class employers' "needs," including their need to indicate their status to others (Dudden 1983). In the South, on the other hand, "African American women constituted the main and almost exclusive servant caste" (Glenn 1992, 8). As a result, the home was "a political figure and space" fraught with struggles between white planter women and their black slaves and servants (Glymph 2008, 3). In the first two decades of the twentieth century, rates of immigration declined, white women found employment in retail, and African Americans migrated to northern cities. As a result, by 1920, African American women constituted a large share of the domestic service workforce in urban areas across the United States. During some historical periods in the United States and Europe, domestic service was a period of the life course limited to adolescence. For African Americans, however, it became a permanent position that had to accommodate marriage and child raising, and they transformed domestic service from live-in to live-out work (Clark-Lewis 1994; Eaton [1899] 1967; Katzman 1978, 72). For both Irish migrants and African Americans, their association with domestic work hardened notions of ethnic and racial inequality, with the servant occupation reinforcing racial and ethnic stereotypes (Rollins 1985). As W. E. B. DuBois wrote about African Americans in Philadelphia, "Household servant work drew a despised race to a despised calling" ([1899] 1967, 136–37). The historian David Katzman stated similarly, "It is difficult at times to figure out whether blacks and immigrants were held in contempt because they were servants or whether urban servants were denigrated because most of the servants were blacks and immigrants" (1978, 221). For both Irish and African American migrants, gradual movement out of this occupation coincided with improved social status and wider social changes (Colen and Sanjek 1990, 8; Katzman 1978).

The twentieth century saw a dramatic decline in the number of domestic servants in the United States, particularly after 1960 (Duffy 2011). In 1950, US-born black women constituted 60 percent of the domestic labor workforce, despite being only 10 percent of the female labor force overall. US-born white women represented another 30 percent and foreign-born women only 10 percent (Duffy 2011). After the civil rights movement, other fields of employment became more open to black women, who represented only 18 percent of domestic servants in 1970 (Rollins 1985). Domestic service was declared dead in the 1980s, replaced in part by jobs in healthcare, service, and commercial cleaning companies, which provided the same services in more impersonal ways (Duffy 2011; Rollins 1985). Yet, since 2000, the United States has seen growth in the number of nannies and housekeepers, as well as an increase in employment in institutional settings such as daycare centers and hospitals, which also provide care (Duffy 2011).

It is in the growing sectors of the economy that migrants find work, and in the United States today, that means the service sector, including health care.[3] Over one in ten employed Americans work in healthcare occupations, composing up to 20 percent of those employed in some metropolitan areas (BLS 2009). Home care is anticipated to expand especially fast. With almost a million home health workers in 2014, the number is expected to grow 38 percent to 1.26 million in the decade thereafter and to be the fifth-fastest-growing job in the decade after that (BLS 2015a, 2015b).

The changing jobs for migrant entry affect the kinds of skills that migrants use and practice, their relations with established residents, and their opportunities for mobilization around wages and work conditions. In the service sector, interactions with customers are more highly valued than in the manufacturing and textile jobs of the past, leading to a stronger emphasis on emotional labor and fluency in English (Hochschild 2003). Cameron Lynne Macdonald and Carmen Sirianni (1996a) have termed service-sector workers "the emotional proletariat": frontline service workers who are required to display friendliness and deference—emotional labor—to customers and are often subject to employers' attempts to monitor and control their performance of friendliness and cheerfulness. Management also plays a particular role in the service economy, either relying on technology to supervise or control workers or selecting "the right kinds of people for the job, often using gender, class, age, and other status markers to serve as a proxy for required personality types" (Macdonald and Sirianni 1996a, 7). Because of gender ideologies in which women are seen as better at emotion management, including friendliness and deference, women are favored in hiring (Macdonald and Sirianni 1996a).

Evelyn Nakano Glenn (1992) has noted continuities in racial and ethnic hierarchies as commercialized service work in daycare centers and food preparation replaced domestic servants. White women are disproportionately engaged in service occupations with a supervisory capacity, a public relational element, and some degree of moral authority: registered nurses, teachers, social workers, and administrative support workers (Duffy 2011). On the other hand, women of color "are employed to do the heavy, dirty, 'back-room' chores of cooking and serving food in restaurants and cafeterias, cleaning rooms in hotels and office buildings, and caring for the elderly and ill in hospitals and nursing homes, including cleaning rooms, making beds, changing bed pans, and preparing food" (Glenn 1992, 20; see also Palmer 1989). However, differences between service work and domestic work also exist, since, "with the shift of reproductive labor from household to market, face-to-face hierarchy has been replaced by structural hierarchy" (Glenn 1992, 32). As a result, many workers prefer service work to domestic service, because workers are not personally subordinate to an individual employer. Instead, hierarchical relations with a supervisor are "embedded in an impersonal structure governed by more explicit contractual obligations and limits," and a work group exists for sociability and support. "While the isolated domestic finds it difficult to resist demeaning treatment, the peer group in public settings provides backing for individuals to stand up to the boss" (23). Even if workplace relations humiliate the worker, "dignity can be achieved through camaraderie and solidarity with coworkers" (Hodson 2001, 3).

Home care represents a return to the conditions of labor that operate in domestic service, in contrast to service-sector jobs. Home health workers work relatively autonomously from their official supervisors: the nurses and coordinators of the agency. Instead, as in domestic service, the patient becomes the supervisor on whose pleasure, health status, and financial well-being the worker's continued employment depends. Although agencies make care more contractual than private arrangements between a patient and a care worker, their orientation to serving patients, rather than protecting care workers, blunts their ability to completely formalize the employment process. Furthermore, unlike the service sector, the management of emotions and emotional affect did not seem significant to my interlocutors, nor did their supervisors or patients attempt to monitor their emotional displays. Jason Rodriquez argues that the widespread sociological literature on emotional labor is "less relevant for the increasing number of workers who have face-to-face interactions with individuals over long periods of time" (2014, 165). Instead, my interlocutors talked about dignity (see Coe 2016c). Dignity, or face, is established relationally and needs ongoing validation from others (Goffman 1956; Rodriquez 2011).

Not all home care workers lack coworkers at the workplace. To my surprise, I found that quite a few care workers care for residents of continuing care communities, where they help people remain in independent-living apartments rather than slipping across the care continuum to more institutionalized and expensive assisted-living or nursing-home quarters.[4] Because other home care workers—usually from the same agency—also work in the same community for other residents, they form a little subcommunity of the facility and meet to chat when the residents have meals or group activities. For example, Millicent worked live-in in one such facility and regularly invited over other home care workers to her patient's apartment for coffee and tea, which she made in Ghanaian fashion with condensed milk. While residents attended a movie on Saturday afternoons, care workers gathered to pray together. When heavy snow fell in late January 2016, making roads impassable for several days, Millicent hosted hourly workers who could not travel home, letting them sleep on the floor of her bedroom in the patient's apartment. She reported that it was great fun, like a sleepover party or a dorm room in the boarding secondary schools common in Ghana; they prayed and ate together (field notes from phone conversation, January 29, 2016). The daughter of another patient in the same facility noted to me that her mother's live-in worker, Linda, who was a friend of Millicent's, similarly invited other care workers to her mother's apartment. The patient's daughter appreciated Linda's social networks—

although not all patients' relatives would have—because she felt that her mother, who had not spoken for two years, enjoyed the social interaction among the care workers. Furthermore, Linda, who was quite short, always had someone else around to help lift the somewhat-heavy patient, a far safer process with two people than with only one (interview, May 24, 2016, Virginia). Mariam accompanied her patient from home into a nursing home, and she would bring big trays of food for those on the unit because "my hobby was cooking" and because she felt so connected to the staff, many of whom knew her from her decade of working as a nurse in Sierra Leone (interview, March 29, 2016, Maryland). For these three women, their relationships with other care workers helped them to do their jobs safely, relieved the monotony of the day with somnolent or nonverbal patients, encouraged them, and allowed them to share information about the home care agency to advocate about their pay and scheduling.

Other live-in workers whom I knew asked hourly workers in the same facility to help them get groceries or meals when they ran out of the food they had brought or could not cook. Some home health workers enjoyed working in a continuing care community more than a private home because they could talk to other workers, even if it was only a brief greeting in the dining room or hallway. Studies of Filipina maids in Hong Kong (Constable 2007), Filipina elder-care workers in Israel (Liebelt 2011), and Caribbean nannies in New York City (Brown 2011) note how opportunities to gather with fellow coethnics and coworkers on days off or during the workday provide relief from the more stifling and restrictive environments of the employer's home, allowing care workers to cook food with which they were familiar, reminisce about the homeland, and share work experiences. In my research, social exchanges with fellow workers were particularly appreciated by those caring for patients with a dementia, some of whom could not speak.

Although work in a continuing care community offers potential colleagues, care workers are also positioned explicitly as nonresidents through their uniforms and rules of behavior. These sites function as private communities for wealthy seniors, with communal spaces carefully managed and lavishly furnished by the facility administration. Care workers, hired privately by some residents, constitute an unmanageable group of individuals entering and exiting the facility. Some facilities contract with a single agency to provide lower rates to their residents and keep tabs on the "outsiders." Another control strategy is to differentiate care workers from relatives or friends of residents through their dress, by requiring a uniform. The livery of maids was used similarly in the history of domestic service (Clark-Lewis 1994; Katzman 1978). Continuing care communities also set rules for care workers that mark them as a particular class of people distinct from residents. In one large continuing care residence in northern New Jersey, where I visited Monica and Janet briefly with the agency social worker, care workers could not use their cell phones, congregate in public spaces, or use the facility amenities available to residents, such as the gym, dining room, and pool (field notes from visit, March 17, 2015). As I saw on my interview visits, almost all the residents of continuing care communities in Maryland and New Jersey are white, with a few Asian Americans, while all the care workers are black. Care workers thus operate like a servant class in continuing care facilities, in which their dress, race, and behavior in public spaces position them as different. Similarly, in order to maintain social-class boundaries, middle-class residents in Turkey use a variety of rituals to stigmatize the servant class that lives in the same apartment buildings (Ozyegin 2001). Despite such public stigmatization in continuing care communities, privately hired care workers also feel less isolated and alone because they are around others in the same position, with whom they can commiserate, share stories and advice, and strategize regarding conditions of work.

Outside these continuing care facilities, home care workers are isolated in patients' houses or apartments, usually in expensive suburban neighborhoods with scarce public transportation and few services or stores within walking distance. Live-in workers find the isolation challenging psychologically because they usually work for several weeks or even months at a time without a break. Several of the live-in workers whom I interviewed referred to their work as prisonlike because of the restrictions on their movement and activities, the result of having to be with the patient at all times. Janet told me, "Live-in . . . is like prison. . . . You can't go visit [other people]; you can't do it. Sometimes you can't talk by phone. You are not yourself" (phone interview, January 20, 2015). In 2015, Janet's four children, aged twelve to twenty, lived in the United States, and she supervised them from work by phone and relied on the oldest children to care for the younger ones. Her husband wanted her to work live-out, but she refused because of the lower pay. By December 2017, she had accomplished her goal of buying a plot of land in Ghana and was now working live-out, bringing more peace to her marriage (field notes from phone conversation, December 31, 2017). The home of the patient, which is the workplace of the care worker, becomes a total institution (Goffman 1961), in which the worker's everyday routines are monitored and exposed to the patient.

Some of the live-in workers felt the need to escape from this space momentarily, whether physically or psychically. Staying in "a mansion" in a suburban neighborhood, Monica said that she took a half-hour walk almost every day when her patient's daughter came by to visit her mother, so that the house would not be "a cage" (phone conversation, December 2, 2014). Another told me she left the patient's apartment in a continuing care facility for a short walk when the patient was taking a nap, even though leaving her patient unsupervised was against agency rules and could result in the loss of her license.[5]

Limited in their physical mobility, care workers use their cell phones to stay connected to children, friends, and colleagues, who can provide emotional support and with whom they can escape momentarily, entering another world in their imagination and reclaiming their dignity. Many welcomed my phone calls for the opportunity of psychological escape. Cell phones also enable them to "parallel manage" their work and home, staying in touch with their children and other relatives in the United States or in their home countries while also being at work (Brown 2011).

As with domestic servants, always being with a patient results in close ties and knowledge of personal information. Furthermore, interdependence and social-class differences—including the direct relationship between the employee's lower standard of living and that of the employer—are much more apparent in domestic work than in service-sector jobs (Glenn 1992). Home care workers are acutely aware of their patients' wealth from the residences in which they are living, whether from the expense of an apartment in a continuing care facility, which may cost $6,000–$10,000 a month, or from the size of the house and kind of neighborhood in which it is located. Housekeeping and elder care generate different kinds of interdependencies. As Hondagneu-Sotelo (2001) notes in her study of housekeepers in Los Angeles, the rules of engagement between employers and domestic workers are unstable and unclear, and employers deal with the confusion by engaging in impersonal and socially distant relations with their employees. Social avoidance may be possible for house cleaners and landscape workers but not for home care workers. Most home care workers physically touch their patients: wiping bottoms and mouths; brushing hair; pulling clothing over shoulders and hips; and bathing, lifting, and turning their patients. They watch to see that their patients have swallowed their food before they give them another spoonful, invite them to notice a flowering tree or chirping bird outside the window, rise at night to check on their patients when they hear a sound, and attend to how they are doing in general. Such intimate touch and close observation are necessary aspects of their work. Similarly, many patients live alone, with relatives busy or residing far away, and they turn to the care worker for interaction and companionship. Home care forces interaction and inclusion but in ways characterized by culturally meaningful forms of social hierarchy and social difference (Buch 2013).

These particular elements of home care—the social-class inequalities, the intimacies and long-term relationships with the patients fueled by constant contact, and the barriers to organizing for better working conditions because of care workers' isolation—lead to grievances about dignity rather than about emotional labor.

Being an Aide in the Nursing Profession

Home care workers obtain a credential either as a certified nursing aide (CNA) or a home health aide (HHA), depending on state regulations. At the time of my research, Maryland and New Jersey required home health workers to have a CNA license, which also enabled them to work in a nursing home. In the middle of my research, Washington, DC, changed its requirements from an HHA license to a CNA license, forcing one of my interlocutors to leave his live-in case for more training and relicensure. Both licensure titles highlight "aide," in which the person presumably being aided is a nurse. This nomenclature signals the hierarchies within the nursing profession, and it is one reason that I use the term "home care worker" rather than "home health aide," the official name of the occupation used in government documents.

The history of nursing in the United States is a history of the struggle to professionalize an occupation associated with feminine work and thus perceived as not highly skilled. Prior to the Civil War, nursing was a low-paid and low-status job associated with working-class women who provided care at home. The professionalization of nursing, which began with the opening of the United States' first nursing school in 1873, offered an opportunity for working-class women to obtain middle-class status, but nurses continued to struggle to gain respect (Cannings and Lazonick 1975; Hine 1989; Reverby 1987). Their status in general became linked to their status in hospitals, which assumed greater importance for healthcare delivery during the Great Depression (Reverby 1987, 180). The development of nursing and hospitals went hand in hand: "nursing schools provided the hospitals with a work force that made their institutional growth possible" (Reverby 1987, 3; see also Cannings and Lazonick 1975). Due to the pressure for cheap labor from hospitals, a hierarchy of nursing staff emerged, in which lower-level staff did the most physical and menial work of caring for patients' bodies in their beds, while professional nurses became administrators and supervisors (Glenn 1992; Hine 1989; Jervis 2002; Reverby 1987). The systematic grading of nursing labor into three ranks—nurses' aides, licensed practical nurses, and registered nurses—was accomplished by the 1940s and has remained intact to this day (Glenn 1992; Reverby 1987). In the end, some nurses became professionals with higher pay and status through the denial of professionalization to others, including those who provided visiting nursing services outside of hospitals in urban homes (Buhler-Wilkerson 2001; Reverby 1987). Educational credentials determined one's place, both within the nursing profession and the workplace hierarchy (Cannings and Lazonick 1975) and in terms of one's social-class position in society as a whole (Collins 1979). The job tasks and level of income associated with a particular occupation are the product of complex social struggles, of which nursing is a prime example (Collins 1979).

Racial differentiation accompanied professionalization. Glenn argues that the occupation of nurse's aide "seems to have been designed deliberately to make use of African American labor in the wake of labor shortages during and after World War I" (1992, 27–28). Previously, in the nineteenth century, nursing schools denied entry to African American women, and so African Americans established their own hospitals and nurse training schools (Hine 1989). As a result of these efforts, nursing "provided the one comparatively open gateway through which young black women of working-poor backgrounds could cross toward digni-fied employment, and a middle-class lifestyle" (Hine 1989, xv). Still, be-cause of numerous barriers, African American women obtained greater access to the lower levels of nursing, which they preferred to domestic service, at a time when they were barred from other occupations (Glenn 1992, 28; Rollins 1985, 195; Tucker 1988).

To this day, nursing is a predominantly white female profession, al-though less so than in the past (Cannings and Lazonick 1975). African Americans in nursing are more likely to be licensed practical nurses and nursing assistants than registered nurses. In 2013, 83 percent of regis-tered nurses nationally were white, and 6 percent were black or African American (Budden et al. 2013), while in 2010, 63 percent of licensed practical nurses were white, and 24 percent were black or African Amer-ican (NCHWA 2013).[6] In 2007, by comparison, a little over 50 percent of nursing assistants and home health aides were white, compared to the 35–39 percent who were black or African American (Khatutsky et al. 2011). In a nursing home in which all three kinds of nurses are pres-ent, these differences result in a staff hierarchy with job titles and lines of authority organized according to race. In one typical nursing home in the Midwest, the registered nurses were white, the licensed practi-cal nurses were white and African American, and nearly all the nurs-ing aides were black women (Jervis 2002). Thus, migrants of color may occupy the lowest-level care positions in an institutional facility, under white nurses, doctors, and administrators (O'Leary 2016; Rodriquez 2014). The differences in kinds of nurses are also indicated through place of employment: registered nurses are more likely to work in hospitals, and licensed practical nurses in nursing homes and home care. For these reasons, in order to maintain their own status, West African nurses may seek to distance themselves at work from fellow Africans in lower-status positions (Flowers 2015).

Nursing licensure varies by gender as well as race and migration sta-tus. Although nursing schools refused to admit men until a Supreme

Court decision overturned that practice in 1981, men have become increasingly attracted to nursing because of its high income and status. Men are concentrated in the more highly paid nursing occupations (Landivar 2013). In 2007, 5 percent of home health workers were male, in comparison to 10 percent of registered nurses (Khatutsky et al. 2011; NCHWA 2013). Migrants represent 28 percent of the home health workforce (PHI 2016) and 17 percent of the healthcare workforce as a whole in 2015 (Altorjai and Batalova 2017). The stratification of the nursing profession thus tracks—and helps reproduce—other forms of social stratification in society. With the anticipated boom in aging, nursing assistance will become an even more important route to either upward mobility or, as I argue, economic stasis.

The Education and Skills for Home Care

As a result of the history noted above, "the nurse's aide job is defined as unskilled and menial" (Glenn 1992, 28), and "home care work, like other caring labor, is underspecified and undervalued" (Neysmith and Aronson 1997, 485). Eileen Boris and Rhacel Salazar Parreñas put it succinctly: "When intimacy becomes employment, it loses its status as a labor of love and becomes regarded as unskilled work that anyone can perform because women have undertaken such activities without payment" (2010b, 11). The patients whom I interviewed suspected that home care workers were not very skilled, and they would often ask me about the education of home care workers, expecting to hear that it was completely inadequate. In the patients' world, in which education determines income, job security, and status, the lack of training explains both the home health worker's low social position and the patient's frustrations with home care.

Depending on the state in the United States, a CNA license requires six to eight weeks of training, including practical experience in a nursing home. The low barrier to workforce entry in terms of time and cost makes the credential attractive to migrants who want to begin working soon after their arrival and may have debts to repay from the process of migrating. The nursing-assistance course in which I enrolled was taught by a registered nurse originally from Sierra Leone, lasted six weeks (eighty hours in total, including thirty-seven and a half hours of clinical practice in a nursing home), and cost $1,025. Although the curriculum covered a wide range of information about aging and chronic diseases, through a textbook and lectures, what I took away from the course were three practical skills: hand washing, lifting, and measuring vital signs. The clinical experience in a nursing home left me physically exhausted, with my hands red and raw from constant hand washing. I admired the nursing assistants in the facility who did their work efficiently and practically, if not always cheerfully. Towels and bedsheets were scarce, and I learned to be strategic about hoarding them in particular places so my patients could have them when they needed them. What the licensure examination primarily measured were literacy skills, rather than a kind heart or practical ability, and so some of my classmates did not pass on the first try, while I sailed through. At the same time, I did not feel ready to begin working after this brief course. Some home care agencies were only willing to employ those who had worked for a year in a nursing home, which provided the appropriate apprenticeship for a range of patients so the care worker could work autonomously, with little supervision, in a patient's residence.

A formal credential and work experience as a nursing assistant or licensed practical nurse do not help one become a nurse. Although registered nurses can acquire a CNA license after the first year of nursing education, obtaining a CNA license does not count toward a nursing education because of the history of distinguishing different kinds of nurses (Cannings and Lazonick 1975). A few special bridge programs to help nursing assistants become registered nurses exist, but most nursing students have to gain admittance to nursing school, through which they obtain a college degree. Completing a noncredit licensed practical nursing program—in nine months full-time or two years part-time—also does not transfer to a registered nursing program (Ducey 2009). Ariel Ducey notes that low-income healthcare workers in New York City have struggled to obtain further education to become a patient care technician or licensed practical nurse, only to discover that the wage and job security was only a bit better than that of a nursing assistant. These educational barriers push workers into what Ducey calls "training without end" (2009, 139). In the 1970s, Randall Collins grew concerned with the ways that credentials produce a stratified society and proposed a common educational sequence for nurses, doctors, and nursing assistants, in which all medical careers would begin with a position as nursing assistant, which could then build toward further nursing and medical apprenticeships (1979, 201). His recommendations, which were never implemented, remain salient today.

Several healthcare experts, worried about the shortage of direct-care workers, propose a career ladder to retain skilled workers (Harmuth 2002). In its report to Congress, the Commission on Long-Term Care (2013, 50) recommends that "paid direct care positions should hold the possibility of advancement and job satisfaction through career ladders and lattices," which allow workers to move upward or laterally along a career path by developing specialized skill sets. The goal is that by acquiring different skill sets, they can then move up from entry-level jobs into higher-skilled jobs in health care. As part of the Affordable Care Act (ACA), six states received funding for pilot programs for direct-care workforce education, several of which included career lattices for home health workers (US DHHS 2011). Progress in this area is therefore happening but not fast enough or at a scale sufficient to affect those I met.

Many care workers wish to continue their education but struggle to combine full-time work with further schooling. Several of my interlocutors had started as nursing assistants in home care or a nursing home and subsequently became nurses, whether licensed practical nurses or registered nurses. These women were young and childless or married to supportive husbands. However, most of my interlocutors had begun but did not complete their nursing education. Usually, they attempted a college degree through a for-profit, online school that accepted them due to low admission requirements and allowed them to continue working full-time. Julie, who had worked as a translator in the US embassy in Congo-Brazzaville and was fluent in English, described her experience of going to school to obtain the credentials for a similar position in the United States. Julie started studying business management at Strayer University, working in home care full-time and going to school full-time. She got a student loan "quick. I said okay." But after one week, "I knew I couldn't go on. I don't want to kill myself." She realized that she did not have the time or energy to do the assignments, and as the main breadwinner for her household (a husband and children), she could not afford to work only part-time (interview, May 6, 2016, Washington, DC). Education is costly in the United States, entailing going into debt and investing considerable time that might otherwise be used in paid labor.

Faustie, who worked live-in while her husband and baby stayed in Ghana, told me,

> My uncle was a home health aide [in the United States], and he told me to try it [home care]. So I entered the field and worked for some time. Then I decided to go back to school. I found it was expensive. Private universities would accept me, but the government universities had too many standards. So I learned that county college would be easier. I got into county college and decided to study biology. I didn't want to become a nurse but pursue medicine, but considering my family and age, I would finish [my degree] in my forties. I would have used my whole life to study and have a lot of financial aid [student debt]. So I decided to do something that would not take as much time. I went for physician's assistant. I am determined. (phone interview, May 7, 2015)

Despite her previous experience as a midwife, she had to return to school. Like her, those who are in their forties and fifties feel that returning to school would be a waste of resources, requiring the rest of their working lives to pay off their student debt. Care workers also have to decide whether to support their own schooling or their children's, and many opt in favor of their children's education. Rather than a route to upward mobility, further education becomes an obstacle because of its time commitment, inflexibility, and cost.

Many feel sorrow about not being able to obtain further education and a better job with higher status and pay. Binta felt that she had been "progressing" as a civil servant in Guinea, but in the United States, she was "stagnating." Binta was explicit about her bitterness with home care and wondered why she continued, given that it was not allowing her to be successful, despite her work in home care for more than fifteen years: "I went to school [in Guinea], but here it [that education] is not considered anything. I support my mother, father, brothers, and son" (interview, December 4, 2016, Maryland). Yet, given the lack of options, she introduced her son, in his twenties, to the agency for which she works, and now he also works in home care.[7]

All jobs, even those defined as unskilled, have a level of competence, such as physical abilities of balance, cognitive processes of memory, and emotional management of self and others (Rose 2004). Care is a conscious social activity requiring attentiveness (Boris and Parreñas 2010b). Furthermore, workers in lower-level healthcare positions are often given complex tasks to perform beyond their training and abilities, in order to reduce costs and as nurses have become busy with recording information (Ducey 2009). Despite their entry-level position, home care workers are conferred much autonomy and decision-making power. They have to be alert to a wide range of chronic and acute conditions of aging, from diabetes and heart disease to dementias. Home care agencies often have a nurse on staff, who is on call for home health workers but is often busy during the day evaluating potential patients or dealing with patients' health problems. Home health workers often rely on their own wit and wisdom—and the advice of colleagues—to resolve problems on the ground, rather than bothering the agency nurse. Ralph Waldinger and Michael Lichter note the level of skill required for the jobs in which migrants are concentrated: "Thus we arrive at a paradox. At the very bottom of the labor market we find workers with little if any formal education, but few jobs that truly lack skill requirements" (2003, 60–61). This statement about the educational background of workers is not so true of my African interlocutors, of whom more than half (thirty-three of the fifty-nine interviewed) had completed secondary school or beyond, including two with master's degrees, five with nurse-midwifery training, three with teacher training, seven with a university degree, and six with technical training in translation, auto repair, or secretarial skills in their home countries. However, it was also true that their educations, like my doctoral education, had not prepared them well for home care, with the exception of the former nurse-midwives. Furthermore, the home health workers did not consider themselves professionals, which would have resulted in a different, more authoritative, and more distant relationship with their patients.[8] Part of their skill was to obscure the patient's reliance on them in order to maintain his or her sense of independence (Buch 2017).

Like other feminized labor, there is an undervaluing of caring skills. Neysmith and Aronson observe, "'Help' turns out to be a complex, negotiated phenomenon—accomplished by means of observation, particular knowledge of the individual, a careful according of self-determination to clients and a large degree of flexibility on the part of the home care worker. Thus, practical help emerges as inseparable from the process of carefully attending to relationship maintenance" (1996, 8). Skill, effort, and responsibility remain invisible to the agency and patient and, sometimes, to the care worker. Ducey notes, "Many allied health care workers experience irreconcilable emotions about their abilities and their work. On the one hand, they feel their work is trivial and that they should seek supposedly meaningful work. On the other hand, they know their work is meaningful but also inexplicably undervalued" (2009, 155–56). Furthermore, there are few norms about what constitutes good care, impeding home care workers' ability to evaluate their own work (Neysmith and Aronson 1996). What someone needs from a care worker is socially determined and constructed, both interpersonally and societally (Thelen 2015).

The skills that the home care workers talked about and used to help one another did not concern health issues—the major topic of the nursing-aide curriculum I studied—but how to handle challenging interpersonal situations, particularly with a patient suffering from a dementia. One difficulty that the care workers had to manage was when a patient pushed them away or asked them to leave the residence, which directly affected their capacity to provide care. Often, the patient was not the one who had asked for agency help; rather, it was the patient's anxious children or overwhelmed spouse. Care workers frequently described being denied entry to the patient's residence or having the police called on them because the patient did not recognize them or refused their care.

One evening, at a suburban Starbucks, surrounded by teenagers flocking like birds and adults hunkered over their computers, I met Beza after she had worked all day. At this, our third interview, Beza told me that she was ready to discuss the negative aspects of care. A short and cheerful woman from Ethiopia, with one daughter in college in New York City, she had decades of experience in nursing homes and home care. She told me the following story, which I have summarized:

> She was caring for a patient who "had Alzheimer's," liked to sing, and had "a beautiful voice." The patient's son gave them money to go to a movie.

They had to drive quite far, and they left halfway through the movie. Once they were out of the movie theater, the patient would not get into the car. "I am not going with you!" the patient said. "You gonna kill me." Finally, Beza asked two gentlemen in the parking lot if they would pretend to be policemen. Beza told them, "I have a lady, and she is upset, and if you say that you are the police and she should get into the car, she will." Beza says she does not know where this idea came from; it surprised her. Her patient believed the men and sat down in the car, and Beza drove her home, without saying anything. When they arrived at the patient's residence, Beza stopped the car, and the patient said, "Get out. Leave." So Beza picked up her personal things from the patient's residence and went out into the parking lot. She called the patient's son for help. While waiting for him, Beza moved her car to another part of the parking lot, to fool her patient into thinking she had left, but she kept her eye on the front door. After forty-five minutes, Beza knocked on the patient's door. The patient said, "Come on in, my friend!" (summary from interview, May 18, 2016, Maryland)

Beza describes being surprised by her idea of asking two strangers to pretend to be authority figures, but I would argue that it resulted from her long experience doing care work, just as Mihalyi Csikszentmihalyi (1990) describes "flow" coming from hours of practice. Beza did not panic, as perhaps a new care worker would, but came up with creative solutions at different points in the challenging afternoon. Beza's expertise entailed "local solutions to specific problems" in which she provided care by trying different strategies (Mol, Moser, and Pols 2010b, 13).

Diane, an experienced care worker from Jamaica, talked about "using psychology." As an example, she reported that she would pretend to cry on the doorstep of a patient who denied her entry. On witnessing Diane's distress, the patient would ask with concern, "What happened?" Out of sympathy, the patient would let her in, and the rest of the time with the patient would go well (interview, January 8, 2016, Maryland).[9] In telling these stories to me, care workers could laugh over what had clearly been stressful situations at the time. They were proud of their level of skill and ingenuity in resolving these problems without losing their job or endangering their patient.

Waldinger and Lichter (2003) explain the paradox of low-educated migrants doing highly skilled work by emphasizing how new workers learn the job through their coethnics. Likewise, the home health workers I interviewed used their social networks to improve their skills. Using their cell phones, home care workers received work advice and emotional support, usually from conationals doing similar work. They shared with one another the strategies that they had learned from others or through their own questioning, insight, and observation.

Associated with women's work, nurturance and care are seen as skills that women naturally have or that they develop through their gender socialization. Similarly, agency staff consider Africans to be naturally respectful of older adults as a result of their socialization in their home countries. African care workers also represent themselves in this way to agency staff, who absorb this message, as well as to patients, who retain deeper reservations about the competence of African care workers.

The Cultural Capital of Being African

Because the home care industry in the United States has no way to measure the quality of care and no clear reward system for good care workers, ethnicity became a mark of quality. In his history of domestic servants in the United States, David Katzman notes, "Ethnic stereotyping was the stock in trade of all employers of servants" (1978, 221). Racialized stereotypes are typical of domestic-servant markets worldwide (Colen and Sanjek 1990), including childcare placement agencies in Canada (Bakan and Stasiulis 1995), maid employment agencies in Los Angeles (Hondagneu-Sotelo 2001), and elder-care agencies in Italy (Ascione 2012) and Chicago (Buch 2015b). In the early twentieth century, southern whites idealized "country blacks," denigrated urban African Americans as servants, and considered African American women to be instinctive, nurturing mothers (Tucker 1988). Given this history, it is not surprising that Africans would also be stereotyped in the home care markets of northern New Jersey and Maryland. Their racialization as African is a form of political othering. Africanness as a sign of difference functions as a variable form of cultural capital; it is valued by agency staff for its association with hard work and respect for elders but devalued by patients. This results in a precarious workplace environment for African care workers, in which they are responsible for overcoming patients' negative evaluations.

Agency staff members with whom I spoke supervised a labor force that was 60–80 percent African. For the most part, they appreciated these workers. They considered them to naturally have the right skills and attitudes for caring for older adults due to their socialization in their home countries. At times, staff members considered these skills unteachable and simply inherent in particular people through their "culture" or "background." They therefore constructed the "labor as effortless and not real work" (Glenn 2010, 180–81). One staff member commented that Africans are very caring toward patients, which she attributed to their background: Africans care deeply for family and are respectful to elders (interview, March 17, 2015, New Jersey). An owner of another agency said that Africans are "very caring, very compassionate" (interview, February 23, 2015, Maryland). At a third agency, the manager explained why Africans were naturally good caregivers. Two weeks prior, he had interviewed a Nigerian with a bachelor's degree in mathematics. He had asked her why she wanted to work in home care, given her degree in a different field, and she had said because of her family. He commented, using this example as proof, that there was "strong elder support [in Nigeria], where the young provide for the elderly." Another staff member at the same agency commented, "The African culture is very strong. They have morals. They do it because of their upbringing" (group staff discussion, January 27, 2016, Washington, DC). An agency owner said, "Africans are more polite, more respectful" (interview, March 17, 2016, Maryland). Finally, one agency staff member appreciated Africans because they accepted all kinds of shifts and jobs, unlike African Americans, she said; they were not so focused on income and benefits, unlike those from the Caribbean; and they stayed in home care, unlike "the Hispanics," who moved into other kinds of employment quickly (interview, April 22, 2017, Maryland). In general, then, my sense was that the agencies highly appreciated their African workforce.

The agencies valued Africans but also differentiated between them on the basis of national origin, which they felt determined personality and tone. Among Africans, Ethiopians were favored over West Africans as "more gentle" and "sweet." One agency staff member said, "The ones who are the most sensitive and the most patient are Ethiopian care workers. They have a soft-spoken nature and a lower tone rather than an excited tone," which she thought was related to linguistic differences. Corroborating her existing stereotype, she was told by an Ethiopian care worker that even if she and her conationals do not understand what the patient says, they smile and face the situation by smiling. She continued, expanding her praise to all African workers: "Some African home health aides are bubbly and do not get frustrated the way some Americans might. For example, a patient might say, 'I don't know you today.' They will be met by a giggle and 'Oh, we saw each other yesterday,' which smooths it over with a laugh" (phone interview, April 25, 2016, Maryland). Another agency owner said she loves Ethiopians as "God's people: kinder, gentler. They wear their hearts on their face. They speak softly." Nigerians, however, "negotiate everything, and they want everything on their own terms. They argue, and it is to their detriment. They can be hostile. We have had to fire several. They have no social skills." Kenyans, on the other hand, are "wonderful" (interview, February 3, 2016, Maryland). Agency staff members use these national stereotypes to determine whom to hire and whom to call when there is work. When they have a new patient, for example, agency staff make a lot of phone calls to various care workers to see if they can take the case. The sequence of calls is determined in part by schedule availability but also by agency favoritism of particular workers on the basis of how they interact with agency staff and patients and whether they tend to accept cases when called.

Those care workers who did not know me very well also tended to emphasize that they had taken care of older people in their own families, which seemed to be what they had learned to say in job interviews.[10] A few agency staff members found the story of family elder care too pat; they had heard it too often to believe it. Care workers whom I knew better also talked about being "humble," "patient," and "respectful" when they compared themselves to coworkers of other nationalities, including more established Americans, particularly if they had worked in nursing homes. At the same time, they emphasized that they did care work to support their families and children. Positive work traits were inculcated, in their view, by the context of need, rather than culture, background, or socialization. Ivy, a nurse in her twenties from Ghana who worked in a nursing home and was quite aware of how she was perceived by coworkers, said, "We don't talk loud [about our grievances about work conditions]; we need to keep working to feed our kids, our mothers, our husbands. She [a care worker] wants her job, [so] whatever you [the employer] want, we will be quiet" (joint interview with Ivy and her mother, December 4, 2012, Pennsylvania). When I first met Regina in 2008, she was forty-nine years old, and her four children (aged seven to twenty-one) were living in Ghana while she worked in home care in Connecticut. She was later able to process the papers for her three oldest children (the youngest was born in the United States and was a US citizen) and bring them to the United States. To support her children and to pay for the expensive process of applying to bring them to the United States, Regina worked in several long-term care facilities as well in home care. She said that the problem that "we Africans" have is "Africans let it go. The white residents don't want to be touched by African care workers because they are black, and the administrators also treat Africans as less than the African-Americans" who know their rights. Only her colleagues from South America understood the closeness of family, said Regina, and why she was working so hard to support her children (interview, October 2, 2012, Connecticut). Janet said, "Africans—Ghanaians—don't want to tell the agency when there are problems because they worry that they won't get the job. They have fear. They don't want to tell them. Because if they don't work, they won't pay the rent" (phone interview, January 20, 2015). Thus, although agency staff members attribute care workers' skills and attitudes to "African culture," care workers themselves consider economic desperation as accounting for their good work. This leads, particularly in comparison to African Americans, to a weaker claim on rights and entitlement in the workplace.

Patients and their families approach aging without much knowledge about paid caregiving because they do not anticipate a need for it or hate the thought of it. Often, the desire for independence and autonomy among American seniors means that transitions in care are sudden and unanticipated and therefore chaotic and rushed (Hashimoto 1996; Kaufman 2005). In general, it is the children or spouses of patients who call agencies, rather than the patients themselves desiring such care. When children or spouses call agency staff to ask about a care worker's help, they are often overwhelmed: a crisis has just happened, or the patient is about to be released from a hospital and sent home. As Elana Buch writes, "Home care can be seen as a kind of liminal practice introduced at moments when older adults in the United States first acknowledge their need for assistance and the ways this threatens their personhood" (2017, 87). Patients' perceptions of care workers are partially shaped by agencies and care workers because they have not prepared for death, frailty, and the loss of independence. Americans resist, rather than celebrate, transformations of personhood associated with aging (Buch 2015b; Hashimoto 1996; Kaufman 2005). This means that aging is a major time for learning, as each person encounters aging for himself or herself, without rituals or signposts to guide the aging life course (Cole 2013; Myerhoff 1984). Some patients and their children receive some information about paid caregiving from within their network. But generally, patients and their relatives are learning about the home care industry during the process of getting help. They find themselves in a new role as an employer of a care worker and might feel anxiety about social class and race, as well as about autonomy and privacy (see Rollins 1985). It is up to the agency staff and the care workers themselves to provide guidance to aging adults about their new role. However, care workers' subservient position and their need to please the patient makes such education difficult and tentative. They are not operating from a position of expert authority, as a doctor or nurse might, but from the position of satisfying a patient.

Thus, at the beginning, patients are often not aware that most care workers are Africans or migrants, and the initial request for care often entails learning that information. The care workers and agency staff had many incidents to share with me where the patients asked for someone "American," which the agencies took as a euphemism for "white," challenging in practice legal notions of citizenship based on the Fourteenth Amendment. Blair Rutherford delineates modes of belonging as "routinized discourses, social practices and institutional arrangements through which people make claims for resources and rights" (2008, 73). Through the understanding that Americanness means whiteness, everyday interactions around home care suggest that political belonging is only available to white people. Thoughtful and patient, Solomon worked as a live-in care worker. He described registering with three agencies when he moved to the Washington, DC, area from Atlanta, where he had worked for more than a decade as a pastor for a Ghanaian church. He first obtained a home care job in a northern Virginia suburb, where he met a woman and her father. When he arrived, the daughter said she was "looking for an American. Now, I [Solomon] am a citizen [of the United States], but I knew what she meant: she wasn't talking about this paper [citizenship]. I went back to the agency and said that the lady was looking for an American white" (interview, March 6, 2016, Maryland). In this situation, formal citizenship—having the right papers—did not confer substantive citizenship, in the sense of the right to work or legal constraints on employment discrimination. Furthermore, Solomon translated the patient's request for an "American" into an "American white," thus recoding citizenship as available to blacks and himself while also, by understanding her true meaning, retaining the discourse that (only) white people are (real) Americans. Historically in the United States, race has been used to assess "the presumed suitability/unsuitability for civic inclusion" (Jung 2006, 407). As has been noted in other works (Balibar 1991; Deomampo 2016), belonging to a nation is partially determined by one's racial categorization.

Patients and their relatives can be explicit about their racial preferences, rather than using the code of citizenship or immigration status to discuss race. One of my white faculty colleagues told me that a friend of hers had called to ask for help finding a care worker for her mother. My colleague had someone to recommend, based on her experience from the care of her own recently deceased mother. In response, her friend told my colleague that she thought that her mother would not want someone "dark," apologizing for saying so but feeling strongly enough to share the sentiment with a friend (field notes, April 19, 2016, New Jersey). A white social worker who helped older people navigate different care options, including using home health workers, similarly reported that "my more usual clients . . . say, 'No, anyone who is not African'" (interview, February 22, 2016, Maryland). Janet said, "Sometimes, they don't like black people. They want a white person" (phone interview, February 6, 2105).

Elizabeth told me an extended story in this vein about a woman she worked for:

> One patient was saying to me, "Pick up the phone and call the police." I asked her why, and she said, "The niggers are here! They are like you!"

I said, "I am one of them." The woman was ninety-six years old. She told me, "You are all right." I said, "You call the police yourself." But she couldn't manage the buttons [on the phone]. I told her I would call the agency for her, and I pressed the numbers [for her] and left the room but listened from the doorway. She told the agency, "How dare you people bring such a person? I am a white lady, and you bring those niggers." The coordinator [Nadine] . . . is white. She blew up! She was giving it to her. They were fighting on the phone. I was listening. Nadine told the rest of the office staff, and they were angry. Nadine said she was going to tell me to pick up my bags and leave. The woman was asking for a white person. But Nadine said, "This is no job for us. I will not let you abuse this woman [Elizabeth]." She told the other people in the office, and their response was, "How dare she!" The woman asked for time to find a replacement. But Nadine said, "Please, with all due respect, no one is coming. Tell Elizabeth to come." Nadine is pissed. Nadine said, "When you [Elizabeth] get off, we are not going to bring anybody. It is all the same [all the workers are the same]: black people." Later, I asked what became of the woman, and Nadine says she doesn't know, because we left [the case]. We don't know what became of her. (interview, February 29, 2016, Maryland)

This was one of the few instances where I heard of an agency staff member supporting the care worker instead of the patient. The punishment for the patient was severe, as the patient was well aware: the agency's withdrawal of care highlighted her dependence on the care worker. The withdrawal of care constitutes the ultimate weapon in the arsenal of care workers, although it simultaneously strikes a self-inflicted blow, as they lose a case. The dependence of patients on care workers and agencies usually results in the grudging acceptance of African or black care workers, carving out a space for an exception for a particularly wonderful black care worker, in contrast to other black workers. Elizabeth was pleased by her ingenuity in handling the challenging situation, in which she capitulated to the patient's request to make a phone call but through which she was ultimately vindicated.

The agency staff members whom I interviewed had even more stories about requests for white or American caregivers than did the care workers. To be sure, most of the agencies' websites and other advertising, such as pamphlets and signs, did not represent the field accurately: using

Figure 1.1: Advertising sign in home care agency window, February 7, 2016, Maryland. Photo by Cati Coe.

stock photos, they generally showed young, female, white care workers wearing scrubs looking into the eyes of older, attractive white men and women, who seemed to be hale and hearty seventy-year-olds.

Agency staff develop a repertoire of tricks to deal with requests for white workers. An agency staff member told me,

> We need to market the care worker to the patient. Many patients will say that they want someone who is not too heavy. They want someone who is white or American, which they sometimes use as code. One woman said that she doesn't want someone African because they can smell them coming through the door. They want someone who is neat and clean, without a lot of jewelry. One man on the phone asked for an American, and I said that I had a man named José, until I forced him to say he wanted someone white. (interview, January 5, 2016, Maryland)

Other agency staff use a strategy of identifying with the patient as a fellow white person. One said, "Some of the clients say, 'I only want a white or a light care worker.' I want one too, but guess what? There aren't any."

She commented to me, "I get that a lot" (interview, February 17, 2016, Maryland). A Ghanaian agency owner used a similar technique, positioning herself as a client looking for child care:

I learned to tell them [the patients, in the initial phone conversation] and let them understand that 80 percent of people doing this job are from Africa. You are not going to get white people who are CNAs. They [whites in health care] are more into the med tech [medical technician] thing and they move quickly into RN [registered nursing] programs. They [white people] don't even try for LPN [licensed practical nursing]. I tell them to let you [the patient] understand and get your mind set. . . . We explain our field to them. I tell them, "If I was letting a total stranger into my home to take care of my child. . . . I understand where you're coming from." I empathize. (phone interview, March 21, 2016)

A Nigerian agency owner told me that her strategy was to present the alternatives to the patient:

The thing is that [without home care] the person will get sicker and end up in a nursing home, where everyone [all the workers] will be black. They [the patients] forget it [that asking for a white person] is illegal. But they are paying money. They know it is not right, but they think that because they are paying, they have the right. I tell them, "It is true that Giant [a large grocery chain in the area] doesn't pick out the apple for you; you can pick the best apple. You get what you want." I don't want them to ride away and say that they didn't like everything the aide did. (interview, February 4, 2016, Maryland)

The salience of the commercial relationship—in which the patient is always right and the complexities of care become akin to a piece of fruit squeezed and examined at a grocery store—puts the agency staff member into a bind of wanting to give the patient what they want (a white caregiver), upholding employment laws that prohibit such requests, and navigating the realities of a workforce that makes such requests hard to honor regardless of the law. Race becomes "a consumable good" like an apple, which the consumer can pick over and choose (Deomampo 2016, 97). As Megan O'Leary says in her study of home care, "The agency, while serving as a useful buffer to the complaints and abuse . . . , views its primary role as catering to the senior citizen client population" (2016, 222).

Another staff member said that patients do not ask the right question about care workers, in that they focus on skin color and race rather than skill, the real consumable good:

> They ask, "Can you find someone with light skin?" I tell them that the staff is based on ability, not the color of their skin. . . . The really big issue for them is not the right issue. . . . The patients ask us, "Where do they come from? Do they speak good English? Do they know how to cook?" I respond, "What do you want them to cook—something in particular?" What they don't ask is, "Do they know how to deal with someone with Alzheimer's?" Especially in this area [Bethesda, Maryland], they ask, "How dark are they?" This is not the right question. (interview, February 3, 2016, Maryland)

The agencies see their job as helping patients focus on the right question, but they have to do so in a placating way because the patient is viewed as a customer, paying money for a service in which they deserve choice and satisfaction. Furthermore, as noted above, some agency staff similarly use Africanness as a defining characteristic, albeit valuing it differently than patients.

Some agency staff deal with patients in a way that tolerates bias and discrimination, positioning themselves as like the white patients in seeking a domestic servant. Others agree with the patient's rationale: because they are buying a product, they are entitled to choose which product to purchase. Some mention antidiscrimination laws, but only a few. Most dodge the racism in an attempt to woo a patient, or they explain the lack of options to the patient. Regardless, they tend not to protect their care workers from racism but instead try to cajole the patient into accepting an African care worker by saying that the patient can interview the care worker or try out the care worker for a day. An agency coordinator from Sierra Leone told me that she would ask patients to "give the person a chance." Then she would prepare the care worker for the job by telling them to talk slowly or that the patient was already biased against them: "The patient is dying to get rid of you. Show them how you make their life better" (interview, May 18, 2016, Virginia). Racism is assumed to come from a lack of familiarity, which the care worker's caring actions and the patient's dependence will overcome. This kind of mediation places the burden of managing racism on the care worker.

Although they vary in their assessment of the African workforce, agency staff and patients tend to agree on one thing in relation to this workforce: the problem of accents. From the agency's perspective, speaking English with an un-American accent is a legitimate reason to ask for an American. An agency staff member said, "Others are more covert [than directly asking for a white person]. They ask for people without an accent. I tell them, 'This is the issue. Most care workers are immigrants.' Some will say, 'I want a Filipino care worker.' I try to say it nicely, using a euphemism. I am a salesperson, but I can't take BS [bullshit]. We talk about it all the time in the office. We get hit by it" (interview, May 4, 2016, Maryland). A staff member at another agency said, "Patients are opposed to having people with different languages come to their houses. It has lessened a little bit, perhaps because patients have gotten used to what is on offer. They say, 'I don't want someone who has an accent because I have a hearing aid.' Or, 'I want someone to cook for me.' We try to work through it" (phone interview, March 15, 2016). Thus, patients try to find the right code language to request a white care worker. Agency staff deal with some of these requests as blatantly racist, while others are viewed as reasonable and deserving of accommodation.

Some patients appreciate African care workers for the same reason that agencies do: they consider Africans to be particularly respectful of elders in ways that mitigate some of the disrespect that they receive as older people in general. However, most of the twenty-five patients or their relatives whom I interviewed appreciated Filipinos or Caribbean people more than Africans. They considered Caribbean care workers to be more outgoing, happy, and full of laughter than Africans. My mother's friend commented that when her mother needed home care in Florida, her mother's friends told her to hire someone from the Caribbean rather than Africa (field notes from conversation, early January 2016, Maryland). A patient's wife, who was quite frustrated with her husband's African care workers, said she found "Filipinas very caring and respectful of older people. There is a difference. They honor older people. They are not subservient, but it is just a love fest, rather than coming with an attitude of 'I have to work. I have to do this'" (phone interview, March 4, 2016). Diane commented that she, as a Jamaican, was treated better than Africans. She obtained more work than they did, she told me, because of prejudice. Patients also commented to her that she was lighter skinned than most Africans (interview, January 8, 2016, Maryland). Unlike agency staff, who make distinctions between different regions and countries, many patients and their relatives do not know exactly where in Africa their care workers come from.

In general, while the racialization and migrant status of care workers as Africans serves as cultural capital among agency staff, it does not do so among the clientele to whom the agencies are beholden. This difference keeps African care workers in a precarious position, in which they have to work harder to please the patient and overcome the patient's distrust and suspicion. Their value is not recognized by patients, and thus their race and migrant status do not serve as stable cultural capital.[11] Race and migrant status thus allow a particular kind of worker to be preferred in a particular employment sector, but they simultaneously function to dehumanize the workforce and render it cheaper and easier to control (Glick Schiller 2012). Inclusion of the care worker at one level (being employed by the agency) is thus accompanied by exclusion at another level (once the care worker goes to a patient's residence).

The Role of Social Networks in the Africanization of Home Care

Africans predominate in home care and nursing assistance in nursing homes on the metropolitan East Coast not because agencies try to hire Africans or recruit them from abroad but because newly arrived Africans are told by those in their social networks to enter health care. This process brings Africans into home care where agencies, now accustomed to their presence, value them.

New migrants' social networks push them into home care because it is a quick way to begin earning money to send back home, as demonstrated by Yolanda Covington-Ward (2017) among African direct-care workers in Pittsburgh and Fumilayo Showers (2013) among West African nurses in metropolitan Washington, DC. Health care "was socially constructed [by West African migrants] as an occupation that was accessible and reliant on incorporating foreign workers" (Showers 2013, 256). Patricia told me, "The person you come to stay with does this job [home health], so they introduce you to the job" (interview, February 7, 2016, Maryland). Caroline joined her parents in the United States from Ghana after a period of separation, which is fairly typical for transnational families (Coe 2013). Her mother already worked in home care, and once Caroline graduated from high school in the United States, she followed in her mother's footsteps.[12] Caroline told me, "You come to this country through your family, and they direct you to the kind of work they know" (interview, March 2, 2016, Maryland). Emily described her brother's wife telling her that "everyone was in home care" and encouraging her to "just try it" (interview, March 3, 2016, Maryland). Twenty-one years ago, shortly after Mariam arrived from Sierra Leone, where she had worked as a nurse, she substituted for her niece who had been hired directly by a patient. The niece got another job "overnight," so Mariam stayed in her niece's original job (interview, March 29, 2016, Maryland). When new African migrants come to the United States, their friends and relatives are already working in home care and encourage them to enter the field.

Some migrants with educational credentials and professional experience arrive in the United States with different occupational expectations but slowly realize that they will have to become nursing assistants. Ivy's mother, who worked in a continuing care community, bitterly commented, "All you have to [can] do here is go through [into] health care," as if elder care was the only kind of employment open to Africans (joint interview with Ivy and her mother, December 4, 2012, Pennsylvania). One afternoon, sleepy from working the night before, Essenam's cousin Justine spoke about her experience of realizing that she could not obtain the same kind of job in the United States that she had in Togo, where she had been an administrative assistant:

A friend told me the only thing you can do [in the United States] is nursing assistance.[13] My father called [from Togo], "Justine, did you find an administrative assistant job?" I said, "Dad, there is no job here for me. They [potential employers] say, 'Because of the accent, or because of this and that.'" I have to take a nursing job [meaning in home care]. (interview, January 14, 2016, Maryland)

Julie, a former translator and secretary for the US embassy in Congo-Brazzaville, described her disappointment with the job prospects in the United States: "In the employment market, whatever I did before, because it was in Africa, equals zero. I needed to start from scratch." With the help of an organization providing job training for low-income residents of Washington, DC, she entered home care (interview, May 6, 2016, Washington, DC). Faustie similarly found that her credentials as a nurse-midwife from Ghana had no cultural capital in the United States because she did not have a bachelor's degree, whereas her friends with the same credential had an easier time in the United Kingdom (phone interview, May 7, 2015). A Cameroonian nursing aide interviewed by Covington-Ward (2017) similarly commented that employers wanted US work experiences and did not pay attention to his master's degree (see also Showers 2013).

Thus, educated African migrants experience downward mobility by entering home care, accompanied by a loss of status. Gilbert, a male Ghanaian live-in care worker, said, "When we from Africa come here, before you go to school and get a job, you have family back home and so you throw away that certificate quick and just begin working" (phone interview, February 19, 2015). After giving me the contact numbers of a few friends working in home care, Binta commented, reflecting on her friends' and her own situation, "We are nothing here, but we were somebody in Guinea" (interview, January 21, 2016, Maryland). When I presented on my research to the African Affairs Advisory Group of Montgomery County, Maryland, a committee member commented that I should consider the "emotional agony" of doing home care in the United States. The care workers expect to be doing something else, she said, and then they "eventually reset their minds," coming to terms with the fact that they will not find other work (field notes, December 2015, Maryland). However, this process of resetting one's mind can be quite painful.

Janet told me a story about a male friend who had been an auditor in Ghana, which she mentioned as a sign of how far his status had fallen through home care:

He said, you know, when he went to someone's house, the man had a gun. He went downstairs, and the man threatened him with the gun.

He put his hands up, and the wife came down, begging her husband, "Please, please." The man said that if she called 911, he would kill this African monkey. My friend told me, "I was praying in my head." The wife told him to go upstairs, and he went upstairs, packed his things and left. He told the agency to bring another person, and the agency said that he should not tell the new aide anything about what had happened to him. He said, "Okay." But he wrote a note in Twi [one of the major languages of southern Ghana], telling the next aide to call him, so that he could warn her. Later, when he went to the agency office, he saw the same aide, and she had a bandage on her hand. He asked what had happened, and she said that the man tried to kill her. He said to her, "I told you to call me." The woman said, "I thought you were going to tell me you loved me, so I didn't want to call you." (phone interview, January 20, 2015)

Janet used the occasion of this terrifying incident to remind him that the job he had held in Ghana was better than home care, which put him in such physical danger. His story indicated that his status was so low that the agency did not protect him or his coworker from violence.

Men are more reluctant to enter the feminized profession of home care and more eager to leave it, choosing security, warehouse work, or even restaurant cooking instead. Two men managed to exit home care work during my period of research: Solomon, university educated in Ghana, had been a pastor and returned to it after several years in home care. Kwadwo, a former teacher, entered politics in Ghana when his party won elections in December 2016. Edem, a recipient of political asylum who held a master's degree in physics and was an intellectual at heart, talked about his experience of entering home health work:

I was looking for a better life [in the United States]. I met a lot of challenges. First, there was the language matter [learning English]. I would have to go back to school. I should study the language for three years. Then I would choose a program of study, and it would take five to seven years to see yourself in a good situation. You know in Africa, we live in solidarity. My parents were in Togo. You are mature [an adult]. People depend on me. I did my calculations [about the number of years of education needed], and I decided to start working rather than going to school. I started working in a warehouse, for Giant Peapod [a home delivery service of a major grocery chain]. I was doing stocking and receiving. I worked there for three years. Then they moved to Baltimore, and I could not go there. I had to change jobs. I accidentally came to this job [home care]. My friends told me this is a good job. (interview, May 25, 2016, Maryland)

Although Edem comments that he "accidentally came to this job," nothing about it seemed accidental. As noted above, those who told me how they had entered the field described friends and relatives who already worked in this field and recommended it to them as a quick and secure way to get money. The agencies were happy when their current workers helped with recruitment and provided them with a small bonus for doing so.

In comparison to men, who switch between home care and other jobs, women tend to stay in the healthcare field and try to become nurses. As noted above, a few women who were married to supportive husbands succeeded in leaving home care and entering nursing. The vast majority, however, struggled to raise their own children, support their families back home, work, and go to school simultaneously, or they determined that they were too old to spend many years on their own education and concentrated instead on that of their children. They ended up staying in the home care field for decades, until they were ready to retire. Oriane, who came fashionably dressed to our interview at a nearly empty mall food court, regretted that when she came to the United States from Côte d'Ivoire, her friends told her that "no man will value you unless you work two or three jobs" and gave her the advice to "work, work, work, make money." Now, twenty-four years later, in her late forties and still working in home care, Oriane felt that she made the wrong set of choices and that "education is the best." "Sometimes, I ask what I have done with my life," she told me sadly. In addition to working in home care, she worked at a nursing home every other weekend to maintain her nursing-assistance license, and "all these little girls are RNs. What have I done with my life?" Ten years earlier, Oriane had taken her children, then aged ten and eight, back to Côte d'Ivoire to stay with her mother while she studied to be a licensed practical nurse, but she had needed more time to study because English was not her first language, and "it was too hard." The four years of full-time education to become a registered nurse felt "too long" to her. Now, she felt that the normal seniority had been inverted through educational credentials, in which "little girls," in the same generation as her children, had more authority than she did. This situation made Oriane feel ashamed, and she questioned her previous choices to prioritize work over education (interview, January 19, 2016, Maryland). Essenam cried in my presence when she reflected about how she had tried to go to community college. As a single parent, she found it impossible to combine school and work (visit, February 23, 2016, Maryland). A few care workers use home care as a stepping stone to further education and better kinds of work, particularly if they are well educated. However, most, especially those women without support from others, realize that they are stuck in this line of work and consider themselves failures as a result. In this way, home care becomes a niche employment field and a dead end for Africans, particularly for women but even for men, who generally have more education than their female counterparts. For many African migrants, it seems that entry-level healthcare work is the only job open to them in the United States.

Conclusion

When Africans come to the United States, they encounter a racialized employment market, in which their Africanness, blackness, and migrant status play major roles in how they are perceived. Due to their desperation to support their families, they are valued by agency staff as dedicated, hardworking, and respectful of older persons. Africans also highlight these qualities when they seek employment. However, these ethnicized qualities are less valued by patients, who ask for someone light skinned, American, or who speaks English well. This situation puts care workers in a precarious situation, in which the agencies fail to protect them from the racism of patients.[14]

African migrants' entry into home care is easy and commonsensical. "All roads lead to Rome," or as newly arrived African migrants are told by those in their social networks, "All you have to do here is go through [into] health care." Those who have dreams of using their translation, administrative assistance, or teaching skills in the United States succumb to the pull of home care. Many become stuck working in home care for decades, without being able to switch to another occupation or advance to nursing, because no educational or career ladder is widely available to home care workers.

The entry into home care thus has implications for the political belonging of African migrants. Valued as respectful and patient, they are included in some ways. For example, agencies employ them, which enables them to earn money for their families. On the other hand, they experience exclusion and subordination in their interpersonal interactions (explored further in chapter 2) and, more impersonally, through the conditions of the home care labor market (explored in chapter 5). They also feel considerable bitterness about their lack of mobility. Some, such as Essenam and Oriane, turn this bitterness on themselves; they blame themselves for their failures. More highly educated migrants, such as Binta and Julie, feel a sense of injustice about their existing educational credentials not being recognized. The racism and humiliation they encounter, coupled with the sense that their occupation is inescapable, make them open to the oppositional viewpoint attributed to subordinate minorities by John Ogbu (1978), as we will explore further in the next chapter.

Interlude

Silences about Servants

Agency and care workers' stories about patients' desires for light-skinned or white caregivers puzzled me. My assumption was that patients of this social class in the urban northeastern and mid-Atlantic United States had experience with maids and housekeepers, who were likely either African Americans (in the 1960s and 1970s) or migrants from Latin America (today). I thought that patients' experiences with "the cleaning lady" or "the cleaner," as they were called, would facilitate the use of a care worker, since they would be accustomed to a stranger in the house. I assumed that white patients would be comfortable around someone of color, so long as that person was in a subordinate position, and that they would have experience negotiating the peculiar tensions of domestic service (Hondagneu-Sotelo 2001; Rollins 1985; Tucker 1988).[1]

These expectations were partly based on my own white family's history of domestic service, a history that may not be generalizable. Beginning in 1930, my maternal grandmother (1904–99), a housewife married to a small businessman, raised her four children in Washington, DC, and Bethesda, Maryland. Initially, when my grandmother had small children, an African American maid lived in a bedroom and bathroom in the basement. In the mid-1940s, my grandmother hired a sixteen-year-old African American named Hattie Jackson to clean one day a week. Their arrangement continued for over fifty years, until my grandmother moved into a retirement community in the 1970s. When my aunt had children of her own, she also hired Ms. Jackson. This intergenerational transfer of servants as family needs changed was quite common, as the literature on domestic servants, as well as slavery, in the South attests (Rollins 1985; Tucker 1988). When Ms. Jackson died of lung cancer, my grandmother and another resident at her nursing home who had also employed Ms. Jackson impressed on my mother that she had to attend the funeral in their stead, which my mother did. My mother thus grew up with a live-out maid in the 1940s and 1950s, but as an adult in the United States, she has never had any servants, corresponding to the relative disappearance of domestic workers in the 1970s and 1980s. Domestic servants reemerged in wealthy and upper-middle-class pockets during the 1990s and 2000s, under conditions of increasing inequality, new migration streams to the United States, and women's increased work outside the home, without changes in the gendered organization of domestic labor (Duffy 2011).

Domestic servants historically did not simply cook and clean but also provided elder care, as is clear from Susan Tucker's collection of oral histories of domestic service from southern women (Tucker 1988). While my mother was growing up, her maternal grandmother lived with her family. That my grandmother disliked taking care of her own mother was part of our family narrative: such care had prompted my grandmother to want to avoid being a burden to her own children, as is a common concern among older adults (Jennings, Perry, and Valeriani 2014). In 1972, my grandparents, who were then in their late sixties, entered a new senior-living community that had opened in 1966 in a suburb of Washington, DC.[2] Despite this narrative of my grandmother's kin care, I learned that during the last six months of my great-grandmother's life, an African American servant slept on a twin bed in her bedroom. The narrative of fifteen years of kin care loomed larger than the six months of paid care. Rather than elder care transitioning from kin care to institutional care to paid care at home, this wrinkle in the story made me appreciate the continuities that underlay the larger changes. Like other white people, I do not talk about this history with my friends; there is shame in these stories, which acknowledge social inequality and racial discrimination. As Ruth Frankenberg noted in her discussion of white women and race so many years ago, "Color and power evasion . . . dominates public languages of race in the United States today" (1993, 189). Silence about servants, including their use in elder care, is part of this evasion.

I began asking patients about their experiences with servants. Many who used home care workers also had cleaners who came in one day a week for several hours. Many did not understand why I was asking about housekeepers, nor did they see the connection between my questions and home care. Home care was conceptually distinct from domestic service in the minds of the patients I interviewed. As the historians Eileen Boris and Jennifer Klein note, "The conflation of home care with domestic labor . . . is historical and not a categorical equivalency," the result of federal legislation that treats home care as domestic work (2010, 188). The legal definition of home work in federal labor legislation differed from the common sense understanding of my interlocutors, for whom these were different categories. Yet in practice, domestic service and care work were elided. Sometimes the cleaning lady became an elder-care worker temporarily. One couple sent their housekeeper to nursing-assistance school to give their live-in care worker a break for a few hours on Saturdays (interview, March 6, 2016, Maryland). Another patient's wife said that she would sometimes ask her cleaning lady to stay with her husband for an hour or so, after the home care worker had left and before the wife could return home from her activity or errands (interview, December 4, 2015, Maryland). My mother reported that many people in her neighborhood gave more hours to their cleaners as a cheaper form of elder care. Cleaners thus fill in the gaps that result from the difficulty of finding elder care in a fragmented system. Patients may also press care workers to become housekeepers.

Relationships between cleaners and their clients may last for decades and are sometimes intergenerational, in that the current cleaner is the daughter or stepdaughter of a previous one. Marie, who had a tense relationship with her care worker Fatu, as described in the introduction, felt more positively about her Latina cleaning lady, who came once a week, partly because the job tasks were more clearly defined (interview with Marie's daughter, January 29, 2016, Maryland). One patient with the most extensive experience of servants, whose father had been a successful businessman in Washington, DC, described having African American servants when she was young. When she grew up and had four children of her own, she had a cook. She described how the cook chose her, a process in which the cook was very much in charge (see also Dill 1994, 93): "The cook worked for my friend and for my friend's son and wife. Then my friend died. My friend's husband was a friend of my father-in-law's. The cook wanted a full-time job and approached me. She interviewed me. She said, 'I know you have a big family,' and she wanted to see everything, so I showed her around. She liked the dog, and the dog liked her. She examined everything, and then said, 'Okay, I'll take you'" (interview, March 28, 2016, Maryland). Later, the cook helped her employer's grown-up son and his wife when their own household became more extensive. This story from the 1940s corresponds to historical research demonstrating that African American women of this period were renegotiating the terms of domestic service to be less subordinate, whether in choosing their place of employment or in negotiating hourly work with multiple clients rather than doing live-in work for one family (Clark-Lewis 1994; Katzman 1978).

If patients have histories with African American maids and cooks, why do they resist African or black care workers? Is caregiving so different from cleaning? I came to realize it is. Older people's vulnerabilities and dependencies are exposed through care. Although housekeeper-client relationships can be as fraught as care worker–patient ones, care—far more than cleaning—challenges patients' sense of autonomy and independence. Studies of maids have shown the ways that employers sometimes ignore them or treat them as if they were invisible (Rollins 1990). Some employers leave the house to let the housekeeper clean and avoid the discomforts of a social relationship that is ambiguous and challenging to manage, hierarchical but also friendly (Hondagneu-Sotelo 2001). These practices are fraught, uncomfortable, and sometimes dehumanizing for workers, but they are far less brutal than the strategies used by plantation mistresses with domestic slaves (Glymph 2008). Tactics of avoidance and invisibility, however, are less available for care work. As one agency staff member said, "caregiving is intimate," involving touching, showering, and toileting (interview, May 18, 2016, Maryland). The care worker cannot be ignored and does her work directly with the patient. Also, older people are more likely to live alone than the mothers of young children who hire domestic servants, and the care worker provides companionship to the solitary senior. The patient's personhood relies on the interactions with and actions of the care worker to a much greater extent than a housekeeper, at least in contemporary households. The history of domestic service also suggests that some families have used maids as a status symbol to showcase their wealth and power (Clark-Lewis 1994; Dill 1994). No patient or care worker indicated to me that hiring a care worker is a sign of wealth or power, although it certainly is. If anything, they saw it as a sign of mortality and loss of mental or physical capability, and thus, as heavily stigmatized.

My own family history and some of my observations suggest that the historical trajectory between domestic service and elder care is a circular one, in which elder care reinvigorates a racialized and feminized servanthood with roots in enslavement. This history makes race and power central to care encounters in the United States. Perhaps this is why patients frequently ask for white or light-skinned caregivers and use racialized insults as a method of control, as we will see in the next chapter. Home care is one site where America's racial system becomes visible. However, just as importantly, I needed to understand the perspective of care workers. What did the circulation of stories about explicit racism amongst themselves and in conversation with me say about their sense of American society and their belonging in it? We will explore these issues in the following chapter.

2

Stories of Servitude

Racial Slurs, Humiliating Insults, and the Exercise of Power

Most of my African research participants in northern New Jersey and the Washington, DC, suburbs told me stories of deliberate humiliation or diminishment. I listened to Ernestina and Patricia, two friends from Ghana, trading "war stories" about nursing-home work with one another in Patricia's apartment in an apartment complex in Gaithersburg, Maryland. Ernestina said, "Someone called me, 'You bitch, you fat bitch. You are my slave!' This was Mrs. Jenkins [a pseudonym; she gives the name to remind Patricia of the exact person], a long time ago. I cried." Patricia turned to me and said, "They call you 'black monkey'" (joint interview, February 7, 2016, Maryland).

Humiliation and aggression are common in health care. Seventy percent of direct-care workers in one survey reported hearing racist remarks from residents of long-term care facilities (Ejaz et al. 2008). In another study, three-quarters of nursing aides in three nursing homes had experienced racial abuse on the job from residents, residents' families, or fellow staff members (Berdes and Eckert 2001). A study of home care services in Canada found that "elderly clients' and families' inevitable frustrations at having to rely on home care services were often directed at their individual workers—the only or closest target." All workers in this study—whether white women or women of color—were "diminished" by their clients for being only "cleaning ladies." "However, for nonwhite home care workers, clients' frustrations could also be articulated in terms of their ethnoracial characteristics. In other words, an additional discourse, concerned not with class but with race, was available as a medium of expression for clients and families who, variously, sought targets for their complaints about meager home care services or who were, in a more diffuse fashion, struggling with their own diminishment as people deemed dependent and needy" (Neysmith and Aronson 1997,

482–83). Care workers at all levels and in all kinds of situations—from hospitals to nursing homes to home care—experience patients' social actions of this sort, perhaps caused by frustration, pain, and anger at their need for care or the humiliating practices of the healthcare institution. However, for black healthcare workers, as Neysmith and Aronson note, anger and humiliation can be channeled through explicit racism. Jemima Pierre (2004) notes that scholarship and popular writing on black migrants often uses the language of ethnicity instead of race, even though they are subjected to the racial order of the United States. Here, I address directly the process of racialization of African migrants at work.

The feminist psychoanalyst Jessica Benjamin would consider patients' humiliating social actions to be forms of aggression central to the making of the self, in which the self projects or repudiates elements of itself in others: "The self is constituted by the identifications with the other that it deploys in an ongoing way, in particular to deny the loss and uncontrollability that otherness necessarily brings. Second, it is reciprocally constituted in relation to the other, depending on the other's recognition, which it cannot have without being negated, acted on by the other, in a way that changes the self" (Benjamin 1998, 79). In the process of self-making, "the self may be invested in depositing its repudiated aspects in the other, using it to represent what is despised or intolerable—for instance, weakness or aggression—and so necessarily casts the other in the role of opposite" (86). This process, in which the self is reciprocally constituted by others, can be especially intense in home care work, in which people interact closely for hours and days at a time. Benjamin's theory of the self would suggest that the very act of caring, through its intimacy and acknowledgment of vulnerability, makes the patient more desirous of engaging in acts of aggression. In the cases described to me by care workers, race was part of a panoply of insults—which included gender, slavery, servitude, and nonhumanness—that patients used to despise and dominate care workers. These were idioms of disbelonging or, sometimes, of belonging through subordination.[1]

I am less interested in the psychological operations that produce these insults and humiliations than in the effects of these interactions on home care workers' sense of self and political membership. Racialization is a political process that operates from "the world historical to the intrapsychic" (Winant 2004, ix). We humans are vulnerable to being deeply hurt by others' actions and responses, and our own sense of self can be affected. As Judith Butler says, "We are not only constituted by our relations, but dispossessed by them as well" (2004b, 24). Patricia related a story that happened "a long time ago" but which she remembered because it hurt her so much. Frantz Fanon has eloquently discussed how being constantly called out as a "negro" or "nigger" by small white children on the street—and considered frightening or amusing as a result—produced dislocation and amputation of his soul, because he desired recognition from others as a condition for participating in the world (1967, 109–40). He argued, "Man is human only to the extent to which he tries to impose his existence on another man in order to be recognized by him. As long as he has not been recognized by the other, the other will remain the theme of his actions. It is on that other being, on recognition of that other being, that his own human worth and reality depend" (216–17).

As represented in the conversation above, Ernestina's immediate response to such an insult was to cry. However, in contradistinction to Fanon, although patients' degradation caused pain, it did not permanently affect the care workers' sense of self-worth. They slipped between positions in which they relied on a patient's recognition at some times but repudiated such a need at others. For example, through telling the story of a patient's insults, Ernestina represented her own painful response to the insult while also gaining validation of her self-worth from her audience. African home care workers' dependence on work makes them publicly accept or ignore these insults; they keep their anger and hurt to themselves or share them only with coworkers and kin. Irene told me that in home care, you have to be "submissive" (field notes from conversation, August 19, 2005, Kumasi, Ghana). However, over time, as these experiences accumulate and occur within the context of humiliating work conditions, care workers become embittered.

The psychological literature has usefully distinguished between shame, in which the person feeling shame considers their degradation to be deserved and feels guilt, and humiliation, which is characterized by "intense other-directed outrage, low guilt, but intense feelings of powerlessness" (Leidner, Sheikh, and Ginges 2012, 4). In the words of Linda Hartling and Tracy Luchetta, "The internal experience of humiliation is the deep, dysphoric feeling associated with being, or perceiving oneself as being, unjustly degraded, ridiculed, or put down—in particular, one's identity has been demeaned and devalued" (1999, 264). The degree to which humiliation is traumatizing depends on several factors, including the public nature and extent of the social fields in which the humiliation is known (Torres and Bergner 2010). The self-worth of home health workers may be denied by patients in the context in which they are working, but such denials do not affect other dimensions of their lives that are more emotionally significant, such as their status with family and friends. Thus, while temporarily undone by humiliation, illustrated by crying, they tend to fend off its significance in the long term, in part by sharing it with friends; they do not experience shame. Although "individuals who have been subjected to the most severe and public of humiliations frequently experience feelings of hopelessness and helplessness" (200), this was not the case among my interlocutors. Although they experienced their patients and patients' relatives as objectifying them, they do not experience *themselves* as objects—as Fanon (1967) argues happens—or at least they did not narrate themselves to me and others from that position. Instead, like the domestic workers studied by Rollins, they highlighted the unjust nature of the humiliation. Rollins argues that domestic workers in Boston are able to ward off these insults because of their intimate knowledge of their employers' faults, their sense of racial and class injustice, and their sense that their real lives are outside their work, in their church, family, and neighborhood: "Free of illusions about equal social opportunity, domestics neither blame themselves for their subordinate economic position nor credit their female employers' superordinate position to any innate superiority of theirs" (1985, 218). For African care workers hopeful about their opportunities in the United States, illusions of equal social opportunity are attractive, although they become freer of such illusions over time. Although they do not take such insults to be true, they consider such incidents to be strongly representative of their overall treatment in the United States.

It is not clear how often these incidents occur, but when they do, they are painful and memorable. The care workers reported crying and being upset. Stories of these incidents are shared among networks of colleagues and friends as paradigmatic of elder-care work in the United States. Some the care workers I interviewed had not had such experiences themselves, but they related the stories that they had heard from friends about demanding or impossible patients, such as the one above. Care workers use such stories to assess their degree of belonging; these incidents illustrate for care workers the larger message that Africans are not treated or accepted as human beings in the United States. These incidents and the stories around them make African migrants feel they do not belong and will never attain a respected status in the United States. But it does not make them feel that they do not deserve respect. Some, who had been doing the work for almost two decades, reported feeling what Judith Rollins calls "ressentiment": "a long-term, seething, deep-rooted negative feeling toward those whom one feels unjustly have power or an advantage over one's life" (1985, 227).[2] They expressed this through bitterness about the failed reciprocity to their labor. Stories about racist insults in care work circulate among home care workers to express and manage such bitterness.

As we have seen in the literature on psychology and political philosophy, recognition has been sometimes used to indicate a stance that is only positive, specifically a recognition of another person as different from the self and with the same claims to autonomy. It is this positive view of recognition that political philosophy has framed as a major goal of a democracy, in the sense that recognition of equal, autonomous, and distinct persons is what a democratic society ought to afford all its members. As older codes of honor were replaced by a universalistic notion of dignity, "forms of equal recognition have been essential to democratic culture" (Taylor 1992, 27). Through the principle of equality of rights and respect, these mutual forms of recognition became embodied in notions of citizenship, "that identity which subordinates and coordinates all other identities" (Holston and Appadurai 1999, 1). Axel Honneth argues that "the justice or well-being of a society is proportionate to its ability to secure conditions of mutual recognition under which personal identity-formation, hence individual self-realization, can proceed adequately" (2003, 174; see also Margalit 1996). Others, in contrast, have highlighted the ways that all forms of recognition, including what political philosophers call misrecognition or nonrecognition and what psychologists call aggression or break down, generate selfhood. Hate speech can therefore be a form of recognition but one that marks the recipient as inferior: "What hate speech does, then, is to constitute the subject in a subordinate position" (Butler 1997, 18). In this latter view, all relations of power, both positive and negative, make up the self (McNay 2008).

In my own understanding of recognition, I tend toward the latter view, in which recognition is not always respectful of equality and difference. The positive sense of recognition, as described by Jessica Benjamin (1998), is too flickering and impermanent—constantly breaking down and in need of repair—to make it the basis of political membership, although it can represent an ideal, psychologically and politically. Instead, like Butler, I see racist insults as a form of recognition that constitutes the home care worker as both different and worthy of being demeaned. Within an interpersonal field of power in home care, racialized insults constitute home care workers as servants and link them to the historical associations of blacks and Africans as slaves and nonhuman. However, home care workers reject such identifications in their own minds, sometimes after a period of vulnerability to the assault. As we will see below, care workers' actions in care encounters span a wide range: from publicly accepting such insults to finding ways to thwart the patient's power by highlighting his or her dependence on the care worker. Thus, care workers are subjected to humiliating recognition, but they also respond to it—usually angrily and bitterly.

There have been many critiques of the philosophical focus on recognition. Scholars have noted that not all struggles against injustice derive from claims of recognition, nor does the lack of positive recognition necessarily drive progressive social change (Aranda and Jones 2010; McQueen 2013). Material class disadvantage does not derive solely from the misrecognition of others as fully equal (Aranda and Jones 2010; Fraser 2003). Paddy McQueen, in his critique of Axel Honneth, argues that "power is infused into discursive and institutional practices of subject-formation. . . . The point is to warn against a reductive theory of recognition that is overly focused on psychological experiences of recognition and thus remains disconnected from, and overlooks or misrepresents, the ways that institutional practices shape our social relations of recognition and intertwine with power at a socio-institutional and discursive level" (2003, 51, 58).

In this research on home care, it is clear that processes of recognition are affected by the social context in which they occur. As labor scholars have argued, the way that dignity is denied varies in different work-places, and the pursuit of dignity is "limited, channeled, and constrained by the surrounding organizational demands and structures" (Hodson 2001, 20). Although inequality and domination are shaped by institutional processes in many areas of American society, such as schooling and the criminal justice system, relations between patient and caregiver in paid home care have not yet become completely formalized, as noted in the introduction. As a result, patients' domination is asserted, in part, through interpersonal relations (see Bourdieu 1991). Furthermore, caregiving relations evoke the legacies of slavery and servitude in the United States, as well as racial hierarchies based on human/animal distinctions, making some kinds of recognitions come easily to patients' minds in conflictual situations.

Through these interactions and stories about these interactions, African care workers are becoming familiar with American racial categories, in which they are black, along with stereotypes about Africans as animals and about immigrants stealing jobs from citizens. These insults incorporate them into American racial categories as "blacks" and into a servant class—social categories that made little sense in their home countries, where ethnic, class, and rural/urban distinctions mattered more than race. As a result, African care workers are becoming more sensitive to the experiences of African Americans, some of whom are their colleagues in nursing homes. As a result, they partially assume the oppositional stance associated with African Americans, as John Ogbu (1978) describes. They take their treatment as indicative of wider power relations in their society and therefore as unjust. The accumulation of slights, insults, and diminutions that Africans receive through their care work affects their sense of political belonging and subordination because it powerfully signals the lack of recognition.

Thus, contra the critics of recognition, recognition is important in political boundary work. Care workers' recognition as "African," "black," "immigrant," and "monkey" in care work encounters makes them feel unfairly excluded from political membership or, at least, makes them feel unjustly subordinate within the political community. Recognition is key to home care workers' understanding of their lack of political membership. They use the language of recognition and respect when they rail against agency policies and the conditions of work. Thus, from my perspective, Honneth's focus on recognition makes sense of my ethnographic experiences. Care workers do feel a sense of psychological injury, not only through the interpersonal interactions discussed here but also by the nature of work conditions, which Nancy Fraser (2003) would term "redistribution." On the basis of this study, similar to Joel Robbins (2009), I argue that redistribution is one aspect of recognition, in that it entails the question of who deserves what.

What I take from the literature on recognition in political philosophy is the significance of recognition for determining political belonging. The use of recognition in both interpersonal interactions and, more widely, in democratic societies allows analysis across scales, following the lead of home care workers who find a parallel between their work and their inclusion in the United States. Furthermore, it enables me to focus on everyday practices by which political membership is determined, both interpersonally and more widely, such as through the invocation of discourses of subordination—through race, gender, class, and human/animal distinctions—to denigrate care workers. Political membership has "moral and performative dimensions" (Holston and Appadurai (1999, 14) that are enacted at multiple levels, including in interactions around care. As citizenship loses its emotional grip as the overarching identity in a globalizing world of greater inequality, other political forms of membership based on hierarchy and domination may reassert themselves. Home care—and the workplace in general—is one site that affords an understanding of how political belonging is changing through ongoing processes and practices of recognition.

Stories of Racial Insults

Care workers told me many stories of explicit racial insults. Only Gita, an Indonesian care worker whom I interviewed as a small comparison case, said she had not experienced racism. Esther had left Ghana fourteen years earlier to escape from spousal abuse in a middle-class household and now had three grown daughters working in Accra and Dubai. The following extended narrative concerns a particular situation in which she was racially insulted:

Esther worked for an agency in a continuing care community with Ms. Smith, a ninety-nine-year-old woman. She worked with Ms. Smith for seven months. Esther said about her patient, "She was so mean, very mean. She doesn't like people of color." I asked if she called Esther names, and she said yes. Esther said, "If you have to, call me names; so long as I can put food on the table of my kids. I needed the money." Esther used to take Ms. Smith to the dining room and watch Oprah at 4 p.m.[3] Esther was "addicted" to Oprah, she said. But one day, Ms. Smith did not stay very long in the dining room. When she came back to the apartment, she found Esther watching Oprah. Ms. Smith was angry. Esther said, "She called me every word in the book. She asked me, 'What is an animal that looks like a human being? What animal is that? I'm asking you.'" Esther demonstrates her stance before Ms. Smith, pulling her arms behind her on the couch as she tells me the story, asking me, "You know how in Ghana we do that?" I nod, remembering it as a respectful pose before someone in authority; standing with one's arms behind one's back is a pose I associate with children and not with a woman in her fifties like Esther. Esther said she responded to Ms. Smith, "Monkey." Ms. Smith said, "You are an African monkey." Esther responded, "I am so sorry, Mrs. Smith." "In the facility, the Africans were so mad. They said I shouldn't have apologized." But Esther said, "I was wrong. I felt less than a human being. I cried." The event reminded her of her abusive husband, whom she had left to come to the United States. "It gave me flashbacks to my husband. I called my sister, and she could tell I was upset." Her sister said she was coming to pick her up right away, but Esther told her, "Wait until my shift is over." She informed Ms. Smith she was leaving by saying, "Good night, Mrs. Smith. You are not seeing this monkey tomorrow," and the patient responded, "No, don't go!" (summary from interview, February 19, 2016, Virginia)

In this case, unlike many others that I heard, Esther did feel that she had erred in watching TV and felt shame rather than humiliation, in part because of the longer history of abuse by her husband, which the insults from Ms. Smith recalled. She felt "less than a human being" rather than anger at being called an animal. By answering "Monkey," she accepted Ms. Smith's naming and questioning of her in this degrading way. At the same time, she presented the viewpoint of her coworkers, other care workers in the same facility, who expressed anger on her behalf and through whom, perhaps, she represented her own anger to me. Esther called her sister, who affirmed her self-worth and offered support. A further response to Ms. Smith, in addition to apologizing, was to leave the case. Leaving, as we will discuss below, is one of care workers' main sources of power, as it reminds the patient of their need for the care worker. Esther was pleased that Ms. Smith expressed her dependence on her with her plea to stay. Although she may have been less than human, the patient still needed her. The plea had no effect; she left anyway.

African care workers describe patients using racial insults not only for disciplinary reasons, as in Esther's situation, but also for the purpose of social distancing, particularly when refusing care, such as not wanting to be touched by the care worker or telling the care worker to leave the residence. These commands impair care workers' ability to do their jobs and therefore directly threaten care workers' primary goal of earning money for their families, increasing the emotional stakes of these encounters. For example, Julie came to work for a woman in a facility:

> The moment Julie entered, the patient asked, "What have you come here to do?" It was the night shift. She told Julie, "You cannot sit in my apartment. Go sit in the hallway." I clarified that the patient had a private apartment in an independent-living facility. The hallway would therefore be like the corridor of an apartment complex, with no place to sit. Julie continued, "I told her I have to be in the room. She told me to 'sit in that corner. You people have to stay with your own species.'" Julie told me in explanation, "She's racist." Julie called the agency in the morning and told them that the patient wants a "white CNA [certified nursing assistant]— not that she will get one." Julie told the agency staff to tell the family to find someone else. "The agency should draw the line on this one [and not work with her]." She told me, "That was the nastiest thing I ever heard— 'your own species.' She was probably racist ever since [from the time] she grew up." (summary from interview, May 6, 2016, Washington, DC)

Emily reported working in the dementia unit of a nursing home, where "they will say things like: 'You come from Africa. Why don't you go back?' [or] 'You take our jobs, so our children don't have jobs.' I [Emily] reply, 'Oh really? Have they applied for nursing jobs?' [Or they will say:] 'You black nigger, get away from me'" (interview, March 3, 2016, Maryland). In the stories that care workers tell, race, humanity, and migration status are invoked as forms of denigration when patients wish to refuse care or to discipline. These strategies of recognition seek to put care workers "in their place," outside the social and physical sphere of the patient. They deny equivalence, mutuality, and intimacy. The insult is painful not only because it comes from the person whom one is trying to help but also due to its repetitive quality. As Butler notes, "Racist speech works through the invocation of convention; it circulates, and though it requires the subject for its speaking, it neither begins nor ends with the subject who speaks or with the specific name that is used" (1997, 34). In addition to assaulting the care workers' personhood, it also materially threatens the care workers' ability to do their jobs and jeopardizes their capacity to support their families.

Sometimes the insult is nonverbal; instead, spatial positioning designates a subordinate position, evoking its significance in the history of racial segregation in the United States. Bathrooms are a key site for such segregation. When I called Irene one day, she told me that a daughter of her patient was upset at her for using the upstairs bathroom at night, rather than the downstairs bathroom. Irene felt slighted and wanted to tell her that she had four bathrooms in her beautiful house in Ghana, but she refrained from doing so (phone conversation, January 6, 2008). In other words, she wanted to use her class status in Ghana to fight against the denigration she experienced in the United States. An agency staff member also talked about patients' social distancing through the use of bathrooms. Some of their patients were "enlightened," the staff member said, but some were not and did not think the care workers were up to "their standard." They had "prejudices." Patients would ask their care workers to sit on the floor, rather than on the furniture, or to use the bathroom in the lobby of the independent-living facility, rather than the one in their apartment (interview, April 5, 2016, Maryland). Justine told me, "A patient told me not to touch anything in the house. I was not to drink their water. I worked for them for four years" (interview, January 14, 2016, Maryland). Commenting on domestic workers in Turkey who live in the same apartment buildings as their middle-class employers, Gul Ozyegin notes, "Stigmatization, by structuring the interactions among members of each class, affirms the social distance that the middle class feels is undermined by physical proximity and the lack of ritualized social contacts" (2001, 10). It is precisely because the care worker is staying in the patient's residence that bathrooms become so symbolically important as a way of regulating the social pollution caused by great intimacy. Both verbal and nonverbal forms of insult draw from a long history of racial segregation in the United States and reanimate it. They are an expression of the power that is continually undercut by the patient's need for care, which requires the care worker's presence.

Stories of Distancing and Other Denials of Care

The care workers, including Gita, reported other forms of denigration that occurred without recourse to racist insults. I met with Valerie in her home in a housing development on the far outskirts of suburban Washington, DC, on one of her days off. Sitting at her dining-room table, she told me about the following incident, which occurred while she was providing care:

> A ninety-five-year-old woman had a patch [for medication], and Valerie asked to clean it. She [the patient] said, "No, don't touch me."
> Valerie asked, "Don't you want medication, for your heart?"
> She said no.
> Valerie asked, "Do you want to die?"
> The woman asked Valerie back, "Do you want to die?"
> Valerie said no.
> The woman said, "Leave me alone. Get out of my face, you good-for-nothing. Trash."
> "I laughed," she [Valerie] told me, and she laughed again in telling the story. (interview, March 15, 2016, Maryland)

Later in the conversation, she told me that one response to the "good-for-nothing" remark would be to say, "I'm good for nothing, but I am here for you." Her immediate emotional response was to laugh, which constituted a rejection of the patient's naming of her; her more considered response was to affirm the patient's recognition of her as useless and highlight the patient's dependence on her. As we shall see, affirmation of the insult, which turns the insult into a harmless remark, is a common strategy for managing denigration while continuing to care for someone.

Although race was not explicitly mentioned in this particular exchange, care workers often suspect that racism is the underlying reason for denigration and distancing, particularly when it involves instructions not to touch the patient or to go away. Sometimes, care workers sense a desire for distance even though the patient accepts their help. For example, Hope said, "Sometimes you can tell that they don't want you to touch them, but they don't say it. One woman in [a retirement community whose name I've redacted] kept saying, 'Don't touch me.' I could tell from her actions [that she was racist]. Later on, when I stopped going and other people [care workers] went, I heard that she asked of me" (interview, May 2, 2016, Washington, DC). Similarly, Janet said, "At times, they don't like me, but [and] they show it with their body language. They don't want me, but they don't have a choice. They won't tell you to your face, but they don't like you. I know. There was one client. She didn't want me to do something, but she has no choice. She said, 'Okay, do it.' She won't say something" (phone interview, February 6, 2015). Such actions by patients create social distance even though care often requires touching and physical intimacy. It may be precisely because of the physical intimacy involved in care that social distance needs to be generated in other ways. Distancing and stigmatization within intimate spaces also generate distance and caution among African care workers about their patients, as well as a disjuncture between their emotional lives and their public persona, which can laugh in response to these attacks or can apologize with humility despite internal anger.

A patient's refusal of care strikes at the heart of what a care worker wants, which is to do and keep her job. At the most extreme, a patient's refusal of care can lead to police involvement and the use of state forms of control. This attempt is not usually successful, because older people are not considered reliable interpreters of reality. Valerie's cousin Victoire reported such an incident when I asked about her experiences doing care work:

> The previous night, Victoire had trouble with her patient. She could tell that her patient was angry when she introduced herself and told her she was taking care of her for the night. The previous care worker had told her

the patient "likes talking," an explicit warning. Victoire was supposed to turn her patient every two hours to prevent bedsores; she knew that the previous care worker had done so at 7 p.m., so Victoire waited until 9 p.m. to do so. At 9 p.m., she tried to turn the patient, but the patient told her to get away from her and called her a bitch. Victoire backed off. Then the patient told her to go away, and Victoire responded that she was there for the patient and had to watch her. The patient then called the police on her. When the police officers came, the patient told them that Victoire had hit her. Victoire explained the situation, and the police went away. The patient called the police again, but they did not come. Victoire said she had heard about patients calling the police on care workers, but she had never experienced it before. (field notes from a visit, March 6, 2016, Maryland)

This patient's tactics directly threatened Victoire's way of making a living. By accusing Victoire of hitting her, she might have caused Victoire to lose her nursing-assistance license. The patient thought that her story would persuade the police; instead, Victoire's story was more convincing. Age was a more significant stigma than race in this case. In conflicts between care workers and patients, both sometimes turn to other forms of authority, such as the state in the form of the police or to the agency—as when Beza, desperate to get her patient home from the movie theater, asked two passersby to impersonate police officers (see chapter 1) or, more commonly, when patients call the police to accuse the care worker of trespassing in their home. Although calling the police did not succeed in removing the her from the patient's house, Victoire felt shaken by the incident and linked it to a wider pattern of stories told by care workers.

Social Distancing through Invisibility

The sociologist Judith Rollins (1985) has described how she felt invisible when she was working as a maid for her dissertation research, in which a mother and daughter spoke about private matters in her presence, as if she were not there. She felt like less than a human being. The home health workers whom I interviewed also mentioned feeling invisible, but invisibility was harder to sustain because they were often alone with their patients, unlike maids whose primary clientele are families with young children. Many home health workers work alone with a single patient, either in a single house, an apartment in a multiunit building, or an apartment in a continuing care community. Among the twenty-five patients (or their relatives) whom I interviewed, eleven of the patients lived alone. When I talked to care workers, they seemed to encounter single-person caregiving situations more often than multiperson households. Under these conditions, invisibility cannot be sustained. Furthermore, the tasks that many patients require, such as bathing, toileting, and feeding, are more personal and require more copresence and interaction than house cleaning or laundry. Still, the home health workers did mention invisibility as an example of humiliation and social distancing. Invisible moments tended to happen when they accompanied their patients in public or when a patient's family members visited, rather than when they were alone with their patients. Invisible moments thus function as another form of distancing, maintained through social interaction and spatial segregation.

Deborah said that she felt like a servant when she took care of someone who needed "total care" and when it was "someone you care about. You get them ready for a birthday or an event. You go to a restaurant, and they tell you to go sit somewhere else [not at their table]. . . . We are human. [It is like:] 'In our home we like you, but this is as far as you can get'" (interview, February 18, 2016, Maryland). Micheline described a similar experience of preparing her patient for a family visit and then being told to leave: "You feel rejected. The person needs you. You know him privately." She explained the rationale behind this action: "It's racism" (interview, May 21, 2016, Maryland). Essenam described another kind of invisibility, in which she had to transfer her patient between wheelchair and car, while the patient and her family toured the monuments in Washington, DC. She expected to take the lead on the transfer but to be assisted by others—including the grandchildren, who were younger than she was—to save her back and knees. But no one helped her. "The whole family will be there. You will be ignored, sitting in the corner. Until the mother needs to be changed, and they remember you. The children pass you without saying 'Hi'" (interview, January 12, 2016, Maryland).

I met Kwadwo for lunch at a McDonald's in a depressed neighborhood of Newark, New Jersey, on one of his few days off from live-in work, after talking to him by phone for six months. Tall and younger looking than his fifty-odd years, he described being ignored by the family members of his patient, which he found insulting. When the patient's children came over, they spoke to their parents nicely, but they ignored Kwadwo. One day the son came with his wife, and although Kwadwo was the first person in the apartment whom the son saw, he walked by Kwadwo without a word and went to his father. Only when the son's wife greeted Kwadwo did the son turn, give a little flutter of his fingertips, which Kwadwo demonstrates to me, and say, "Oh, hi." This came nowhere near the formal greeting, accompanied by a handshake, that Ghanaians expect. On another occasion, the daughter of Kwadwo's patient and her family came for a visit. They wanted to have lunch in the dining room of the continuing care community, and they asked Kwadwo to take the patient there in the wheelchair, which he did. He received no invitation to join them for lunch; in fact, he said he would have refused an invitation, but he wished that one had been extended. He went back to the room, and the daughter's family did not come back to the apartment to say goodbye to him. These slights were too much for him, and he told the agency he wanted to leave the job (summary of conversation over lunch, August 4, 2016, New Jersey). He felt that the children of the patient should appreciate his care and should show it by treating him as a person (see also O'Leary 2016, 173–75).

Nonrecognition through invisibility means that care workers do not belong in the social circles of their patients. In general, these moments of invisibility happen when care workers are no longer needed, for example, when they have brought the patient to the dining room to have lunch or have changed their patient. They are not greeted as full persons. These slights signal to care workers that they are not respected as persons or as caregivers. As we will see, such treatment raises concerns for care workers about reciprocity.

Patients' Stories about Racism, Aggression, and Distancing

I asked patients and their relatives about racism and aggression because they were so much a part of my conversations with care workers. Only a few family members talked about their relative's racist or humiliating behavior. Susan, for example, had employed care workers for several hours a day to care for her husband, who suffered from a dementia, until things became so bad that she put him into the dementia unit of their continuing care community. When Susan had care workers for a few hours, she wanted them to take her husband out of the condominium so that she could handle the housekeeping and accounting, tasks that were overwhelming in his presence. Like the uncomfortable and distant relations between domestic workers and employers described by Hondagneu-Sotelo (2001), she also found that she did not know how to interact with the care workers in her own house. For example, should she offer them a drink from the refrigerator when she got herself one? All in all, it was easier for her if the care workers and her husband left the residence to give her respite. Susan described how, one day, her husband had used racism as a strategy to return home:

> After a while, he didn't want to go out. Home was a security blanket. He told aides, 'I want to go home,' and they would come back, and I would tell them, 'I need the time.' I needed him out of here. He said once to two aides, 'I don't like black people.' He was not racist or at least not more racist than white people are. [The aides brought him home and reported what he had said.] He told me he was deliberately trying to get them upset so they would take him home. I made him apologize to the aides; I was struck that he understood [that his statement would work; she was monitoring his mental decline]. This strategy didn't work for him [because of her scolding], so he didn't try it again. (interview, April 21, 2016, Maryland)

Now that Susan's husband had declined to the point of being in the nursing section of this continuing care community, she visited him often and saw how other patients treated the care workers: "The aides face these racial things. There is one woman on the dementia unit who is nasty and says things like, 'They scraped the bottom of the barrel when they chose you to work here.' Or, 'You are the lowest and most ignorant of your class.' They [the aides] see the bad behavior of patients, and they have to roll with it" (interview, April 21, 2016, Maryland). She contrasted her husband with the "nasty" patients in the nursing home; for him, racism was a strategy to get what he wanted rather than an internal quality and, after being rebuked by his wife, he did not use this strategy again.

Still, the incident highlights how racist speech is a strategy available to white patients for trying to get their way with black care workers.

Other spouses and children described more ongoing anger and insults, which they attributed to a dementia. They highlighted how their spouse or mother had changed. One husband described how painful he found it that his wife was "nasty" to her live-in care worker. She was hostile and quick to lose her temper; she swore and called the care worker "a bitch." She had always been quick to anger but never like this, he told me. He tried to intervene when his wife insulted their live-in care worker, Hope, because his wife did not treat him similarly. He recognized his dependence on Hope for help caring for his wife, and he could not permit his wife to drive her away (interview, May 2, 2016, Washington, DC).

Jane also felt the onslaught of her husband's anger but, in contrast, was impressed that the care workers could take it: "I'm so offended [by his behavior]. When he turns it on me, I scream! But as for the aides, it's amazing what they can absorb. They are experienced." I asked for an example of what her husband would do, and Jane referred to the previous night, when her husband had been swearing under his breath, saying, "Asshole, asshole" (interview, May 20, 2016, Maryland). Another woman whose husband "abused" (her word) his care workers realized that her relationship with him would be ruined if she tried to care for him, and so she let the care workers do so. She said, "He didn't want anyone touching him. And I thought to myself, 'If I don't have to do these things, I can continue to have a good relationship with him.' Otherwise, it would be poisonous." I asked her if she had tried to care for him, and she said she had not: "I never wanted to test it. I suppose it was cowardice" (interview, January 14, 2016, Maryland). Care workers absorb the more challenging aspects of care, so that the relationships with family members can continue to be pleasant and conflict free. The literature on domestic service makes a similar argument that the use of paid household workers allows couples to avoid conflicts over domestic work (Hochschild 2003; Hondagneu-Sotelo 2001; Rollins 1985). These two wives experienced the relief care workers gave them by absorbing the anger of their husbands. By giving the labor of care to a third party, the wives avoided marital conflict. In contrast to these two wives of patients, who appreciated that the care workers absorbed the brunt of their husbands' aggression, the husband of a female patient was less subject to abuse from his wife and tried to protect the care worker from his wife's rage.

Finally, a daughter described her mother as sometimes "raging, angry, and kicking, screaming, and biting," whereas "earlier in our life, she was our German shepherd. She was the one who fixed things. She was a calm person. Now I wonder, was she calm inside too? She was someone who filled up the holes. She didn't panic; she was practical." When I asked her about her mother today, she said that her mother seemed "cruel" rather than "racist," but the cruelty felt racist too, because she sometimes would mock the way someone spoke. The daughter described, "She was in her chair saying, 'Bwla bwla bwla' in a mocking way (like 'nyah nyah nyah') and going on and on." Because her care workers were migrants from Sierra Leone and China who spoke English with a non-American accent, the daughter said, "The mocking feels racist to me. She'll mock me a little bit [too]. Like I say, 'It's time to go,' and she'll repeat [mockingly], 'Time to go.' She is belligerent. She is mercurial. It comes and goes" (interview, May 9, 2016, Virginia). Because of her position and relationship, like the husband above, the daughter did not receive the same degree of attacks ["a little bit"] that the care workers received, and she was better positioned to fend off her mother or transform the mocking into a game, although some care workers do this also.

Later, after her daughter left, I sat with the mother and her care worker, Yaema, for another hour. I witnessed the mother refusing a cup of tea for being too hot and then, after waiting too long to drink it, she complained that it was too cold. After Yaema patiently warmed the tea in the microwave, the mother went through this sequence again: complaining that the tea was too hot and then, after waiting too long to drink it, that it was too cold. This was not explicitly racist, and the mocking tone the daughter described was absent, but it was certainly imperious. It required Yaema, almost six feet tall with wide hips, to rise several times and to walk to and from the kitchen, an adjacent room. Yaema responded calmly and patiently to these requests, more patiently than I would have, moving back and forth each time between the microwave in the kitchen and the rocking chair in the living room where the mother was sitting and chatting with me. She may have been especially patient because of my presence. But the daughter had commented on Yaema's patience, which she had explained by saying that Yaema "remembers her [her mother] as she is from before." (Yaema had cared for her father three years earlier.) Afterward, the daughter wrote me an email to say that it had been a particularly good day for her mother.

Kin stories of racism did not fully align with care workers' stories. Kin stories highlighted changes in patients' personalities; they described general aggression and downplayed explicit racist insults. I learned from their stories that care workers sometimes served as a buffer for patients' aggression around care, allowing kin to maintain a good relationship with the patient despite personality changes that the kin were mourning. Care workers seemed more subject to aggression than kin, perhaps because of the lack of a long-term relationship or lack of status, particularly race status, or because they were not protected by others. Both care workers and kin used the word "nasty" to talk about racism, insults, and anger (see also O'Leary 2016, 194–95), and I learned to inquire about these incidents by asking care workers if anyone had been "nasty" to them.

Is an Aide a Domestic Servant? A Slave? Conflicts about the Definition of Care Work

The stories I heard from patients and care workers did align over conflicts about household labor. From patients who accepted care work, I heard stories expressing irritation and frustration at care workers about their activities. Patients were irritated that the care workers were not *working* but just sitting, watching TV with them or talking on the phone, when the patients were spending so much money or feeling weak. Although patients did not use such language, through their criticisms, they positioned care workers as domestic servants and appreciated care workers who responded to such recognition as a domestic servant by assuming general household labor. Many care workers refused such a designation, however, turning to agency staff to support their refusal.

Patients praised care workers who did house work in addition to caring for them personally. Emily was a licensed practical nurse who had been hired to empty and change her patient's colostomy bag, a task that requires careful attention and skill because of the risk of infection. This task needed to be done several times a day, taking only a few minutes but at irregular intervals. Therefore, a nurse was on hand twenty-four hours a day. Instead of focusing on Emily's highly skilled work, the patient praised her for doing "everything: the laundry, the trash, she takes blood pressure and vital signs, and keeps the records. . . . She even does some of the cooking now" (interview, March 3, 2016, Maryland). Similarly, Sharon's son praised Essenam because she did "light cleaning and laundry, perhaps to keep busy. We thought this was part of what we were buying, but the other two aides balked" (interview, January 17, 2016, Maryland). Thus, the patients and their kin appreciated care workers who assumed household work on their own initiative and functioned as domestic servants in addition to providing personal care to the patient.[4]

Another son said that his mother was somewhat imperious with the care workers in maintaining a social boundary and a distance. He said, "She works hard to train them. One aide came in to be a 'lady's companion,' sitting and chatting with her," but that was not what his mother wanted. He did not know where this "aristocratic" tendency in her came from, as she had been raised in a working-class household. However, his mother had always been very strict and was a former teacher. Also, because the care workers were quite expensive, she did not just want them sitting around doing nothing: "So she trains them to meet her standards." In connecting me with his mother and her care workers, the son was a little anxious about what the care workers thought of her (field notes from conversation, December 24, 2015, Maryland).

Given patients' frustrations and requests, care workers, not surprisingly, complained to me about the extent of the housework that they took on. Like domestic workers (Rollins 1985), care workers described being run around and becoming exhausted from the pace of demands. Deborah said, "The bad clients let you know you work for them" (interview, February 18, 2016, Maryland). Faith, an older woman who previously worked in hotel management in Nigeria and generally enjoyed working in home care, said, "Some clients are naturally very demanding. They don't want to see you sitting down because they are paying you. So you become exhausted" (phone interview, January 2, 2015). Ohemmea said that sometimes the children of the patient lived with the patient, and so the care worker ended up working for them too, even though they were not sick and were not the care worker's responsibility (phone interview, December 24, 2014).

Live-in care workers, who were paid a daily rate based on ten hours of work, complained about being on call twenty-four hours a day. Janet told me why she preferred live-out work to live-in work: "With live-in, you work 24-7, and they only pay you for ten hours. They don't even pay for twelve hours. They say that you sleep eight hours. Meanwhile, the patient thinks they are paying for 24-7: 'Bitch, I pay you for twenty-four hours. If I call you, I [you] have to come'" (phone interview, January 20, 2015). Monica said that she used to have a patient who beat her with her shoe, waking her up early in the morning, around 5 a.m.: "She wanted me to wake up and said I was being lazy. I told myself, 'I only need something from her; I have to be obedient and get it'" (phone interview, September 10, 2015). The "something" she referred to was income.

Care workers sometime use the language of the job description to refuse particular tasks that they find strenuous or unnecessary, although they often do other household chores that they prefer or do not mind doing, as has been well documented in other studies of home care (Buch 2014; Neysmith and Aronson 1996). Millicent told me about a "big house" where she had to cook and clean—a private job that she had not found through an agency and, therefore, where she was more vulnerable to employer abuse. She told me that she "worked like a donkey" on a Friday, when they were preparing for Passover (phone message, April 23, 2016). Almost every day, she had to do laundry, including washing the patient's comforter, since her patient went through four sheets a day as a result of her medical condition. The patient did not want Millicent to use the dryer, and she found it tiring to hang the heavy comforter on the line. Millicent was "exhausted," she said. Although she enjoyed cleaning and kept her own house very neat, when the patient asked her to clean the windows, Millicent refused, saying it was not her job (field notes from visit, May 17, 2016, Maryland).

Hope told me a similar story of declining to assume some cleaning tasks, although she also took on others. She used to care for a man who was living with his wife in an assisted-living facility. When she first arrived, cleaners came regularly. Hope then overheard a conversation between the couple, in which the wife told the husband that she would cancel the cleaning. He asked why, and she said she would do the cleaning with "the help of Hope." Hope said, "I didn't care. But then the woman wanted me to clean like the cleaners, vacuuming the pillows of the sofa and high up and dusting the lamps. I told her, 'I am a CNA [certified nursing assistant] to help with the ADLs [activities of daily living].' She got angry and called the office." The agency nurse told the patient's wife that Hope could leave for another position. The woman said, "No, no, no." I asked if the agency intervention resolved the conflict, and Hope said yes. Also, the children told their mother, "We know that Dad is difficult, so keep Hope, and we will pay for the cleaners." Still, "I chose once a week to clean the man's bathroom." He showered every day, which she noted because of the amount of labor it entailed; some patients are bathed only once or twice a week. On Fridays, she vacuumed the man's bed and the kitchen, and she cleaned her own bathroom. "We [CNAs] do light cleaning, but not heavy cleaning. So the agency was on my side" (interview, May 2, 2016, Washington, DC). However, from Hope's report, it sounded as if the agency offered to replace her with another worker who might be more amenable to the wife's demands, rather than reiterating the job description of a home health worker. Furthermore, the children also helped resolve the situation by offering to pay the costs of cleaning. Hope successfully used her job description, including its healthcare acronyms (of CNA and ADLs), to renegotiate her role in the household, although she continued to do more than was contractually required.

In complaining to me about their work, care workers sometimes used the language of slavery to justify their refusal to do certain tasks. This idiom had moral force—slavery is widely acknowledged to be wrong—and also indicated the level of denigration felt by care workers. Paulina was remarkably open about sharing her experiences. She had escaped from a difficult childhood with little education into a difficult marriage with a Ghanaian migrant in Italy. Joining him in Italy, she could not afford to buy food for her three young children, so she sent the two oldest to live with her mother in Ghana and the youngest to her sister in Germany. Leaving Italy because of the lack of work, she arrived in the United States, first working as a hairdresser in Atlanta before coming to northern New Jersey and working live-in, which she did not enjoy as much as hairdressing. Regarding home care, she told me,

> "They treat you like a slave. They think they're paying you. Every two minutes, they ask you to do something. There is a care plan [set by the nurse or social worker at the agency], so you don't have to do everything for them."

I ask, "What happens if they ask you to do too much?"

Paulina says, "You think they are sick [with a dementia], but they know what they are doing. You tell the supervisor this and this. The supervisors don't care about you. They just care about the client. It is painful. A lady [a friend] called me last night [to talk about her case]. She was with a Jewish family." Paulina paused to ask me, "Are you Jewish?"

I said I was not, with some trepidation about what was to come.

She said, "They treat you like you're a slave. To get them dressed up takes two to three hours. They say, 'Get me this, get me that.' You can't sit. Feeding them is also difficult. The job is not hard, but they make it hard.'" (phone interview, February 6, 2015)

Victoire related working for only four hours for a man who had just been discharged from the hospital. During this shift, she had not even had time to drink a glass of water. When she was asked to return the next weekend, she told the agency that she would not go there again because, as she told me and possibly the agency staff, she was not "an *esclave*," or slave (field notes from visit, March 6, 2016, Maryland). Elizabeth said about her nursing-home experience, "They regard them [the workers] as slaves. . . . It's sad. Some of us are coming from good homes, beautiful homes. But we are treated [here in the United States] like we are nothing" (interview, February 29, 2016, Maryland). Solomon said, "They may think you are a slave. They look down on the job" (interview, March 6, 2016, Maryland). The imagery of slavery and servitude is available to both patients and care workers for evaluating and commenting on the caregiving relationship. Patients want care workers to also be domestic servants, and they appreciate those who recognize themselves in that description and take on household tasks. Care workers use the language of slavery to refuse this recognition and highlight its injustice.

Most poignant for me was Kwesi's description of work. Aged sixty and from Ghana, he had previously lived in the Netherlands and the United Kingdom before coming to the United States; his wife was also a care worker in Pennsylvania. Working live-in for a couple in Maryland, Kwesi traveled with them to Florida for the winter. He told me in Twi, "This work is not good work. They don't respect you, even the ones you look after. Like a maidservant (*abaawa*), you stay with them. You don't see your wife; they don't listen to you. Even if you eat, you are not full.

This work affects your mind. It is depressing. They take us as a maid-servant. They scold (*tia*) you" (interview, February 8, 2016, Maryland). I was deeply moved by an older man describing himself through the gendered term of *abaawa*, which is associated with an adolescent girl. Doing this work overturned the respect that he felt was due by virtue of his age and gender. Kwesi's friend from the same town, through whom I had met him, thought it was time for him to retire back to Ghana because of the physical and psychological toll of the work, although his current patient was easier than his previous one, "an Alzheimer's man" (field notes from phone conversation, January 18, 2016). Kwesi did indeed seem tired of working in home care, as expressed through the term *abaawa*.

Sometimes, the care workers complained to friends and to the agency that cleaning was not part of their job description and used the language of slavery to complain about the lack of respect and the exhausting work-load. When they used such language, they signaled that they refused to be recognized in such a way. At the same time, they recognized that they might need to meet the patient halfway to get what they needed from the situation, namely the money to support their families. Here, they used the language of obedience and submission. Although other studies have described the extra tasks of care workers as a gift (Buch 2014), my interlocutors discussed it through the language of domination rather than as a freely chosen gift in the context of ongoing reciprocities.

"Being the Boss": Exerting Control by Being the Employer and Home Owner

As the care workers tell it, patients exert control not only through rac-ist insults but also through a discourse of "being the boss," which is justified by being either the employer or the homeowner. The US Con-stitution partly bases its formulation of the limited role of government through rights to property, which it seeks to protect, and thus prop-erty has functioned mythically and powerfully in Americans' views of freedom and autonomy (Nedelsky 1990). Because of the assumption of owners' rights to control their property in the United States, working in another person's house puts the worker in a subordinate position, under the constraints of the rules and regulations of that house. Generally, the care worker is expected to accommodate "the house" and its owner, who is positioned as the employer and patient simultaneously.[5] Thus, while housemates might be expected to make reciprocal adjustments to one another, that is not the case for live-in home health workers and their patients.

Thus, in care, the house can function as either an intersubjective space (Jackson 1998) or a place for the denial of intersubjectivity, in that one person's autonomous personhood reigns over another's, thus denying the other's humanity. In particular, home health workers have to adapt to the food and sleep routines of the patient, two activities most associated with home. As noted earlier, in some situations, they can cook in patients' homes; in others, they are only allowed to heat up already-prepared food. Workers also have to accommodate the sleep patterns of their patients, particularly if they go to bed late or rise early. Paulina talked about a beloved patient whose family often visited, making it hard for Paulina to get enough sleep:

> The woman had two daughters and a son. . . . They would all come [by] at 9 p.m. and drink tea and listen to music and talk. They would stay until 11 or 12 at night. I didn't know what to do. In the daytime, I can't rest. My friend said to me, "You don't have to stay with them [in the evenings, when the children come]. Go and rest during that time and tell them to call you when they are ready for their mother to go to bed." I told them [the children], "I am so tired. I will take a nap." And I did so. I was in the same room as the mother in the night. So she would yell for me, and I would never sleep. But napping in the evening, I was able to get an hour, an hour and a half, or two hours of sleep. (phone interview, February 6, 2016)

As this incident shows, friends, many of whom are also home health workers, help one another figure out how to take care of their own needs within the constraints of another's routines.

In disputes, the owner of the house sometimes makes overt claims to control what happens in the house, against the care worker's preferences. Ownership, and the accompanying claim to control the space, arise in situations of conflict (Busse and Strang 2011). For example, Jane told me about her husband, a patient: "He tells the caregivers,

'This is my house! Who are you to tell me what to do?'" Jane commented that he could not treat her similarly because she was an owner of the house too (interview, May 20, 2016, Maryland). In another example of this phenomenon, a care worker, Janet, felt unsafe when she arrived at a male patient's house for the first time and learned that he lived with his middle-aged son:

> Her bedroom was between the bedrooms of the father and son along the hallway. She decided to protect herself at night by placing a chair against the door of her bedroom. On the fourth night of her stay, at 1 a.m., the son knocked on her door and said that his father had to use the bathroom.[6] The son asked why she had placed a chair behind the door, and she responded, "I like it that way." She told me, "He said I can't do it, 'Not in my house.' So in the morning, I called the agency and said I had to get out today. It was an emergency." The agency responded so that she was able to leave the house and situation that day. (phone interview, February 6, 2015)

The son's overt claim to control the domestic space signaled to Janet that her rights to safety would not be respected.

Care workers find new cases stressful because they have to adjust to a new set of routines. Monica told me, "Sometimes when you go to someone's house, everyone is different. You feel lost and need to put one and one together" (phone conversation, February 26, 2015). Irene said, "You try not to change them. You clean the place but don't change the way they arrange their things." Such changes would have made the patients frustrated because they were used to living independently (phone interview, November 28, 2004). In discussing how she could not mention Jesus's name in a Jewish household, Elizabeth commented, "You're in their home. Whatever they say goes" (interview, February 29, 2016, Maryland). Thus, in situations other than when they feel threatened, care workers tend to accept their subordination to the patient as legitimate when it is based on the patient's ownership of the living space, something also noted by Elana Buch (2017) in her study of home health workers in Chicago. Working in another person's home, which functions as the care worker's workplace, thus serves to deprive care workers of rights they might have in a more public workplace.

I heard about far fewer incidents in which a patient used the discourse of employment rather than home ownership in a conflict. For such patients, "being the boss" did not mean following impersonal workplace regulations, which define roles and protect workers from abuse, but that they had authority and the right to command others. One such story came from an agency owner, whose interview I summarize here:

> What happened today is that in a couple married seventy years, the wife declined and went into a nursing home. An aide had gone to assist them and continues to help the man. They went to visit the wife in the nursing home today. The wife wanted to return to her room, and the husband pushed the wife in the wheelchair. There was a lip at the door, and he should have pulled the wheelchair backward, rather than forward. The aide tried to correct him, and he yelled at her, "I am the boss here. I pay the bills." She responded, "Yes, Mr. Bill. She's your wife. But the nurses on the floor released her to me. I just want you to know." He is ninety-three years old, and he told her, "I'm sorry." The nursing aide called the agency owner to inform her of this incident. My informant told the aide that the husband was experiencing "separation anxiety" from his wife, and therefore the aide should be patient with him. "It could be any other person next to him that he would take his pain out on," she said to me, "but the caregiver is the next one there. They are available, and the client has control over them. It is just natural." (interview, February 4, 2016, Maryland)

In this secondhand account, the care worker claimed the legal authority and expertise of the nurse—entrusted temporarily to the care worker—to counter the husband's claim to authority as the employer who assumes financial responsibility. She considered his right as a husband to determine his wife's care to be legitimate but did not accept his authority as her employer. The agency owner encouraged her to be compassionate to her patient and accept his impatience and irritation.

Paulina told me a story from a friend of hers in which the patient also positioned himself as the employer:

> Her friend was saying on the phone, "I can't do this." She went to take care of a man, and the man asked, "Do you know what you're here to do?" She said, "To take care of you." He said, "To clean my shit!" She said, "Why do

you say that?" He said, "I'm the boss. You have to listen to what I say. When I am inside the bathroom, you have to wait outside." Paulina told her friend to keep quiet and go home when she could. She told me, "At times you listen to people and hear sad things." (phone interview, February 6, 2015)

The man used his position as employer to justify demeaning Paulina's friend by speaking explicitly about his feces—the dirtiest and most polluting aspect of care work—perhaps metaphorically to signal all the kinds of "shit" that she had to take from him. He refused the care worker's framing of the relationship as caring for him and instead exerted his power, under which she had to respond to his actions and on his time frame. Paulina counseled her friend against complaining, but at the same time, she felt grief about this situation in particular and care workers in general.

Thus, patients try to exert control through the language of home ownership and being the boss, in addition to the language of racism and denigration. Their authority as the home owner is often taken as legitimate by care workers, who largely accept this recognition, while patients' authority as the employer is more often refused by care workers, who perhaps see the agency as the primary employer.

The Significance of Seniority

For patients, care may evoke resonances with race, slavery, and domestic service. They may seek to exert control through racist and sexist insults, humiliation, or discourses of being the boss. Likewise, African care workers liken their treatment to being domestic servants and slaves, terms used to identify the feelings and relations generated by care work. However, another form of control exists for many African care workers that is not significant for patients and their families: seniority. In care workers' eyes, older persons can legitimately direct their juniors, who owe them respect, obedience, and domestic labor. A younger person acts morally by treating an older person with respect, garnering status by acting appropriately toward older adults. By doing so, he or she also gains blessings and patronage from the older person. From the perspective of many care workers, it is the patient's seniority that justifies the care worker's care, just as children sweep or run errands for adults. Domestic service, in this perspective, is a stage in the life course, associated with childhood and adolescence, rather than a permanent status determined by race or social class.[7] As noted in anthropological work on youth in Africa, "The movement from childhood to adulthood is a movement not just between developmental positions but between positions of power, authority, and social worth" (Christiansen, Utas, and Vigh 2006, 12).

In conversations with me, care workers emphasized their patients' ages, especially those in their nineties, an advanced age that is somewhat unusual to encounter in their home countries. Such reminders of age helped them adjust emotionally to being outwardly subservient and respectful in interactions with their patients. Esther's bodily response to her patient's scolding—like a child being scolded by an adult—signaled her age status relative to a ninety-nine-year-old woman. Priscilla said, "Some people call you names while you are wiping their backs [bottoms]. But you can't say anything bad to an adult." Trying to show understanding, I responded, "Someone senior." She continued, "You also stay in the job, because of wanting your children to become more and better than you are" (phone interview, February 15, 2016). Home health workers thus preserve their self-respect by acting patiently with an abusive older person and refraining from talking back. As Priscilla clearly said, their economic needs and their hopes for their children also motivate them to accept, at least publicly, insults and names.

However, this same attentiveness to age status means that what is acceptable from an older patient is not tolerated from someone whom the worker perceives to be of the same age or younger. Many patients' children are technically senior to the care worker; a patient in her nineties might have children in their sixties or seventies, for example. However, in general, care workers feel more slighted by the actions of younger members of their patient's family. Janet talked about a particularly humiliating incident. Her patient had an appointment at the hospital. Janet was supposed to bring the patient there and meet the daughter by the hospital door at 1:30 p.m., for an appointment at the same time. Janet was waiting outside for the daughter at the right time. She said,

> I got a text message from her, saying she was there. I told her, "I'm outside." When she came, she was acting like I delayed them for the appoint-

ment at 1:30 p.m. But I was outside already. She just talked to her mother and didn't say anything to me. I followed them. The way she was talking to me!—like I was a baby. Her mom knew I was upset. I went to the bathroom to cry. The appointment with the doctor was at 1:30, so why is she coming late? Later on, the daughter called the office [of the agency], and she herself said to me, "I'm sorry." (phone interview, February 6, 2015)

Janet commented, "At times you will be treated so badly, you are crying." I made sympathetic sounds. She said, "You will cry. They won't treat you good. But you can't refuse to work because of your kids." She continued to make general reflections on care work: "When you are working for people, it is not always good. When you are doing this job, sometimes the way they treat you, you know it is not from the heart. They smile, but it is not from their heart. Some people do it from their heart. They know you are taking care of their mother or father. Others, they feel that they are paying you to do it. I don't like it. I tell the company [agency] or go to some [other] place" (phone interview, February 6, 2015). It is when children or grandchildren—those in their age cohort or younger—treat them badly that the care workers feel particularly demeaned. Such anger at the children may be a way of protecting the care worker's view of the patient as good, a necessary condition for caring for the patient. Furthermore, the patient may be more appreciative of care and more sensitive to the care worker's feelings than the children because of the intimacy generated through care. However, from the care worker's perspective, the children ought to respect the care worker for doing what would otherwise fall on them.

Although age is significant to the care workers, it is not for the patients and their families. Race and social class are permanent identity positions, transmitted through the generations, in which the care worker is in the same position relative to all members of a family; age, on the other hand, is a variable, relative position in which patients and their children are positioned differently vis-à-vis the care worker. Although care workers learn and come to understand the racial hierarchy embraced by their patients—and its force in the United States—patients do not have to learn the age hierarchy held by their care workers, perhaps because the patients are its beneficiaries. Jane, in her early seventies, wrote me an email in which she spoke explicitly about the status of older people in the United States, on the basis of what her husband's care workers from East and West Africa had told her: "In the USA, older people become invisible. It is obvious to me. I feel it and accept it as normal and do not personalize it. At big parties—younger people look right past you. You are of no interest in any dimension. As a grandparent, you are loved, and valued for your services and love to the little ones, but outside of the immediate family (e.g., cousins, etc.), you are forgettable. I am not complaining about this" (email, December 15, 2016). Thus, she felt that her invisibility as an older woman was natural. She did not use her age, but instead her status as their employer, as a way of controlling her care workers. At the same time, the care workers responded to her and her husband as older people deserving of respect. It served as an element of power in patient–care worker interactions, which care workers used to control their emotional reactions but which patients did not directly rely on to exert domination.

Recuperating Dignity

A number of psychological studies have examined responses to humiliation, which include moving away (e.g., withdrawal, avoidance, isolation), moving against (e.g., aggression, retaliation), and moving toward (e.g., affiliation, joining a gang), to create a sense of self-worth and a feeling of power (Hartling and Luchetta 1999). Three routes to recuperating dignity came up in my conversations with home health workers: leaving the case (moving away), resignification of the racism, and connecting to the home country (affiliation). These strategies are shared within the social networks of home health workers, who maintain connections to one another through phone calls, short overlaps during shift changes, and face-to-face interactions in continuing care communities. Care workers who overlap briefly in the care of a patient often exchange phone numbers so that the new care worker can ask the more experienced one questions about how to care for a particular patient. Conversations with other workers—outside the dining rooms of facilities, for example—or social intimates also provide a social interaction in which one is acknowledged as a human being.

I did not hear of explicit moments of "moving against" or retaliation, although it is natural that care workers would not have shared these with me. At the same time, leaving a case is both a moving away and moving against, in that it highlights the patient's vulnerability to the care worker and functions as retaliation, although the care workers did not speak in such terms. Leaving also forcefully dramatizes the care worker's definition of the situation: that the patient needs the care worker. After Esther said she was not returning because the patient had been so angry at her for watching Oprah, the patient said, "Don't go." No doubt, in response to Esther's exit, the patient's relatives and the agency staff scrambled to find a replacement.

Leaving

One response to assaults on dignity is leaving the patient and the case (see also Andall 2000, 158). In order to leave, live-in home health workers need a place to go that is always available, since they may need to leave in a moment of emergency or crisis, as when Janet was afraid of the patient's son. Some have a room in the house of a friend, although they are unlikely to feel "at home" there. All the live-in home health workers I have interviewed maintain some kind of landing pad in case they need to quickly escape from a humiliating or dangerous situation. For this reason, live-in home health workers do not save much on rent, if at all.

Irene reported to me that, luckily, she has never been so in need of money that she could not leave a case, but she knows other women through her social networks who have stayed in humiliating circumstances because of their financial situation. Irene said that as a care worker, you cannot be "in a desperate situation" financially, because you need to be able to "walk out." She talked about one live-in situation in which she was substituting for a seventy-two-year-old Ghanaian care worker with bad knees. The patient's house in upstate New York was so cold that she had to wear her winter coat indoors.[8] The patient told her to take the coat off. When she refused, the patient asked what she could do to send Irene back to Africa, and Irene told her to call immigration and get a witness. Irene was in fact a US citizen, and she called the patient's bluff. The patient happily asked a friend to come over, and the patient then insulted Irene. Irene felt that if they called the police, they would succeed in getting her in trouble, perhaps not with immigration but for some other reason. Irene worried that the police would believe

two senior women, so she kept quiet. Then, surprisingly, the friend be-
rated the patient for insulting Irene. The rest of the weekend went well,
because the patient left Irene alone (field notes from visit, August 14,
2005, Kumasi). Irene told this story in a spirit of self-congratulation.
Because she had been willing to leave the case, she had stood up to the
patient—and she had continued working!

Leaving came up fairly frequently as a strategy for resisting humiliation. Priscilla told me about a previous patient, who had been easy to
care for. However, the patient's daughter would drop by and was not
happy if Priscilla was just sitting. The daughter would beckon Priscilla
with her finger, as if to say, "Come here." Priscilla found that very disrespectful because the daughter was her "age mate." So she finally left
(interview, February 26, 2016, Maryland).

However, care workers sometimes feel that they have to come up with
a good reason to leave—one that will persuade the agency that they deserve another case. They are careful about what they tell agencies; if they
seem unrealistic in their expectations, they might not receive another
assignment. Essenam went to help someone "on the weekend who was a
slave master." She laughed as she told me this and explained,

> I was on my feet the whole time. The dishwasher was full of dishes, and
> he wanted me to take them out and clean them all by hand. I did it. Every
> little thing. I would finish one [task] and would do another. It took the
> smile off my face. He asked, "What's wrong?" I said, "I'm tired. I need to
> sit." He said, "I'm sorry." But five minutes later, he wanted something. I
> did four loads of laundry. I don't know if the whole week he doesn't have
> anybody. So when they called me about the following weekend, I said no.
> But the coordinator said that he likes you. So I went. I found him in bed
> smoking.[9] So this was a good reason to stop. I finished the weekend, but I
> told the coordinator, "I can't stand the smoking." She asked, "Do I put [on
> your record], 'Do not send me to that case'?" I said, "Yes. Because you are
> there, they are paying by the hour, and they want you to be on your feet
> from first to last." (interview, January 12, 2016, Maryland)

Care workers have to manage their relationship with the agency as well
as with the patient, in particular by showing that they are not refusing a
case without a good reason.

Leaving depends on the agency's ability and willingness to find a replacement. Leaving a patient without permission or before the end of one's shift can result in suspension of the care worker's license, a point emphasized forcefully in an agency orientation that I attended in November 2014. Some agencies are more responsive than others to care workers' requests to leave. Agencies struggle to find substitutes for live-in care workers because live-in work is not attractive to most workers. Sometimes workers have to invent stories of sick children and emergencies to put pressure on the agency to let them leave. In a negative feedback loop, agency staff tend to be suspicious of workers' stories and complain of workers who claim that they need to attend the funerals of an unrealistic number of parents.

Home health workers also tend not to tell their patients that they are leaving permanently, nor do they complain to patients about the inappropriate behavior that makes them want to leave. Instead, they act as if they are leaving for a short break or for personal reasons. Leaving is a sign of powerlessness consistent with the feeling of humiliation, in that one recognizes that one cannot change the situation and thus does not directly confront the patient. Judith Rollins has observed a similar practice among domestic servants, whose "ways of coping with employers' degrading treatment have been effective, then, in protecting them from the psychological damage risked by accepting employers' belief system but have not been effective in changing the behavior" (1985, 231–32). Leaving also has another cost for care workers in that it means that they lose income from not working and cannot contribute to their house-building projects or their children's well-being, jeopardizing their dignity in the other social contexts in which they operate. Finally, while leaving in response to a patient's refusal of care seems, on its face, to honor the verbal request and bow to the patient's power, it also functions as retaliation by reminding the patient of the ways they are dependent on the care worker's labor.

Resignifying Racism as Dementia

Care workers use several mechanisms to resignify racist insults, as noted in other studies (O'Leary 2016). Some care workers attribute a dementia to the patient, thus diminishing the status of the patient as mentally unfit and without agency. As Jason Rodriquez argues, agency is "a moral—and pragmatic—concept, used as a resource and deployed in the process of making meaning" (2014, 151). Others reframe the racist insult as a neutral statement of fact or reject it by laughing. Still other workers rise above the insults, generally through a religious worldview. No matter which narrative care workers use to explain this behavior, care workers have to find a way to take the sting out of racist behavior to continue caring for the patient.

Care workers account for the racist and humiliating behavior ("foul words" and "nastiness") of patients in a variety of ways. Perhaps because they are working one-on-one and outside the context of an institution such as a nursing home, the variation in interpretation seems wider than has been discussed in some studies of nursing homes (Rodriquez 2014). Following the justifications of agency staff, some invoke dementia, saying, "You are dealing with dementia. The brain is not working right," or "They don't know what they're saying," or they are not "mentally okay" (interviews in Maryland with Edem, May 25, 2016; Emily, March 3, 2016; and Micheline, May 21, 2016). Through this resignification, the status of the patient declines and the agency of the patient—in conveying anger, aggression, and the desire to control—is muted and able to be dismissed. Others use dementia more subtly, saying that while the patient must have been racist or unkind their entire lives, the dementia has destroyed social filters and inhibitions, so that the patient now expresses feelings about which he or she used to be more circumspect. For example, Julie told me, "If a client is talking that way, in a nasty way, they say it is because of dementia. It is not true. I think that they were that way before. You cannot blame dementia" (interview, May 6, 2016, Washington, DC). Still others said it was because "of the era" in which the patient grew up, thus suggesting that the passage of time will naturally take care of racism and relieving the patient of responsibility for acting in that way (interviews in Maryland with Agnes, April 23, 2016; and Micheline, May 21, 2016). Others, in response to this discourse, noted that some people from the same era do not use such language, so it must have to do with their "mindset" (phone interview with Berenice, September 8, 2014).

Many care workers brush off racist insults in ways that allow them to maintain their dignity. They do not minimize the racism, only its ability to affect them. Laughing in response is a way of demonstrating power and infantilizing the patient. The care worker cannot be hurt by what the patient says. She can treat what is intended as an insult as if it were merely a factual piece of information or a source of pride—responding, for instance, as Zainab did, "I'm black. Thank you." However, insults used to make her cry: "They would say, 'Go back to Africa. Monkey!' Now, I laugh. I say, 'Yes, I'm black'" (interview, May 27, 2016, Virginia). Belinda related, "Some [patients] are very nice, some are *nasty*. I have been called, 'You nigger.' I respond, 'I'm a nigger?'" (interview, May 14, 2016, Pennsylvania). Thus, while some refuse the terms of the recognition, as Judith Butler (1997) notes, others accept them by revaluing the names as positive and not insults. In particular, by laughing, they demonstrate that this name (and the patient) has no power to hurt them. Janet said, "At times, we cry. The way that they treat you. But we have nowhere to go. We don't have a choice. I have to laugh" (phone interview, December 31, 2014). Unable to leave, care workers use a different form of power instead: they laugh.

Care workers also frame themselves as superior to the insult and more Christian, meeting anger with love. Beza spoke about her long experiences in nursing homes: "'You nigger,' they say, 'Get out.' 'See you later,' I respond, 'I love you. See you later.'" She laughed as she related this paradigmatic incident (interview, February 1, 2016, Maryland). Valerie said, "Some people are racist, and they don't want you to touch them. You use your good heart and do it anyway without judging them" (interview, March 15, 2016, Maryland). Religious responses to care work are certainly a source of strength for some care workers, which allows them to care despite explicit racism and mistreatment.

Conclusion

One afternoon in May 2016, I attended a lecture on dementia by a geriatric psychiatrist at a memory-care unit in an assisted-living facility in Maryland. I learned many things from her presentation, namely that dementia has multiple manifestations and causes. As a result, psychiatrists are now speaking about dementias in the plural.[10] Most of the audience members, as far as I could determine from their questions and my brief conversations with them before and after the presentation, were kin caregivers of someone with a dementia. They had many questions for the speaker concerning specific drugs, making the conversation hard to follow for someone who, like me, was not familiar with the various medications. After the talk, I approached the psychiatrist with a question too sensitive to ask publicly, in this forum of patients' kin. I explained that I was doing research with African care workers and many talked about racist insults. Many blamed dementia for these insults. I asked if there was a connection. The psychiatrist surprised me with her response. She thought that African care workers experienced racism because they tended not to look people in the eyes and spoke abruptly, without conversing with the patients. All these factors made patients uneasy. So the care workers needed to be trained better, she concluded. Since there were others waiting to speak to her, I did not have a chance to follow up on her statement, but I stepped away deeply troubled by her blame of the care workers. She did not draw on her professional expertise to talk about the neurology of dementia but instead discussed the care workers' skills. I was struck by how blind she was to African care workers' experiences. Instead, she only imagined what patients felt. Although their perspectives are important too, patients' concerns about care workers are well represented in the literature and public discourse about care because of patients' higher status, education, and class and racial positioning (Michel and Oliveira 2017). Her comment strengthened my resolve to represent care workers' experiences in this book.

Racist insults are only one way by which patients exercise control over their care workers. Sexist insults, monkey analogies, references to migration status and domestic service, treating them like strangers in the house, and excluding them from social circles through invisibility are others. These are forms of recognition or lack of recognition that position care workers in particular ways, by distancing and dehumanizing them. African care workers respond to these subject positions differently, finding some legitimate and others humiliating.

These forms of recognition in interpersonal interactions signal a lack of political belonging. This is clearest in the insults about migration status, in which a care worker's formal citizenship is belied by interpersonal relations in which a patient feels he or she can threaten a care worker with deportation. However, this is also true of insults that deny African care workers' full personhood (referring to them as animals or members of another species) or that treat them as belonging to a subordinate group (domestic servants, slaves, or employees unprotected by workplace regulations). These workplace interactions indicate to African care workers that they are not fully accepted or valued in the United States, despite their formal citizenship or the fact that labor rights accrue to persons, not solely to citizens.

Care workers mainly respond to these kinds of recognition with avoidance and escape, leaving a case without clarifying to the agency or the patient why they are doing so, or putting up with the case because of the need to support their families. Sometimes, they resignify the recognition by laughing in response and framing it as a dementia, an explanation contested by other care workers. In the next interlude, we will see one other strategy for recuperating dignity: building a house in Ghana. As a result, political belonging to the home country is strengthened by the experience of care work in the United States; dignity can be recuperated in the home country, at least in care workers' imaginations.

Interlude

Longing for a House

If I have money, I would like to go home. . . . I still have a
dream: I am living in a house, with a successful husband. But
how will it happen? It is like a fantasy, but I have been seeing
it. It's like I am living it. [In the dream,] I have a successful
husband, with the kids jumping up and down on the couch,
and I am busy, just coming home from work, and I need to
clean and cook. You are not living in it, [but] you are seeing it.
So I work hard and hope. I just want to be home, with a nice
house, working hard, with an intelligent, successful husband.
—Monica, phone interview, February 26, 2014

Many home health workers told me about their longing for a house at
"home." A house in their country of origin operates in complex ways for
home care workers in the United States. First, the house serves as a sign
of success after years of degradation in others' houses. It shows that the
humiliation was worth it. A house represents the fruits of their labors.
Second, it allows them to retire. A house signifies the end of work, a
time of rest and being at home. For my interlocutors from Ghana, similar to migrants from Mexico (Pauli and Bedorf 2018; Rouse 2005; Smith
2006), home was associated with sociality—a sociality with kin enabled
by houses—in comparison to the work-dominated and time-limited
social world of the United States in general and the isolation and long
hours of home health work in particular. Anticipating an upcoming
visit to Ghana, Millicent said she would spend all her time visiting her
friends and relatives and cooking for those who visited her (field notes
from phone conversation, May 12, 2015). In her late thirties, Monica
imagined Ghana as a space for family, with happy, energetic children
and a supportive, income-generating spouse.

Although most Ghanaian migrants aim to build a house in Ghana, I argue that care workers fantasize about houses in Ghana because of their lack of autonomy and status in their work. Feelings of humiliation can be lessened through trying to attain the culturally designated goal of one's own house in Ghana. Knowing that she had a four-bedroom house in Ghana, Irene said, helped mitigate the humiliation of being restricted to a particular bathroom in her workplace in the United States. Millicent's emotional life seemed more oriented toward monitoring her construction project from afar than toward her patients. Building a house in Ghana is a kind of displacement, to use Freud's terms, a shift to a new set of goals or emotions to allay anxiety about the original, unwanted feeling—for Freud (1977), aggressive or sexual feelings. Ghanaian home health workers displace the humiliation, powerlessness, and anger they experience at work into a longing for a house of their own, "at home" in Ghana. That care workers fantasize about a house is not surprising given its significance within the economy of dignity in Ghana and in the Ghanaian diaspora. Their emotional energies and finances become oriented toward house building, and their wages go into land, cement, reinforcing iron rods, and roofing sheets. A house in Ghana is considered the polar opposite of the houses where they work: as full of sociality, rather than long hours of isolating work; as restful, as opposed to exhausting and sleepless; and as enhancing their dignity, rather than degrading it.

These psychic processes of attaining dignity in Ghana because of humiliation in the United States occur for many Ghanaian migrants in the United States, but such processes are particularly intense for care workers because of the nature of their work. Migrants orient to Ghana because of a lack of belonging in the United States, despite living and working there for thirty or forty years. Those without status in one social field can try to use their status in another field to offset that lack of status. Transnationalism provides one way that people might do so. Elena Theodorou (2011) discusses how Pontian children in Greek Cypriot primary schools use their parents' transnational actions, properties, and networks as shields against their local social marginalization. Rhacel Salazar Parreñas (2001) describes the fantasies of reversal of Filipina domestic workers in Rome and Los Angeles, as they dream of attaining higher status when they return to the Philippines. Yet there are limits on the extent to which transnationalism can reverse the lack of status abroad, if one does not gain the social and financial resources to obtain honor at home.

Most displacements are ultimately not emotionally satisfying. Fantasies may be more satisfying than messy reality (Frank 2002). Although having a house generates status, building a house involves humiliations for people already sensitive to status threats from their work. In June 2015, on a Sunday afternoon, I accompanied Millicent on a visit to her building site in Kasoa, a suburb of Accra. With us were her youngest daughter, then age twenty; her sister's son, who was overseeing the construction; and his wife. Millicent had come to Ghana for two months to supervise the building of her house and to enroll her daughter, who was living in Ghana, in SAT preparation classes in anticipation of her coming to the United States to start college. The construction of the house, associated with her future retirement at the age of sixty-five, and the launch of her youngest child into successful adulthood were Millicent's major projects. The emotional significance of these goals and the limited time available during her stay in Ghana meant she was deeply affected by the ups and downs of these projects.

The sun beat down on the scrublands of half-completed houses and empty plots of land. The sandy road we walked along was occasionally filled with large pools of water that we had to bypass by going through the tall grass on the side of the road. On the way to the construction site, dressed American-style in white culottes, sandals, and a gauzy red top, Millicent lamented all she had gone through and the expense these problems had caused: the delivery of sand along poor roads made worse by the rainy season, and an unexpectedly high water table, which meant the foundation had to be specially reinforced. To build the house, she was drawing not only on her wages from live-in work but also on an inheritance she had just received.

When we arrived, Millicent and her nephew inspected the site, pleased that the foundation had been completed the day before. Her daughter and her nephew's wife, neither of whom had visited the site before, lessened the sense of accomplishment by commenting on the small size of the plot.[1] Although I was impressed with the plot and foundation after hearing Millicent's struggles, I was less familiar with "the cultural code to 'read' the local hierarchy of wealth" (Hatch 1987, 49). They all seemed able to imagine what the three-bedroom house would

Figure 1.1: Millicent's daughter standing on the foundation of the house, June 21, 2015, Kasoa, Ghana. Photo by Cati Coe.

look like better than I could. Sufficient by my standards, by theirs, the house seemed too small for attracting dependents and indicated that Millicent was not a successful migrant. I took a picture of Millicent's daughter standing on the wall of the completed foundation. The photo seemed to me to be a wedge of time, bringing the future into the present (Nielsen 2014), because she, with her siblings, would probably inherit the completed house.

As we were leaving the building site, a muscular man called to us and ran down the road after us until we stopped and turned around. Known locally as a "land guard," who guarded plots of land from being illegally built on, he had prevented work from proceeding on the site a week or so earlier. Now he threatened to remove the workers' tools the following morning unless he was paid his protection money. Millicent's nephew placated the land guard and made a phone call to the person whom they had previously paid the equivalent of almost $1,000 to say that the land guard still needed his share of the funds. During these negotiations, Millicent complained to me—quite upset and not very quietly—about how the land guard was just taking her money without doing any work for it. In essence, she saw him as demanding money to protect us from his own capacity for violence. It was as if she were seeing the money she had accumulated over the past few years, through her many hours of labor, being frittered away before her eyes, taken without cause by a man whose only labor was to run after us on a hot day and act in bullying ways.

After the land guard left, appeased that his money would be forthcoming, the nephew's wife complained that the land guard should not have called after us without any honorific or salutation because it was disrespectful; he had used the equivalent of "Hey!" In the eyes of Millicent and her relatives, Millicent's status as a migrant did not gain her respect in this interaction but rather seemed to initiate unfair, blatant, and disrespectful attempts to gain access to her wealth. And yet, despite these depredations to her status and her hard-won financial resources, Millicent remained excited about the progress of the house. She was glad that the land guard had stopped us, rather than the workers on Monday morning. She was willing to undergo a certain level of degradation, so long as the house's progress was not delayed. And yet, she also responded with ambivalence: perhaps she would rent out the house rather than live in it because of its many problems.

Millicent's experience showed that building a house can make one subject to other kinds of humiliation or, perhaps, that one must submit to humiliation to gain status (Lucht 2011). It showed that Ghana is not always a space of sociality, characterized by visits among friends and family. Instead, Millicent spent much of her time in Ghana managing the construction project in the burning sun and feeling worried about how things were proceeding. Home health workers often seek to recoup their dignity transnationally, by building a house in Ghana. Yet as low-wage workers, they cannot afford the large plot and house expected of transnational migrants.

The retired Ghanaian home health workers whom I know end up living in Ghana. Of the three I have visited in Ghana, two lived in houses they had built, and one lived in a family house in a room given to her by her brother. All three were relaxed, happy, and supported by their kin, and so, at least in the long run, their dreams of dignity had been realized.

3

Making and Breaking Practical Kinship

Affectionate Names, Social Occasions, and the End of Life

Although home care work generates political exclusion, it also creates opportunities to produce intimate bonds that form the basis of partial political inclusion. Patients and care workers alike discuss close attachments through the language of kinship. Kinship is used as a register of intimacy and mutuality, unlike the language of racist insults and human/animal distinctions that generate social distance and exclusion. Kinship is invoked through the linguistic use of kin terms, as well as through nonlinguistic signs of kinship, such as gift giving, emotional and material support, and attendance at ritual events. For example, Beza spoke of a former patient for whom she had worked for four years, "She was like my mother, the mother I never had," and commented that she used to visit the patient's grave on every holiday until she moved away from that particular town in Pennsylvania (interview, May 18, 2016, Maryland). Beza had been fostered by a wealthy and important family in Ethiopia, for whom she had worked as a domestic servant and whom she accompanied when they relocated to the United States. For her, her biological mother existed only in her imagination; the patient whom Beza described was the mother she would have liked to have had, a mother of fantasy.

Kinship, like national belonging, is a way of sorting humanity and distinguishing those for whom one is compelled to care from those for whom one is not (Edwards and Strathern 2000; Fausto 2013). "Like all systems of subjectivation, kinship limits the possibilities of the self and its relations to others. It also produces such possibilities" (Faubion 2001, 17). Kin terms are used linguistically to indicate "intersubjective belonging" (Stasch 2009, 129) and mutuality of being: "kinsmen are persons who belong to one another, who are parts of one another, who are co-present in each other, whose lives are joined and interdependent" (Sahlins 2012, 21). This language of mutuality is formulated in genealogical terms (Shyrock 2013, 276) and is extended to include others as "a *logic* of relations which may be at work in any domain—genealogy or terminology, politics or economy, ritual or food sharing" (Hamberger 2013, 306). Thus, kinship is one way of formulating belonging, including political belonging through metaphors of blood and national brotherhood (Borneman 1992). Belonging to a family forms the basis of belonging to a nation (Deomampo 2016, 126), in which families confer citizenship and identity. There are other discourses that do so—such as race and geographic origin, as noted in chapter 2—and which are also used in political discourse to distinguish insiders from outsiders.

"Kinning" refers to the active process of making kin relations through linguistic and nonlinguistic signs (Agha 2007). Kinship is thus active, rather than given, and a verb, not a noun: to kin and, concomitantly, to de-kin. Studies of adoption illuminate processes by which adopted children are stripped of their biological parentage (de-kinned) and kinned by their adoptive parents (Howell 2006, 2007; Yngvesson 2003). Processes of care, such as feeding and coresidence, establish belonging through kinship (Carsten 1997; Marshall 1977; Weismantel 1995). Persons actively kin one another outside the norms of biological kinship, which are so hegemonic in the United States, through adoption, surrogacy, and gay and lesbian constructions of family (Howell 2006; Pande 2014; Weston 1991; Yngvesson 2003). Furthermore, kin made through biological ties can be de-kinned and drop out socially, although these processes often go unremarked upon (Edwards and Strathern 2000). Official and dominant versions of kinship in the United States highlight the ways that biological connection and formal marriage make kin, but kin terms and kin behavior are used more widely and diversely for practical ends in everyday situations (Bourdieu 1977).

It is not surprising that care would generate the feelings of intimacy and closeness that people name as kinship. My interlocutors used kin terms only to indicate positive relations, despite the fact that kin relations can certainly incur conflict and tension (Brightman 2013; Lambek 2011).[1] They could have drawn on the language of friendship, but they did not, speaking to the depth of feeling and closeness established through care. As other studies have noted (Stacey 2011), care workers' talk about kinship with patients reinforces their social value. The use of kinship idioms indicates respect for the care workers' dignity, in contrast to the use of racism or insults, which generate social distance and exclusion (as discussed in the previous chapter).

In fact, in using kin terms, differences of race and social class as cultural categories are ignored discursively rather than addressed directly. This was somewhat surprising to me, since studies of interracial and international adoption have shown how adoptive families emphasize the birth country and "birth culture" of the adopted child as part of the process of kinning, while simultaneously occluding the birth parents (Howell 2006; Leinaweaver 2013; Yngvesson 2003). For example, Norwegian parents adopting from South Korea might go for a week-long tour of South Korea with their adoptive children to give them a sense of their heritage, or they might send them to Korean language and heritage classes in Norway, organized for children adopted from Korea. Processes of kinning between home care workers and their patients, in contrast, tend to mute cultural differences. Kinning masks relations of power, even though terms of generation (e.g., parent-child) and affiliation (husband-wife) do refer to unequal relations, with different persons accorded different statuses and roles .

Kin terminology is routine between domestic servants and their employers in numerous contexts. Most domestic servants in urban Ghana, for instance, use kin terms to refer to their employer, as a sign of respect. Scholarship on domestic service has noted that kinship functions as a mechanism of control. Kinning has led to the exploitation of Filipino care workers, who did more for their patients than if they had thought of the relationship as a contractual one (Tung 2000). Therefore, some domestic servants dismiss kin terms: "Today, when employers use the ideology of family membership ('she's one of the family') to soften the edges of exploitative capitalist wage relations, workers reject it" (Colen and Sanjek 1990, 4). As these studies document, kinning in domestic service can exploit workers and empower their employers.

However, others note that domestic workers find kinning useful also. In his study of domestic servants in Nepal, Saubhagya Shah (2000) argues that kinship is a device by which a servant, who is often a child or adolescent, can orient to an unfamiliar household. David Katzman, in his history of domestic service in the United States, notes that the social-class difference between employer and employee tends to preclude a family relationship, yet domestic servants may wish otherwise:

"Servants . . . tended to feel ambiguous about depersonalizing household work. Many would have preferred a familial relationship in service if it was genuine and reciprocal" (Katzman 1978, 182). When they realized that such a relationship was not possible, they "sought the more impersonalized and specialized work roles of the industrial and commercial worlds" (183). In her study of home care workers in the United States, Tracy Karner (1998) argues that kinship idioms help both the patient and the care worker: they allow the patient to maintain a cultural ideal of family caregiving and place kin expectations on the home care worker, while giving the home care worker a sense of meaning in the work (see also Stacey 2011). Even in institutional environments such as nursing homes, care workers describe residents through the language of kinship and consider the treatment of residents "like kin" to constitute the highest form of care (Berdes and Eckert 2007; Fisher and Wallhagen 2008). Given how working for money and caring for family are ideologically distinct in the United States, even though they intersect in multiple ways (Zelizer 2005), care workers position themselves as moral human beings through the language of kinship, emphasizing that they care out of love rather than money.

What is clear is that evoking kin relations—or, in contrast, more impersonal and commodified relations—can be used by care workers and their employers in the negotiation of a relationship in different social contexts. Judith Rollins (1985) argues that intimacy between employer and domestic servant in Boston is stronger in instances of greater racial segregation, with clear differences between subordinate and superordinate, whereas more impersonal relations occur in situations of greater equality. In contrast, Shah (2000) argues that in rural areas of Nepal, servants are incorporated into households through specific kin roles, but middle-class, urban families use an ephemeral domestic-familial rhetoric, such as "a member of the family" or a "person of the home," rather than specifying a particular kin term, such as "son" or "daughter," thus maintaining class distinctions.

Kinning has a long history in domestic service, which is now being extended to and by home care workers. My interlocutors appreciated, rather than rejected, kin-like relationships. The employer-employee relationship was not a mode of protection against further demands but made them feel uncomfortable or like a commodity. Furthermore, given other experiences of humiliation and disrespect, they found kinning respectful and enjoyable (see also Liebelt 2011; Parreñas 2001). Patients, on the other hand, seemed less comfortable with kinning because of the reciprocal obligations it entailed. To my surprise, I found that male patients were more willing than female patients to kin their care workers.

At the same time, it became clear to me that African care workers are practical kin, not official kin, meaning their kinning with patients is limited. Asif Agha discusses the "tropic" (i.e., trope-like) use of kin terms in which "performed relations are partly non-congruent with presupposed roles and relations" (2007, 370). Such tropic uses need to be ratified by others in order to become routine. Care workers kinned through such tropic uses of kinship are informally and temporarily adopted, but they are never treated as equivalent to official kin. In distinguishing official from practical kin, Bourdieu cautions that one should not emphasize official kinship practices over practical ones, as this can lead to considering "a mere ideological screen as the norm of practice" (1977, 43). The reverse—of privileging practical arrangements of kinship at the expense of official ideology—also constitutes a danger, in that the social uses of practical kinship, as a way of maneuvering around the limitations of official kinship, are downplayed. Furthermore, the state is an arbiter of kinning: rights that accrue through official forms of marriage and descent, such as citizenship, do not extend to informal, temporary adoptions or marriages for the purposes of providing care, as is the case with practical kinship of care workers. Thus, practical kinship rarely leads to political belonging, both officially and through social practice, because of its temporary and contingent quality.

Between African care workers and their patients, kinning does not happen to the extent seen in studies of the international adoption of children or between nannies and their wards. First, although kin terms are used by care workers and patients, they are often used in a superficial or joking way, indicating their tropism. Second, although care workers are sometimes given the kin term of "daughter" or "wife," they are not treated as equivalent to official kin (the biological daughters or current spouse). Care workers do more daily labor and personal care than official children and do not inherit like official children. Although they may be given a substantial gift of cash or a less significant gift of other used household items, such as furniture or clothing, at the death of the patient, their inheritance is framed as a gift or an act of generosity, in contrast with the inheritance of official children, which is anticipated and even seen as an entitlement. Furthermore, the patient may make sure that "the rightful inheritors"—the official children—agree to any major gift for the care worker, because the gift comes out of their inheritance. The relationship between the care worker and the patient's official kin often—although not always—terminates upon the patient's death. Thus, this research supports Daniel Miller's assertion that, despite its flexibility and negotiability, kinship remains normative, with a "highly prescriptive set of behaviors that arise from the formal relationships constituted by kinship" (2007, 540). For example, in a study of inheritance in England, he notes that "inheritance practices show an almost obsessive concern with kinship as formal and normative" (537–38), wherein kin have primary rights over nonkin. Thus, although elder care was commodified in the households I examined, income continued to be pooled primarily by official kin, contra Immanuel Wallerstein's assertion (1991), rather than determined by care activities. Although care workers and patients used kin terms and engaged in kin behavior with one another, this was a tropic, unroutinized form of kinship, as became particularly clear with death and inheritance.

Even if the patient accepts the care worker as a special person in their private interactions, those in the patient's social network must validate that perspective—or at least act as if they do—when the patient invites care workers to special occasions on birthdays or to a restaurant, the kind of inclusion whose absence was painfully noted by care workers in chapter 2. Care workers' kin status, including their acceptance as social equals and members of the patient's social network, is not solely determined by the patient's actions but also ratified by the patient's official kin and social network. In the situations discussed here, the patient worked to secure others' acceptance of the patient's definition of the relationship; the care worker also had to negotiate the social awkwardness of these public interactions. These public affirmations of patients' mutuality with care workers are sometimes part of larger projects by patients to create a circle of support among neighbors and friends, beyond official kin (see also Buch 2017).

The kinship relationship between patients and care workers is practical, rather than official, for several reasons. From an official perspective, "adoptions" between care workers and patients remain informal because there is no way in the American legal system for adults to make one another kin outside of marriage (Borneman 1992); only children are eligible for adoption and, even then, only under certain circumstances. Thus, there can be affection and gratitude between patient and care worker, shown through the use of kinship terms, but nothing in the way of conferring citizenship, legal status, or rights to material benefits. Additionally, the presence of official kin, such as biological children or spouses, prevents patients from fully kinning their care workers. For patients, the official rights of children, grandchildren, and spouses to kinship and inheritance would be whittled down by the inclusion of new kin members. For many care workers, the fact that the work is helping them support their families similarly makes them quite pragmatic about their relationships with patients and keeps their own official kin—their children, siblings, and parents, in particular—foremost in their minds.

Finally, while all relationships will come to an end, the fact that caregiving relationships are initiated by patients' frailty means that an awareness of death and loss looms over the interactions, bringing an intensity, sweetness, and sense of meaning to the relationship, while also reminding care workers to maintain an emotional distance. Adoption is intended for the long term, and there is hope and joy in seeing a child develop in capability and personality. The elder-caregiving relationship, on the other hand, is one that entails seeing another kind of change, usually of decline and vulnerability, ultimately leading to death. This has its own sacred moments, but caring for someone who is dying is also hard, emotionally and physically. The awareness of the relationship's end makes the kinning between care workers and patients less like permanent adoption and more like surrogacy, in which a woman is pregnant for nine months with the child of another. Amrita Pande (2014), in her wonderful study of surrogacy in India, describes how surrogate mothers and biological mothers sometimes establish kin relationships with one another, a few of which continue after the baby's birth but most of which abruptly end—from the surrogate's perspective—after the baby has been born, signaling the end of the practical reasons for kinship. As Bourdieu says, "Not only does practical kinship wither away when there is no practical purpose left, but it can also conveniently be 'disowned' if the need arises" (1977, 34). Biological parents can disown the surrogate mother after the baby is born and are within their contractual rights to do so, legitimizing such a sharp break. However, Pande notes, the surrogate mothers often anticipate that the relationship will continue after birth and that they will accrue more benefits to themselves, which is one reason that they agreed to the surrogacy in the first place. For home health workers, relationships with their patients last a more variable amount of time, because death, unlike pregnancy, proceeds more unpredictably. When the patient dies, the home care worker can be either dumped like a surrogate mother, as no longer needed, or publicly acknowledged and appreciated by others. The patient's death is also when some official kin recognize the extent to which the care worker is a kin member.

Kin Terms as Care Workers Use Them: As Address, Emotional Labor, and Sign of Acceptance

Care workers use kin terms as a form of respectful address, calling older female patients "Ma" or "Mama," for example, as they would do with older women in their home countries. This naming is not kinning per se, even as it evokes affection and kinship. For most of my interlocutors, such kin terms were simply meant to be respectful of another person's seniority, rather than indicating a kinship relation. They considered such terms more affectionate and less distancing than other terms of respect, such as "Ma'am" or "Sir." However, some patients took offense at these terms, thinking that greater intimacy is meant (also see Buch 2017).

Care workers also use kin terminology to help them respond properly to the patient. As has been noted in studies of nursing-home care (Berdes and Eckert 2007; Fisher and Wallhagen 2008), care workers associate the best care with kinship and affection. Thinking of their patients as their own kin helps them do the emotional labor of being cheerful and tolerant, despite the frustrations of the job (Hochschild 2003; O'Leary 2016). When I asked Hope about her experiences as a care worker, she said that when she took care of someone, she would think, "That's my mother. I was not able to be there for my mother, so I take the client as my mother. If it is a male client, then I remember my father. It is all from my heart. I do it with love. I do it with joy" (interview, May 2, 2016, Washington, DC). Hope was finding this mode of operating particularly challenging with her current patient, who constantly insulted her, but she continued to try to do so, praying and reflecting on her actions at the end of the day. Other care workers responded similarly: "Me, myself, I take them as my own grandparents, with all my heart" (Leticia, interview, December 29, 2015, Maryland), and, "I put myself [them] in the shoes of my father or grandfather: what will I do?" (Kwadwo, phone interview, January 27, 2015). These care workers saw or tried to see their own parent or grandparent in the place of the patient, creating an equivalence between them and displacing the identity of the patient. Thus, the memory of their own kin helped them treat their patient well—kindly, calmly, and affectionately. The care workers tended not to say that the patient *was* their mother or grandfather. Instead, most but not all used analogical words (e.g., "like," "as," "in the shoes of") that showed the distinction between official and practical kin.

The care workers usually had a favorite patient from their past who treated them "like family." Relationships described in this way were often ones in which they cared for someone for years, sometimes as a live-in care worker, reflecting the ways that kinning is enabled by care over time. Most of the care workers had one such patient in their decade or more of care work; it was not experienced with every patient but generally with only one or two. They contrasted these relationships with more usual work-oriented relationships, in which they were treated like an employee and in which they did not become emotionally involved with the patient. Linda told me about a patient who had recently passed away, after four and a half years in her care: "She was like my own mother. She didn't complain. Everything you do, she thanks you. If she has an accident on herself, she says, 'Thank you, thank you'" (interview, January 11, 2016, Maryland). Thus, for Linda, the respect and recognition she received from her patient—the opposite of the humiliation discussed in the previous chapter—made the patient like her own mother.

Emmanuel, a tall, polite man in his early thirties from western Kenya, worked in home care to pay off several years' worth of tuition from an American university, which he had attended as an international student six years prior. He would receive his bachelor's degree when he had finished paying the bill. For the past six years, he had taken care of a man as a live-in care worker. Emmanuel spoke about how he became close to the patient and the patient's children over time: "We became family.

I saw them most of the time. I communicated with them. They trusted me a lot. I was in charge of most of the stuff—the appointments to fix the house [for example]." They no longer saw him as "an employee"; they were "comfortable, so they talk to you when they need to. There is full trust." After his patient died, Emmanuel continued living in the patient's house for several months afterward, while the patient's children organized its sale (interview, January 13, 2016, Maryland). In contrast to the patient who called her a monkey, Esther described her current situation in which she took care of an older couple: "You meet people who treat you like family. For the last six years, going to work I feel like I am going to my own parents' house. I cook; I am free [a Ghanaian expression meaning easy and comfortable]. I don't see it as a job" (interview, February 19, 2016, Virginia).

As has been noted in the literature on domestic service (Colen and Sanjek 1990; Tung 2000), "becoming part of the family" can also be a means of exploitation, in that it encourages workers to go above and beyond the contractual obligations of the employer-employee relationship. For my interlocutors, kinning accompanied a willingness to do more for the patient, whether cooking, cleaning, organizing appointments, shopping, and supervising home repairs. They went above and beyond their job description as a nursing assistant. The care workers did not consider these situations to be exploitative, although one could see them that way, but as a way of showing love. Justine told me that "some clients are very, very nice and understand you. They treat you like a human being. In these houses, I overwork. I take care of their house like my house" (interview, January 14, 2016, Maryland).

Paulina spoke about her previous live-in experience with a Greek patient, aged ninety-four:

> I always felt I am like her daughter. I was like her little baby. I didn't think I could do it at first. They would drink tea and leave all their things there. My friend told me, "You can't have everything 100 percent; sometimes, you get 60 percent. You take it like that. This is the family." So I took it like that. I would clean and do everything. They treated me like family. I couldn't tell them, "This is not my job." I am taking care of everyone. They would be thinking, "You are so mean" [if I did not do the work]. I have to take care of them. (phone interview, February 6, 2015)

Many adult American children, using a similar kin metaphor, would have found this arrangement unfair. They would have asked their siblings—particularly their sisters—to take on equal shares of the household labor. However, because of the significance of seniority in Ghana, as the youngest, "the baby" of the household, Paulina was able to reconcile being a daughter with doing all the household labor. As noted in chapter 2, Paulina also described how she slept badly at night, because of the nighttime needs of the patient, and so when the adult biological children would come over and chat with their mother, she would take advantage of the opportunity to lie down and rest. By assuming the household work and withdrawing during moments of kin sociality, she did not behave like family or a daughter but like a domestic servant.

Thus, the distinction between practical and official kin seems clear, despite the use of kin terms by care workers. Care workers enjoy being treated like a daughter or cooking in "their parents' house," even though these relationships only approximate, and are not equivalent to, relationships between care workers and their official kin, or between patients and their official kin. Furthermore, the kin terms that care workers use, which highlight generational differences and seniority, show the ways that hierarchy and mutuality can coexist.

Paulina was also given a new name by her former Greek patient. Usually the patient would call her "Michelle." Paulina told me she would ask her patient, "Did you forget my name?" And the patient would respond, "No. I like Michelle Obama, and I like you." Sometimes, the patient called Paulina *kori mou*, or "my daughter" in Greek. Paulina said that the patient explained the name, "You are my daughter." Her current patient had renamed her "Missy" (phone interview, January 15, 2015). Paulina's different names positioned her in different ways: (1) as the famous and admirable African American first lady—a flattering comparison that nevertheless raises the question of whether the patient thought of all black women as being similar to one another; (2) as an intimate kin member whom the patient assigned a deeply meaningful name in her native language, which was nevertheless unfamiliar and required translation for the care worker; and (3) as a servant or young person. Paulina objected to these name changes, preferring her own name, but also accepted them within the context of care. With others in her social network, she brushed off her renaming. "At times, at home," she said, "you are laughing about it."

Renaming care workers is a sign of power, reminiscent of the kind of identity stripping or social death associated with slavery, in which the slave master gave the slave a new identity (Patterson 1982). Similarly, in this context of renaming, kinning does not seem so kind but incorporates the care worker into the patient's social network and worldview, while denying the care worker's separate identity—what Jessica Benjamin (1998) would consider an aggressive act of incorporation rather than recognition of the other's separation and autonomy. However, in general, the care workers appreciated kinning, even if they worked harder for the patients they kinned and were kinned by. They labored to put themselves in a position to be kinned, which resulted in deeper and closer relationships and a sense of meaning and respect in their work.

Patients' Use of Kin Terms: Practical Adoptions and Marriages

Care workers tend to refer to patients as parents or grandparents, noting the significance of generation, in which the patients' senior status requires the care workers to offer them respect and labor. Patients, on the other hand, more usually use same-generation terms through marriage and sibling metaphors (brother, sister, wife), perhaps to smooth over the unequal care relationship through a kin relationship of greater equality.[2] A few patients use both cross-generational and cogenerational terms in tandem.

Joking about marriage and sexual relationships constitutes one way that patients use kin terms to refer to care workers. These jokes prompted me to ask care workers and agency staff about sexual harassment—a common complaint among domestic workers in Ghana (Coe 2016a), as well as in the history of domestic service in the United States, particularly for African American adolescents and women (Tucker 1988). However, the few care workers who reported being sexually harassed told me that they had been threatened not by a patient but by a kin member, such as the patient's husband or adult son. Agency staff members considered sexual harassment to be rare, although they admitted that care workers might not report all such incidents, for fear of losing their cases.

Some relationships are easier to subsume into jokes about marriage. The presumption of a heterosexual relationship means that it is more easily posited between a female care worker and a male patient. It is never a joke between two women or two men. Furthermore, marriages across social classes and age differences in the United States are more acceptable if the woman marries up in social class and age (known as hypergamy), rather than vice versa. This dominant view makes it seem acceptable for an older, wealthier male patient to marry a younger, poorer female care worker. In addition, the sexuality of older men is more accepted than that of older women.

Susan told me that her husband had said to her, "I will marry Aminata [the care worker] if you die." Susan told me she was "thrilled" with this statement because it confirmed that he really liked his main care worker, and it indicated his cognitive abilities: he knew he would need help if she died. When her husband moved into the dementia unit of the continuing care community, his relationship with Aminata continued because she worked there also, although she was not employed by him. Aminata "fuss[es] over" him, Susan told me, and he still knew her name, despite forgetting many other things. In February, in the days leading up to Valentine's Day, Aminata asked him, "Who is your valentine?" and he responded as she wished: "Aminata." Aminata had been "priming the pump" for several days for him to answer this way, said Susan (interview, April 21, 2016, Maryland). Susan only expressed pleasure that someone working in the dementia unit cared for him and kept him connected to the social world. She did not seem to be threatened by this practical kinship, perhaps in part due to her husband's physical and mental decline and because Aminata did not take it seriously but as a game, despite her own recent widowhood.

Yanna Meyer, another woman whose husband needed substantial care, told me that recently both she and the care worker, Diane, had been trying, with difficulty, to get her husband out of bed. He said, "There goes Meyer with his two women." Concerned that Diane might be offended, Yanna reported with relief that Diane understood her husband's sense of humor and laughed with them. "We all laughed," said Yanna (interview, January 7, 2016, Maryland). His joke relieved the frustration all were feeling in the moment.

Talk of marriage by older female patients poses more problems. Learning of my research project, a middle-aged woman from my mother's Quaker meeting told me about the young man caring for her husband's mother.[3] The mother-in-law "titter[ed]" to her daughter-in-law that she had a boyfriend: the care worker. Although she spoke in a loud enough voice for the care worker to hear, he did not seem to mind but just smiled. The older woman's mind was so far gone, her daughter-in-law thought, that she did not see how strange it would be for her to have a young man as a boyfriend. She just saw that he took her out to the movies and attended to her needs. The idea of a boyfriend animated her, and so the daughter-in-law saw no harm in it, particularly since the young man did not seem to mind (field notes from conversation, January 3, 2016, Maryland). Because the mother-in-law was not joking, the daughter-in-law and the care worker smiled at each other in solidarity, unlike in the situation with Yanna's husband, where everyone laughed. Furthermore, the daughter-in-law highlighted the relative ages of the care worker and the patient, which went unremarked in stories of male patients, as a way of signaling the degree of the older woman's dementia. The men who spoke about marrying their care workers, on the other hand, were viewed as lucid and socially appropriate in those moments, despite their dementias or cognitive difficulties at other times. As has been noted elsewhere (McLean 2007), the activities and interactions of other persons can support or undermine the personhood and agency of a person with a dementia. The social network of male patients generally supports the social appropriateness of their kinning, while those around female patients consider such statements to be signs of their mental decline.

I heard a third story of an implied relationship from a patient's daughter, who lived with her mother and a live-in care worker from Ghana. When the daughter was away for several days on a trip, both her brother and the care worker called to report that the mother, a widow, thought the care worker and the brother were having an affair. On hearing the news, the daughter reported: "I burst out laughing." The family "joked about it afterwards," knowing it was false (phone interview, May 31, 2016). This patient's attribution was dangerous, because of the marriages at stake. Both the son and the care worker needed reassurance that it was a ridiculous claim and they were not under suspicion. The patient kinned her care worker by imagining an affair with the son. Because both the patient and the care worker were women, the patient attributed the care worker's closeness to a male proxy, her son, rather than directly to herself. Furthermore, because both the son and the care worker were already married, the patient framed it as an affair, an illegitimate sexual relationship. The patient combined a generational relationship with an affiliative one, becoming her care worker's unofficial mother-in-law.

Because of the age differences and the ways that care workers always use a generational relationship (descent), I wondered why marriage (affiliation) comes to patients' minds. Perhaps they imagine marriage, rather than adoption, because it establishes a relationship between unrelated adults, whereas adoption is only legally possible between an adult and a minor—and even then, only under particular circumstances in which the biological parents are deemed incapable or have died (Coe 2016b). Although some care workers feel treated "like a baby," the care workers' adulthood in the eyes of patients may preclude the metaphor of adoption. Furthermore, some of the physical and intimate forms of caring and companionship (such as going to the movies together, talking and laughing together, or cooking for the patient) may feel more like a romantic relationship than a parent-child relationship. At the same time, marriage is more problematic than parenting to describe a caregiving relationship. First, according to US marriage laws, a person can have only one legal spouse at a time, whereas one can have multiple children and parents. Thus, because of existing marriages, the second female patient had to presume an affair between the care worker and her son; Yanna's husband had to joke about having two women; and Susan's husband had to raise the emotionally difficult issue of his wife's death to consider marrying Aminata. Second, the hegemony of heterosexuality requires the patient and care worker to be of different genders, whereas a model of parenthood is more flexible, allowing same-sex as well as cross-sex combinations. Since 90 percent of care workers are female, and since more women than men over the age of seventy-five receive home care assistance (Jones, Harris-Kojetin, and Valverde 2012), marriage is a problematic relationship by which to kin care workers and is most discursively available to older men cared for by women.

I learned of only one official marriage between a care worker and a patient's kin member. Binta, a divorced mother in her fifties, had married the son of a patient who had passed away. Binta's new husband, who was at least a decade older than she, became sick too, and she ended up caring for him; he was alcoholic and suicidal, she said. Meanwhile, his sister lived in their mother's house. Binta's husband had power of attorney for his mother, and he wrote his sister a letter saying that if he died, his sister should sell the house and give Binta, his wife, a portion of the proceeds.[4] However, after his death, her sister-in-law did not give Binta anything. Binta said, in her usual forceful and direct way, "I didn't take it to court, because I know that in court cases everything goes to the white people." Also, Binta collected everything from her husband's apartment and shipped it to her stepson in another city, so that she could not be blamed for taking his property. The stepson neither acknowledged receipt of these items nor thanked her. She had no relationship with her stepson, she said, because of his mother's anger against her former husband (interview, January 21, 2016, Maryland). Thus, even in a situation of formal marriage, Binta's rights as a wife were not socially recognized, in that she inherited none of her husband's property on his death and did not establish close relationships with her husband's son and sister. Furthermore, she attributed her loss of the inheritance to the racism of the US legal system, in which she would not have had a chance of success. However, the state recognized her marriage to the extent that she received US citizenship through it and was able to apply to bring over her teenage son from Guinea.

I only heard about kin terminology from patients and their kin when it was taken lightly and when the care worker was appreciated. However, care workers sometimes told me that the practical kin relationships threatened the positions of official kin. Care workers sometimes reported jealousy on the part of patients' wives as a reason why they treated the care workers in humiliating ways. An agency staff member from Sierra Leone and the agency owner, in a joint interview, commented on the complex feelings that adult children may develop about a care worker: "Sometimes children are jealous because Mom and Dad are so close to the caregivers, if they are out of state and don't have time to be close. Others are making the decisions, when they should be making the decisions. They feel guilty about this" (joint interview, May 18, 2016, Virginia). These emotional concerns by official kin, in which they feel they are not living up to their obligations, may be one reason why they deny the kinship status of care workers. This point shows that kin relationships between care workers and patients need to be recognized as significant by others to be sustained, including in public situations.

Kin Terms and Kin Behavior in Public Situations

Male patients—whether single or married—kin their care workers more often than female patients do, despite the fact that women are typically the major laborers in the work of kinning, through sending Christmas cards and keeping in touch with distant kin (Di Leonardo 1987). Women with conflictual or absent kin relationships, whether patients or care workers, are drawn to creating satisfying kin relationships through paid care. Whatever their gender, relationships with care workers can be validated or denied by others in their social network.

John, an eighty-three-year-old widower who was somewhat estranged from his two adult sons, talked about his live-in Ghanaian care worker, Joseph, repeatedly as a "brother" and once as a "soul mate" (phone conversation, January 27, 2016; visit, April 13, 2016; interview, April 22, 2016, Washington, DC). I sensed that he described Joseph in such strong language to defend his interpretation of their relationship, because he anticipated doubt and social distancing, which he had encountered elsewhere in his social network (but I hope not from me). They had been together for three years. John had worked at a high level for the federal government and in higher education, and he continued to attend prominent social and political gatherings. He invited Joseph on these outings, and he told me that Joseph often accompanied him, as if Joseph had a choice. John's friends had become familiar with Joseph; the women would hug him, John said, as a sign of Joseph's acceptance as a coequal and member of the friendship network. Joseph sat by John's side at important events, including fancy dinners. Although John emphasized these activities to me, Joseph was less enthusiastic, although he did describe his excitement at meeting Hillary Clinton and attending concerts at the Kennedy Center, a beautiful performance space in Washington, DC.

On one of these social occasions, Joseph told me, one of John's friends asked Joseph if he wanted to go back to school. Joseph responded that he could not be in the classroom and work live-in simultaneously but that he would love to become a registered nurse. Joseph reported that John overheard this conversation and responded, "Don't worry. I'll get you [in] somewhere." John recommended that Joseph research a particular online university with which John was financially and professionally connected. John called the dean and was able to obtain a 50 percent tuition reduction for Joseph, with John paying the remainder. Joseph is now studying health care, not nursing, through this university (interview with Joseph, April 22, 2016, Washington, DC). Thus, although John presented the kin relationship as one of brotherhood or soul mates, in practice it seemed like the relationship between a father and son, in that John was willing to pay for Joseph's education.

Joseph told me that he had lost his own father, a doctor, when he was in secondary school. His seven siblings were split up to live among various aunts and uncles, a typical strategy in the wake of parental death in Ghana (Coe 2013). His father's death meant the end of Joseph's education. Rather than continuing his education, Joseph decided to become a carpenter so that he could begin supporting his younger brothers and sisters, as the oldest sibling should. Later, two aunts in the United States applied for Joseph through the diversity visa lottery, and he migrated as a young man. In his forties, he has never married, but he is close to many kin members in the United States and in Ghana, including the aunts in the United States who helped direct him into nursing-assistance work. When I talked to him, he had recently reconnected with a childhood sweetheart with whom he had had a child (unbeknownst to him at the time), and his emotional life was now wrapped up not with John but with his newly discovered son and his former sweetheart, both in Ghana. Although it appeared on the surface that John replaced the father whom Joseph had lost—or at least helped him continue the education that had ended when Joseph's father died—Joseph did not present John as his father. Instead, when talking about the education that John was providing, Joseph told me, "I am like an investment to him." Joseph's education seemed more important to the highly educated John as a sign of both his own generosity and Joseph's intelligence. Joseph seemed less enamored of his online education and instead focused on his son's nursing education, about which he asked my advice.

A longtime friend of my mother's lived in the same continuing care community and knew John as an acquaintance from the dining room and through her friends. She told me that "the young man" (Joseph) did not even present himself as John's care worker but instead as his student and protégé. Having lived in Ghana herself as a member of the diplomatic corps, she knew Joseph came from Ghana. But she found their relationship odd and hard to parse. In particular, she was not sure how sick John was and how much care he needed (field notes from phone conversation, January 19, 2016). Thus, John's and Joseph's representations of their relationship within the social spaces of the continuing care community obscured John's dependence and Joseph's work role, maintaining a particular social personhood for each but making others feel uneasy and uncertain about them.

Kinning does not just go one way. In other words, it is not just the care worker who is incorporated into the patient's family or social networks; the patient can also be incorporated into the care worker's kin. The kinning between Jane, a woman in her early seventies, and Micheline, a woman in her early forties and one of Jane's husband's care workers, also became public. Jane told me that Micheline was like her sister or daughter. Micheline was somewhat unusual among my interlocutors in that financial reasons did not force her to work. Her husband, from Burkina Faso, worked for the World Bank. Micheline was a homemaker during the week but worked in home care on the weekends when her husband was free. At Micheline's request, Jane had twice attended Grandparents Day at the school of Micheline's children, aged six and eight, because the children's official grandparents were in Burkina Faso and Burundi (field notes from phone conversation with Jane, May 2, 2016). As Micheline said to me, in explanation, "Who else will go?" (interview, May 21, 2016, Maryland). I do not have any information on how the school personnel, other grandparents, or students responded to Jane's presence. However, since she had gone more than once in this capacity, it must not have felt too uncomfortable.

Practical kin relationships can be affirmed at celebrations associated with official kin, such as birthday parties, weddings, and funerals. Are care workers companions and guests equivalent to the others, or do they attend as care workers assisting an honored guest? Beza showed me photos on her phone from her weekend: she had gone to the ninetieth birthday dinner of a patient she cared for two days a week, whom she feels that no one but herself is taking care of. One photo showed the patient, her two sons (one mentally disabled and living in the same facility as his mother and one living abroad), a daughter-in-law, and a grandson, as well as the patient's lawyer, the privately hired care manager, and Beza herself (field notes from interview, May 18, 2016, Maryland). I was interested to see that Beza was not the only person of color at the party, as the son living abroad had married a woman from China. Furthermore, Beza was dressed up rather than wearing scrubs or casual clothing, as she would normally do while working. Beza also accompanied her patient on vacation to help her. In March 2017, Beza took a cruise to the Caribbean with this same patient and sent me photos of the shrimp and alcohol they consumed and the tourist sites they visited, with Beza pushing her patient in a wheelchair.

If patients attend a family event, particularly one requiring travel out of town, care workers often need to accompany them. Care workers, as practical kin, thus help their patients maintain their official kin connections at ritual occasions. One agency owner in Maryland described the first care worker she ever hired, a man from Tanzania who drove his patient to his grandchildren's bar and bat mitzvahs in New York (interview, January 20, 2016). Mariam attended the wedding of a patient's granddaughter in Cincinnati, Ohio. "We traveled together [from Maryland] in an airplane and stayed in a hotel." Like other wedding guests, Mariam gave the newlyweds a wedding gift: "I made them a nice gift of a tablecloth and napkins from Africa." However, there was some conflict with other family members about Mariam's attendance: "I heard him [the patient] tell the son that 'if Mariam doesn't go, I'm not going.'" Mariam thought that perhaps the daughter-in-law (and mother of the bride) was not happy with her presence, but the daughter-in-law never said anything about it directly to Mariam, and "they were very nice in their behavior." Mariam told me that she thinks that if she "comports" herself, "no one can throw you away." She was the "only black there" at the wedding, except for maybe the driver or photographer; on reflection, she recalled that the driver was also a black woman. Mariam sat in the reception hall with the other wedding guests, and her patient tried to make her feel welcome and equivalent to the other guests, rather than a servant. He told her, "You're an African queen. Don't wheelchair me; we can hire someone else to do it." Mariam commented to me, "He was so nice with me" (interview, March 29, 2016, Maryland).

Kwadwo similarly described to me how nice his current patient was. His patient always wanted him to have dinner with him in the dining room of the continuing care facility, even though the patient could feed himself. When Kwadwo agreed, the patient introduced Kwadwo as being from Ghana to the other residents sitting at the table, and they asked him about Ghana. Their impression was that Ghana was very far away, signaling his foreignness. The day before I talked to Kwadwo, a friend of the patient was having a birthday party, and the patient wanted Kwadwo to sit down at the birthday party. However, Kwadwo excused himself, thinking it would be too uncomfortable, and left the friends to talk amongst themselves (phone interview, July 28, 2015). Kwadwo appreciated the level of recognition he received from the patient but was also attuned to the potential for discomfort in these social occasions.

Practical kinning constitutes new forms of belonging that usually ignore class, race, and migrant/citizen identifications without addressing them directly. Exceptions include the reassuring statement from Mariam's patient that she was an African queen, when Kwadwo's country of origin became an interesting topic of conversation, and when Joseph's hopes for social mobility were raised by John's friends. New forms of kinship are practically constructed through elder care and are honored at ritual occasions, such as funerals and birthdays. Care workers, as practical kin, are included with some discomfort and tension. When multiple paid staff—such as lawyers and care managers—are treated as guests and practical kin, the incorporation of care workers, such as Beza, is easy. On the other hand, care workers' participation in public celebrations may mean that they are either the only person of color present or the only person of color who is not providing a service, as with Mariam at the wedding in Ohio. In these situations, their status as guests is challenging to sustain, requiring constant recuperation and reassurance from the care worker and patient.

Kin Behavior through the Materiality of Care: Education

Patients are much wealthier than their care workers, who often struggle financially. Patients have often retired from a profession and value education highly. Some come to know their care workers well and recognize their talents, including how their previous education and work experiences are not commensurate with their current work in the United States. Many patients would like to help their care workers become successful in the United States and encourage their further education, even to the point of paying for it. In a sense, paying for or encouraging the care worker's education allows the patient to bridge social-class differences and pass on some aspects of their own social class to their beloved care worker. It represents kin behavior of a parent to child, a nonlinguistic sign of kinship. Agency staff members confirmed that they have heard of care workers whose education was paid for by patients, although it is not common. My sense is that the younger care workers were more likely to receive gifts of education, because they were seen as having the most promise.

As described above, John was paying for Joseph's education through an online university, which allowed Joseph to simultaneously care for John and go to school. Other patients give the gift of education in their wills, so that their own care is accommodated in their lifetime and they can be certain about the financial resources for their own care before providing substantial gifts to their care worker. Deborah, who had attended university in Ghana before she came to the United States, was surprised to discover, after a beloved patient's death, that he had set aside some money for her education. Uncertain about the terms and amounts, she quickly scrambled to make use of it by enrolling in an online university. Although the money ran out after a semester, it stimulated her to continue her education in community college, which she has sustained in the year since his bequest (interview, February 18, 2016, Maryland).

Other care workers were simply verbally encouraged by their patients to pursue their education. In her early twenties, Caroline was having a rocky time finding her path. Taking a break after high school in the United States, she became a home care worker like her mother, although her mother worked live-in and Caroline worked hourly. When I met her, she had been studying at community college for three years and anticipated several more years before receiving her associate's degree. She had just switched her major to psychology from nursing. (Nursing was "the path laid out before me" by her parents, she said.) She also had to coordinate her classes with her work schedule and go to school part-time; her patient Jacob, a former journalist, accommodated her school-related absences, although he liked her better than any of his other care workers. When I had a joint conversation with Caroline and Jacob, he said he wanted her to become a doctor, given "her energy and IQ." Caroline told me in response that he was her "biggest cheerleader" (joint interview, March 2, 2016, Maryland). It was clear that although Jacob greatly appreciated Caroline's care, he also wanted her to make more of her life and that he did not value the skills involved in care work very highly.

The Symbolic End of Practical Kinship

The deaths and funerals I heard about usually created connection and recognition of the close relationship between care worker and patient. Care workers are sometimes invited to funerals and publicly acknowledged for their care. Sometimes, relationships with the children or spouses of patients continue after the patient's death; sometimes, care workers receive a large gift on the occasion of the patient's death—a symbolic portion of the inheritance. Death is a difficult time for all kin, when kin relationships shift, regenerate, or disintegrate. Likewise, they are a significant time for practical kin, such as care workers. They not only mourn a person's death but lose their job, leading to a period of financial instability that may last some months before they find another permanent, full-time case.

Some care workers maintain connections with a patient even after a transition to another care arrangement. One daughter described how as her mother declined, her mother moved from living in the daughter's house into a nursing home closer to where her son lived, an hour away. The daughter and the former care worker, Sandra, drove down to visit the mother several times in the nursing home. The mother was "thrilled to see her [Sandra]" when we came down. "She loved to talk about [Sandra] and about her home," where they had all stayed together, with Sandra and the mother sharing a bedroom. Furthermore, the care that the mother received in the nursing home could not compare to what Sandra had provided. By the time her mother died, Sandra had returned to Ghana, and the daughter let her know the news by email. "[Sandra] was one of the first persons I emailed. Emailing her was a part of the finality of my mother's death. It was an important part of my mother's passing." The daughter seemed to have trouble finding the language to describe the depth of her feeling and said simply, "She was so much a part of my mother's last days" (phone interview, May 31, 2016).

Care workers are often invited to funerals, and most attend, unless it conflicts with a new job. When one of my interlocutors died, three of her care workers attended the funeral. They were the only black people in attendance, and two sat together in the back of the room while Emily sat in the front near the deceased's husband and son, whom she knew well from her months of providing care. They were all dressed in funeral clothes, in dark-colored skirts and dresses, rather than work scrubs. Although they were not acknowledged publicly and did not speak about the deceased, as other friends did, they did not seem awkward or uncertain. They knew the deceased's friends at the funeral because the same friends had visited the patient at her house before she had died. However, the care workers clumped together in a group during the reception, and they did not linger but left quickly after a few moments, without staying to eat or drink. I also did not know where to be, flitting between my mother as a neighbor in attendance, the spouse and child of the patient, whom I knew, and Emily, the care worker I knew best (field notes from funeral, May 5, 2017, Maryland). At Sharon's funeral, Essenam was not able to attend and was not mentioned at the funeral or reception. Instead, neighbors and family friends praised Sharon's son for taking care of his mother so well, as if Essenam did not exist (field notes from funeral, August 11, 2017, Washington, DC).

I heard about care workers' attendance at funerals from patients and care workers alike. These funerals were mentioned because they were highly significant, in that the care worker played an important role, unlike the funerals I attended. Julie told me about her attendance at the funeral of a patient, where she took on the role of comforting her former patient's husband: "If I had white skin, you would have thought I was family—although I came in scrubs, so everyone knew I was an employee. He [the husband of the deceased] would turn to me and cry on my shoulder, and I would hold him. At the funeral home, I stayed by the father. He needed a shoulder to lean on, to cry on." She noted that her own husband paid the family a visit after the funeral, which "the man's children appreciated," although he could not attend the funeral itself (interview, May 6, 2016, Washington, DC).

The attendance of two live-in care workers at a funeral out of state was described to me by a friend of the deceased, who had given them a ride to the funeral and found the fact that the care workers traveled three hours to the funeral quite moving (field notes from phone conversation, January 13, 2016). I later was able to speak to one of the care workers (Linda) and to the daughter and son of the deceased. From all sides, the care workers' attendance was in line with other caring actions and consolidated the closeness between the patient's official and practical kin. The daughter of the deceased told me how pleased she was that Linda and Linda's friend, another care worker in the facility, were present at her mother's death: "I was glad that she wasn't alone." When the daughter arrived, Linda and her friend were crying. The daughter made phone calls to her siblings, and Linda informed her own children. To the daughter, Linda's phone call "speaks to the level of connection and that we were part of a broader family." What consoled the daughter about her mother's death was, "She [her mother] was with people who loved her when she died. She was not in a cold hospital setting; she was not alone. She was with people who loved her" (interview, May 24, 2016, Virginia). Linda, who had worked for the patient for more than four years, could not work for two weeks after the patient's death because it upset her so much. She would have taken more time off, but she had to return to work to pay her son's tuition at community college (interview, January 11, 2016, Maryland).

Likewise, Deborah went to the funeral of her patient and was mentioned in the obituary; as noted above, she received money for her education from this patient. She realized how much she adored her patient only when he was dying: "I cried. I cried. I prayed. I told God, 'You can't take him right now.'" She said to me, "You never realize how much you care until the person dies. 'We were close, your father and I,' I told the children, 'but I didn't know I loved him.'" After his death, she took two weeks off to mourn his death. On her next case, after four months, the patient died. "I thought, 'No, not again, not again, not again'" (interview, February 18, 2016, Maryland). All care workers I talked to had one such death that mattered deeply to them, from which they required an emotional break before they could take on another case and reconnect to another patient. However, economic pressures meant that many could not mourn for long; they had to find another case to pay their bills and support their own official kin.

Attending the funeral is also an opportunity to find a new position. Private duty aides, working on their own without an agency, have trouble finding a new job. Adimu, a charismatic private duty worker from Tanzania who is adored by her patients, described how she was passed around within a social network of senior friends and was snapped up by a new patient after one patient's funeral (field notes from visit, March 22, 2016, Maryland). Through this network, she was also able to find employment for her unauthorized friends and relatives. Kwadwo described how he was acknowledged and thanked at the funeral by the deceased's son: "He told all the people at the funeral and lunch [afterward] how if they needed a caregiver, he could assure them that I am a caregiver." The patient's son gave Kwadwo $2,000 and asked if he wanted any furniture from his father's house, but Kwadwo, who usually worked live-in, declined the offer of furniture (phone interview, April 26, 2015).

I was first clued into the significance of funerals and death by a conversation with one of the live-in home health workers with whom I had bimonthly phone calls over the course of a year. When I first talked to Monica, she was taking care of a female patient and was generally content with the situation. But because of the way she was treated when the patient passed away a few months later, she became very angry with the patient's family and with care work in general. Monica's anger arose from the fact that she was dismissed from work when her patient entered the hospital a few days before she died. Speaking to me, by chance, on the day of the patient's death, Monica said, "All the homes I have been in where the patient has died, the patient is in the hospital, you stay in the house and do everything with the family. You go to the funeral. You are a part of them. After they bury the patient, you pack up your things and you ask to leave. But for this one . . ." Monica sensed that the patient was dying, although she did not say so to the patient's daughters to protect their feelings. She wanted to be there during the patient's death because of their closeness. "I didn't get a chance to see the last breath of the woman. Perhaps it was because I was the only black person there." She was upset that she was dismissed at this significant time. Furthermore, the agency had told her about her last day rather than the patient's children communicating directly with Monica. "The agency was the one to tell me. It is like I was a total stranger. I feel I know them, but I don't." And even communication about the patient's death felt cold and impersonal. "The daughter [just] texted me and said, 'My mother is gone.' I didn't see the patient dying [as Monica had in other cases]. She was in the process of dying" (phone interview, January 2, 2015).

Monica's feelings about what happened at the patient's death made her reinterpret what had happened previously, highlighting elements of the relationship that had similarly degraded her or positioned her as "nothing." In particular, she felt like the family had treated her as an employee doing a useful job, rather than as a human being who cared for their mother, taking the place of a daughter who could not provide care. This felt disrespectful. "It's like the family needed me; that's why you accepted me. They needed me. But once they didn't need me, they dropped me. . . . But here, it's like, they needed me, but they thought she was dying and so they didn't need me. Because if they thought she would leave the hospital, they would have kept me. It's like an insult. One is not respected. I can say it: it's like an insult to me. It's like they needed me before, but now they don't." She said later in the same phone call, "It is like a slap in the face. I wanted to see this woman's funeral and where she is buried. Yes, they are . . . paying me, but I'm giving myself to her. She [the daughter] can't take care of her own mother. In the final analysis, I am not important" (phone interview, January 2, 2015). Two weeks later, she seemed even more angry: "We are human beings. I could see she wanted to mop me on the floor the first time [she met me]. It was a mansion. The daughter was the VP [vice president] for a company and had a high position. I was a black girl from Africa. She thought I was nothing; I was from Africa. So when she says 'Sit,' I have to sit. It distressed her that I had come to her mother's beautiful house to be in charge" (phone interview, January 16, 2015).

From an employer-employee standpoint, the daughter's perspective might seem totally rational: the home care worker was unnecessary once her mother had gone to the hospital with an illness from which she would not recover. But from the Monica's perspective, she saw the dismissal as an insult in which she was not considered fully human. While the patient was alive, Monica had felt appreciated—particularly by the patient, whom she described as sweet and full of gratitude. Now, Monica

MAKING AND BREAKING PRACTICAL KINSHIP | 157

looked back at the relationship with the daughter and could only see disrespect: "In this house, Thanksgiving and Christmas were nothing. You are nothing. In other places, on special occasions, people show their appreciation [with money and gifts]. Here, they didn't even say 'Happy Christmas.' . . . You have to be careful with people like this," she noted to herself as much as to me (phone interview, January 2, 2016).[5]

Monica commented, "We are not animals; we are human beings. And even animals feel things" (phone interview, January 16, 2016). Months later, even as she moved to other cases, she remained deeply hurt by what had happened with this particular patient's death. Although she had been extremely fond of the patient, she felt that the patient's children had perceived her as a household instrument (a mop) and an employee. In Monica's view, her care was reciprocated by the patient but not by the daughter, something that became visible when the patient was dying and the patient could no longer define the relationship.

Monica reacted strongly to the sudden end of kinning, in which she felt deeply insulted and demeaned, eliciting a process of exclusion, rather than inclusion, in several dimensions: (1) as an employee and not kin or, perhaps more precisely, not one who loved and was loved; (2) on the basis of social status and the wealth of the patient's family in relation to the race and geographic origin of the care worker ("I'm a black girl from Africa!" she said); and (3) on belonging to the human race, although even animals' feelings might have been acknowledged more than her own, she felt. Thus, as Bourdieu (1977) suggests, practical kin can be disowned when they are no longer needed. Amrita Pande (2014) examines a similar process of disowning of kinship in surrogacy. Although Monica wanted to remain close to her patient when her patient required hospitalization and died, the patient could no longer set the terms of the relationship. Instead, her daughters began to interpret the relationship with Monica as an employer-employee one, rather than one of mutual affection. Because of Monica's lack of formal power, through the contractual nature of the relationship, and as practical kin rather than official kin, her interpretation of and desires for the situation did not have influence. As Monica noted, this experience was unusual in her seventeen years of care work, and it was extremely painful, contributing to her desire to find a way to leave care work and return to her children in Ghana, which she did in January 2016.

Practical Kinship after Death

As noted above, one of the challenges of establishing kinship relations in home care is the constant awareness that the relationship will come to an end. Although all relationships will end—whether through death, conflict, or drifting away—in this case, the relationship is usually initiated when the patient needs assistance in some way, and thus the cognitive and physical decline of the patient—leading to physical death or the social death of dementia—cannot be ignored. Because of their numerous experiences with death, care workers are particularly alert to signs that the relationship or case will end, although they hope it will last as long as possible so that they are not out of work or have to mourn another powerful connection. In most situations, the patient's death ends the practical kinship. In extraordinary cases, such as those I describe here, kin relationships with care workers continue past the patient's death, albeit in more muted and distant ways, as if care workers were extended, official kin who lived far away.

Sometimes the knowledge of impending death elicits enormous tenderness and self-sacrifice on the part of the care worker, rather than a withdrawal for emotional protection. In a conflictual marital relationship and with two teenage sons whose education was her main goal, Valerie worked in a nursing home and in home care part-time. She told me about a Frenchman she cared for as he was dying:

> It was like they were old friends, and they talked and talked in French, with which both were more comfortable than English. He asked her to come by in the morning to prepare his breakfast. Valerie would leave her house at 6 a.m., go around the Beltway, the main highway circling Washington, DC, and stay until 1 p.m., when she went to work for an eight-hour shift in the nursing home. She would cook him lunch and dinner while she was there. He needed insulin shots and an enzyme before he ate, to absorb food. He did not like his other care workers. She did the work from the heart, she said, without getting paid; she said that the money he would pay her did not suffice to satisfy her. The family reimbursed her for the food she bought, and two family friends forced upon her, in combination, $600 for her transportation costs. He lived seven to eight months, dying in February 2014. The man was "like my husband,

my father, my brother," she said. "The whole family was like family." (field notes from visit, May 10, 2016, Maryland)

His dying in middle age lent poignancy to the relationship. After his death, Valerie's relationship with his young adult daughters continued. More than two years after his death, she reported on the recent visit of one of his daughters to the United States:

> His two daughters, age twenty-four and twenty-eight, are in France. The younger one visited two weeks ago and called Valerie to say she was in town. Valerie came by with a plate of food—fish and vegetable kebabs—because the daughter always liked Valerie's food and does not like meat. Unfortunately, when Valerie arrived, the daughter was on a quick errand to the supermarket, and Valerie, on her way to work, could not wait, so she simply left the food. The daughter later thanked her, sending a photo of the plate, which Valerie showed me, and a meaningful note about how "heartwarming" the food was. (field notes from visit, May 10, 2016, Maryland)

As described in earlier chapters, cooking familiar food and having it satisfy another person marks a close connection. Furthermore, through the plate of food, Valerie signaled her knowledge of the daughter's tastes and thus their intimacy. It was a maternal act and sign of care.

Other care workers described maintaining relationships with a particular patient's relatives, through a yearly lunch or ritual phone calls, generally initiated by the official kin. Mavis described a relative of a patient who still got in touch, seven years after the patient's death (interview, March 17, 2016, Maryland). The children of Victoire's former patient, for whom she cared for two years, still called her (interview, March 6, 2016, Maryland). Yaw received Christmas cards from the relatives of a patient from twenty years earlier (interview, May 14, 2016, Pennsylvania). Ohemmea, a queen mother for a small, impoverished town in Ghana who supported numerous children and grandchildren there, described a strenuous situation wherein the patient could not sleep and wanted to go to the bathroom every two hours at night. Two other care workers had already abandoned this case as too difficult. The patient lived with her husband and her daughter, who had just had a child. Ohemmea said she was just supposed to look after the patient and not the rest of the family. However, when the laundry basket overflowed, not just with the patient's clothes, she washed all the laundry. The patient's husband asked her about it, and she told him it was not a problem. When they had finished eating, she washed everyone's dishes nicely, until the day that the patient died. She also looked after the grandchild and gave the baby cloth as a present, as is customary in Ghana, which surprised the patient's husband. They called her after the patient's death, and when they found out that she lived nearby, he and his grandchild came by for a visit. Thus, she saw her willingness to step in to care for everyone in the household as eliciting affection in response, including a personal visit by the patient's widower and grandchild (summary of phone interview, February 19, 2015).

Binta also told me about being invited to tea by a couple, relatives of a patient who had since passed away. They asked about her goals for 2016, and she replied that she wanted to go on pilgrimage to Mecca, as is a Muslim's duty, but did not have the money. Both of her parents had gone on the hajj to Mecca; she had paid for her mother's trip from her home care work, while her father had financed himself. The couple asked for another goal, and she said to get "a good job," like the white-collar job she had had in Guinea. The next day, the couple called to tell her how well she had taken care of "our mother, like your mother." Apparently, they had installed a hidden camera, which showed them Binta's good care. (Binta did not mind the camera when she heard of it.) They offered to pay for her transportation to Mecca, as well as her food during the hajj, perhaps because it would be less complicated than launching Binta into the same social class she had occupied in Guinea. Binta cried and accepted their offer. The only obstacle was that Binta had to pay off some debts before she went, because one cannot go on the hajj with debt, but she felt confident she would (interview, January 21, 2016, Maryland).

Despite these stories, most care workers and patients' relatives described the relationship as ending at death. Sometime after her husband died, a woman told me about calling one important care worker when she was moving out of the house and into a continuing care community. This particular care worker had organized the other care workers and served as the general housekeeper or manager of the care in the household during her husband's illness. This care worker was present in the house on the day her husband died, came the following day to help her, and attended the funeral. But, she described, all her husband's care workers went on to "the next thing in their lives" (interview, January 14, 2016, Maryland). Suddenly, all those who supported her daily activities disappeared. Thus, if kinship existed in the caregiving relationship, it tended to end at the death of the patient or, as Monica found out, a little bit before, when the relatives no longer saw the practicality of the kin relationship.

Practical Inheritance for Practical Kin

When the patient dies, care workers often receive something, whether cash, used household goods, or even cars or houses. This is a token, a gift acknowledging the emotional depth of the practical kinship, but not a true inheritance equivalent to what the official kin receive. Furthermore, care workers do not have any right to these gifts; official kin may contest them. I heard about these gifts from agency staff and care workers.

From an agency staff member, I learned that the Tanzanian care worker mentioned above, who drove his patient long distances to celebrations of his grandchildren, received an antique car "with the consent of the client's two sons." The care worker sold this car to help supply water to his hometown in Tanzania and built a clinic and a church, said the agency owner. She also commented, "Some clients want to leave their houses to their caregivers, and the adult children are up in arms. The clients sign an agreement with us not to give everything to the caregiver" (interview, January 20, 2016, Maryland). Another agency owner reported that a judge willed his modest house to his care worker when he and his wife moved out of the house to live nearer to their daughter, an attorney. "They were all clear on it" (interview, March 15, 2016, Maryland). Their occupations were mentioned, I think, to indicate that everyone, including the daughter, was wealthy enough to not need the "modest" house.

Care workers do not expect houses or cars, but they do anticipate a large cash gift from wealthy families. This gift tides care workers over for the few weeks or months before they receive another permanent case. Sometimes, they use the gift to make a major purchase, such as a house or a car. From care workers, I usually heard of gifts of several thousand dollars, but one agency owner reported that he knew of a gift of over $50,000 (interview, March 17, 2016, Maryland). One reason that care workers told me of their patient's wealth, as measured by the size of their house and their former occupation, was that they expected, sometimes erroneously, a wealthy person to be more generous. As noted elsewhere in the literature on domestic service, the attraction to wealthy employers is due to the potential rewards of high salaries and fringe benefits (Dill 1994). It is a measure of how the relationship retains personalized elements despite the formalization and contracts generated by the agencies.

For example, Mariam took care of a former psychiatrist who was very emotionally and financially generous with her, including calling her an African queen at his granddaughter's wedding. "He was rich," she told me, noting that he had a two-bedroom apartment in the independent-living facility, rather than the cheaper one-bedroom option. During his lifetime, he had paid for her groceries when they shopped together. "He loved me. He said I was like no one in the family, because I cared for him." On his birthday, he would give her $5,000. With a son who was a (wealthy) doctor and a daughter who was a (middle-class) teacher, he told Mariam that if his son-in-law had been rich, Mariam would be rich, but as it was, his daughter and grandchildren needed to inherit his fortune. He wanted to buy Mariam a house, for which she would pay him back without interest. "But it never happened because the children didn't like it. He left me money, but I never got it. I know how much he loved me." She knew he had left her money because after the funeral, the son told her that after the lawyer talked to the daughter, she would call Mariam. But the daughter never called. One day, as they were packing away the patient's things, the daughter asked Mariam, "What shall I do?" Mariam said she would think about it, and she made up a figure. "I came up with: 'I have worked for him for three years, so please give me three months' pay.' That seemed reasonable. She gave me $3,500" (interview, March 19, 2017, Maryland). Mariam did not feel that this gift equaled what her former patient willed to her, given his previous generosity, but it was all that she felt she could legitimately claim from the official kin.

If care workers do not receive a cash gift upon their patient's death, then they feel unappreciated and disappointed. Millicent complained about one patient's death, mainly because she thought the family deliberately killed her patient by withholding food and water. In addition, despite having a large house, they did not give her "a penny." Normally, she told me, she gets $5,000–$10,000 on a death. But in this particular case, the money was "getting finished," so the family wanted the patient to die, she thought. Millicent was also not invited to the funeral, which was unusual in her experience (field notes from phone conversation, December 4, 2016). Although Monica did not mention it, the lack of a gift may also have played a role in Monica's disenchantment with her patient's death, given that she thought both her patient and the daughter were well to do.

Sometimes, a patient's relatives are aware that the patient's death has created unemployment. Needing help after the patient's death, they pay for the care worker to sort and tidy the patient's residence. Many care workers are offered used household goods and furniture, which they generally ship to their home countries or distribute among their networks. Some are allowed to live rent-free in the apartment or house until the family has a chance to sell it; such was the situation of Regina when I first met her in 2008. Because of the depressed housing market in Connecticut at the time, the family waited more than a year to sell the house. Regina appreciated saving money on rent, although she still had to pay the utility bills through the winter. However, these acts are gifts rather than obligations, even though care workers may come to expect them, just as waitstaff expect tips.

Inheritance is significant not only because it differentiates official from practical kin. It is also a key way that wealth accumulates (Piketty 2014). Care workers' partial inheritance from their richer patients helps distribute this wealth more widely. Sometimes, the gift is large enough that care workers can use it to help create a little upward mobility by investing in a house in the United States or in Ghana or to be a patron in their hometown through providing water or other services. Practical inheritance depends on the generosity of the patient and their official kin and can easily be denied or reduced. If care workers were accepted as official kin rather than simply practical kin, such inheritance would make a substantial difference in their lives, including changing their class position. Through their construction as temporary and contingent kin, care workers' inheritance of the social class of their patients—whether materially or through education—is illusive.

Conclusion: Care Workers as Practical Kin

This chapter has focused on the ways that care creates belonging, in the sense of attachments, identifications, and routines. Home care brings workers into the most vulnerable and intimate of personal situations, which can create emotional connections and a sense of interdependence. Processual approaches to kinship have highlighted the significance of care in making, breaking, and negotiating kin relations. Patients and care workers learn to share bodily, familiar routines concerning food and leisure activities, as I describe in the next interlude, just as parents, children, and spouses socialize one another into particular tastes and routines.

In the case of African care workers in the United States, however, I argue that care makes practical not official kin. Care workers sometimes receive a financial gift or support for their education, which approximates a parent's bequest to a child but is not equivalent to it in either emotional or monetary terms. Care workers and patients alike use kin terms such as "younger brother" (said defensively), "second wife" (said jokingly), or "like my husband, my father, my brother," which indicates its tropism and lack of social ratification. Multiple terms are used, indicating social participants' uncertainty in using kin terms at all to represent the care relationship.

Time is central to processes that create belonging. Care practices become routinized over long periods of time—months, if not years—and identities stabilize. People grow accustomed to one another and are better able to anticipate and respond to one another, even as both are changing over time. Among my interlocutors, practical kin relationships arose only in care situations that lasted more than a year. Time is also important because the death of a patient usually causes a sudden end to the practical kin relationships, with only a few family members and care workers willing to sustain these relationships at a lower pitch of intimacy—through an occasional meeting, Christmas card, or phone call.

As Helma Lutz (1993) has pointed out, we expect the integration of migrants to occur in part through workforce participation, but a racialized labor market and hierarchical places of employment often impede such integration. Here, I have discussed cases in which care workers felt included through kinning, in which the migrant care worker came to participate in the life of a more established resident through bonds of mutual affection and a sense of interdependence, although not always as a coequal. These incorporations into another's life and the outreach to care workers' own official kin make African care workers feel appreciated and welcome in the United States. Kinning is generally not an occasion for material or emotional exploitation (Stacey 2011). Instead, care workers use a large gift to support their hometown or as a down payment on a house in the United States. The gift can also set a few on a potential path of upward mobility out of home care through further education. Kinning becomes a way by which intimacy can be recognized in relations of differing power and privilege.

However, the political belonging generated by kinning between care workers and patients is limited. This kinning is practical, not official; it is undercut by laughter, the lack of formal pathways to cement and publicize the relationship, the reactions of other friends and relatives to the care worker's presence, and the care worker's obligations to support their own official kin. The ending of practical kinship makes some care workers feel politically excluded—Binta, by a court system that she felt would never rule on her behalf, and Monica, who called herself a "black girl from Africa" as a result of being suddenly dropped from a case as her patient's health declined. Care workers similarly evaluate the reciprocity in their relationships with patients, the topic of chapter 4, as a sign of their belonging and whether they will receive fair treatment in the United States in response to their care.

Interlude

Playing Tennis

As my mother and I arrived at the tennis courts of the local elementary school one balmy Saturday afternoon in March 2016, I recognized Caroline and her patient, Jacob, playing together on one of the courts. I had met with them together once to talk about my research and home care. Jacob was a tall slender man of ninety years and recent widower. Caroline was a strikingly beautiful young woman from Ghana of similar height. After greeting them cheerfully, my mother and I settled in to play on the second tennis court. Since I rarely had the opportunity to play tennis, a lot of balls rolled and bounced between the two courts. Caroline was practicing her serve, with Jacob returning it. Although Jacob missed a lot of shots and moved very slowly, they seemed to be having a wonderful time in the breeze and bright sun. They stayed at least half an hour. Both were wearing athletic clothing, with Caroline's tennis outfit particularly new and colorful.

Seeing a care worker from Ghana play tennis with her patient surprised me. First, most patients requiring care workers are not in good enough physical health to play tennis. Second, my experience in Ghana had taught me that very few Ghanaian women are athletic. Men prefer boxing and soccer, although some upper-middle-class men and women patronize the few new fitness clubs for jogging and weight lifting that have opened in the capital. Furthermore, most of the care workers I knew were consumed by work. For these reasons, it was surprising that Caroline had learned a sport like tennis.

One of the things that kin do is shape one another. They influence one another's tastes—in food, music, and leisure activities—by introducing them and making these activities meaningful by spending time doing them together. This shaping of one's bodily dispositions, or "habitus" (Bourdieu and Passeron 1990), occurs not only in childhood but across the life span. The inculcation of bodily dispositions happens over time, through practice and routinized behavior. It thus represents a deep level of intimacy, which calling someone "daughter" or "spouse" may allude to. I was particularly sensitive to this point regarding tennis; a member of my family could not have chosen another sport.

Because of the ways that they were raised and the experiences they have had over their lifetimes, care workers and patients often tend to like to do different things. They enjoy different kinds of food, as noted earlier. Rather than mutual accommodation of differences, care workers are expected to adopt their patient's routines and habits. One man appreciated Hope's care for his hostile wife but was disappointed that Hope was not interested in learning card games. He called gin rummy "a simple game," but Hope did not remember the rules unless he was also playing and reminding her of how to play. He was disappointed that it was hard for care workers "to take on active things," such as puzzles or cards, with his wife. Usually, they just watched television with her. His concern stemmed from his desire to staunch his wife's cognitive decline by keeping her "intellectually active." He complained, mildly, "I do have to do a lot of stuff that caregivers who were more American might do" (interview, May 2, 2016, Washington, DC).

The issue is not simply that of being American but also having a particular class sensibility. Gin rummy is like tennis for me in its embedding in family routines and interactions; I can recall hours of playing gin rummy with my cousins during rainy summer days. The physical and leisure activities that patients tend to mention from the past are those of the upper-middle class or wealthy: tennis, swimming, horseback riding, classical music concerts, crossword puzzles, and jigsaw puzzles. Patients have become accustomed, and have learned to value, these activities over their lifetimes, sometimes through their spouse or children or sometimes in their own childhoods. Age has eroded their ability to do many of the leisure activities they did earlier in their lifetimes, depriving them of pleasures they have learned to enjoy and requiring them to learn new ones.

Jacob was exceptionally physically healthy as a ninety-year-old. He swam every day at his continuing care community's swimming pool and took exercise classes. He had previously taught swimming and been a lifeguard, in addition to playing tennis regularly. Mentally, however, he was beginning to forget things and became agitated about doing so, hence his need for Caroline's care. Jacob's daughter, Lucy, felt that his overinflated sense of himself as fit derived from his dementia (interview, May 21, 2016, Maryland). From my perspective, physical activity warded off his anxiety about cognitive decline, about which he spoke and joked almost constantly.

I was curious about why Caroline decided to learn to play tennis. Caroline explained, in a private interview, that one day she was complaining to Jacob about not getting exercise, perhaps because Jacob always talked about his physical activity. Jacob encouraged her to exercise more. She began to consider the possibilities. Caroline had played tennis and volleyball in high school in the United States, and Jacob advised her that tennis would be a better option because volleyball was a team sport. Plus, Caroline knew that Jacob had once played tennis. Caroline began taking tennis lessons; when she finished one set of lessons, she began another. Tennis, like other sports, requires practice to learn, and she put in the time and energy. "I love it," she told me (interview, July 12, 2016, Maryland). When I visited them in Jacob's apartment in a very wealthy continuing care community, Caroline was less serious about tennis because they interacted through banter, with Jacob assuming an avuncular role. She told me then that she had started learning tennis because she looked so athletic that people thought she must be physically active; besides, she looked good in tennis clothes. When I asked them about the important qualities of nursing assistants, Jacob mentioned that one requirement is that nursing assistants not want to be rich, and Caroline joked in response, "Everyone needs money to buy tennis racquets" (joint interview, March 23, 2016, Maryland). She reconfigured leisure activities as not solely the domain of the wealthy but also the right of care workers.

Four months later, in July, Caroline told me that they had played again on another public court, and she was continuing her tennis lessons. During the same summer, Jacob began teaching Caroline to swim in the nearby YMCA; as a care worker, she could not use the swimming pool in his continuing care community. I wanted to join them one day for a swimming lesson, but our schedules never coincided. In March 2017, when I visited them again, they had stopped playing tennis together but hoped to resume their swimming lessons when the weather again warmed.

Caroline's adoption of Jacob's sports enabled them to have joint activities that they both enjoyed. She supported a particular kind of personhood for him, in which he was fit and had something to offer, such as teaching her how to swim or returning her practice serves. She was not solely helping him get through his daily activities and reminding him about the loss of his abilities. For her part, she could look attractive according to American aesthetics of beauty that emphasize athleticism and fitness. She could assume the leisure activities of another social class, that of her patients. Furthermore, their joint physical activities seemed to be an outgrowth of their practical kinship. Caroline had cared for Jacob's wife for a year, until she passed away, at which point she shifted to Jacob's care. He was still in mourning, and Caroline, who knew his wife very well, could participate in such mourning, telling stories about his wife and his devotion to her. Caroline joked one day in front of Jacob, "I was indoctrinated into the family" (joint interview, March 2, 2016). Another time, she commented that Jacob and his wife were "extended family." Caroline reported that Jacob's wife once said that Caroline was better than family; this was the best compliment she ever got (joint interview, March 16, 2016). Jacob's daughter, Lucy, commented that sometimes Caroline said that she was the "adopted daughter" in contrast to herself, his biological daughter who was very involved in managing his affairs and cared for him on the weekends (interview, May 21, 2016). Joint leisure activities emerged from the practical kinship that Caroline struggled to find the right words to describe.

I met only one other care worker who seemed to take leisure as seriously as Caroline and who considered the money she earned to be appropriate for purchasing fun. Deborah was also from Ghana, but unlike Caroline, she had arrived in the United States not as an adolescent joining her family but alone in her early twenties. From a middle-class family in Ghana, she made sure to take time off from work to travel with friends to Philadelphia, Florida, and New York City (field notes from phone conversations, December 5, 2016, and December 31, 2017; field notes from visit, March 17, 2017, Maryland). She explained that she had learned about the importance of vacations from her care work; her older patients taught her to "enjoy your life" because time goes by very quickly (interview, February 18, 2016, Maryland). Caroline and Deborah seemed to be assuming a different class sensibility than the migrant one

I knew, one in which having fun through travel and exercise was important, even if it meant spending hard-earned money. They were adopting the habitus of the middle- or upper-middle class of their patients. In this, they were somewhat unusual.

More common was simply a sharing of perspectives and histories between care workers and patients. Some care workers talked about learning how to succeed in America from their patients. Micheline said, "I meet different people with different backgrounds. I am not from here. I learn American culture. I bring information back to my husband." I asked for an example. She responded, "How to invest in college education for your children. All the loans; all the travel. For example, one client said she had taken her children to all the fifty states so the children can see. We can [do the same] little by little. We went to the Grand Canyon last year. We are open." Travel is one of the forms of cultural capital associated with the middle and upper-middle class in the United States (Lamont 1992). Furthermore, on the basis of conversations with her patients about finances, Micheline and her husband also opened a college fund for their son who was born in the United States. She concluded, "We know we need good credit. I know a lot of immigrants who don't know the system. People are willing to share different experiences, what worked and what didn't" (interview, May 21, 2016, Maryland). Thus, Micheline seemed to be using her patients' experiences and advice to help her raise children in the United States. She felt as if she was learning "the system" in the United States, particularly how to become upwardly mobile through her children's education, both in school and through vacation travel.

Some particularly open and curious patients have their horizons expanded through their care workers, but in ways that are less routine altering. Jane, for example, learned of the horrors of genocide in Burundi from Micheline (field notes from phone conversation, May 20, 2016). She expanded her knowledge of foreign events, but such knowledge did not change her practices or behaviors. Although she considered such knowledge interesting and mind expanding, she did not treat it as significant to her everyday life. In general, patients do not know very much about their care workers and do not care to learn more. Only occasionally will they taste the care workers' food as a sign of their openness and flexibility.

Thus, care work provides some opportunities for adoption of another person's way of life, reinforcing the kinning between care workers and their patients, shown most particularly between Caroline and Jacob. Younger female care workers seem more open to reshaping their routines according to direction from their patients, including taking on some aspects of a middle-class or upper-middle-class American habitus of travel, college funds, and exercise seen as fun, healthy, and beauty making. Patients, on the other hand, learn very little from their care workers. Thus, unlike kinning more generally, the accommodation to new leisure routines seems to only happen in one direction, when it happens at all.

4

Reciprocity

Who Deserves What, and on What Grounds?

Over the summer of 2016, Jane's husband, a tall, slim man in his early eighties, grew more violent toward his care workers. Jane explored putting her husband into a memory-care unit designed to handle patients with dementia, at the cost of $125,000 a year.[1] However, none would take him because they did not have the staffing he required and could not handle his aggression, despite its prevalence among people with a dementia.[2] Jane decided to rent a separate apartment for him, while she remained in their current residence, and hire round-the-clock care, which would be cheaper than memory care. However, after a six-week stay in a facility to monitor a change in his dementia medication, where he was mostly restrained, he returned home with problems with balance and urination, the latter resulting in a new catheter. After the stay, he needed five times as many care workers, including two care workers at all times to change the catheter safely because he would not cooperate with the procedure. In a phone call in March 2017, Jane said that for the past six months she had been running "a small business" of ten care workers (field notes from phone conversation, March 5, 2017).

Two weeks later, over lunch in a small café in Maryland, she explained further: the original two—Micheline and Edem—had cared for her husband for three years and were from an agency; the rest were recruited privately through word of mouth. She told me she gave the private workers W-2 forms and paid their Social Security contributions. She paid the new private care workers $22 an hour, she said, because she was formerly an economist and wanted the care workers to be happy, but she did not know whether Micheline and Edem were jealous of the new care workers, whose wages were higher than their own. She knew that $22 an hour was above the going rate, because one of them also worked for a continuing care community at $12.50 an hour. "It is costing a fortune," she said. "He [her husband] is bleeding money," about $500,000 a year, she estimated, but he had the money to make the current arrangement work for another year or so.[3] Not only did his care feel like a small business in terms of the paperwork it generated, but Jane also relied on the skills she had used to manage others in her career. She said that she had always disciplined others awkwardly, in part because her supervisory persona was incompatible with her gender socialization. She did not mind using her work skills in retirement, but she did not like managing others (field notes from visit, March 16, 2017, Maryland).

She was frustrated too because she expected better care, given that she was paying above the normal (albeit low) wage rate and spending so much of her husband's savings. The most important care worker, Edem, was "indispensable" as he was the only one willing to pull her husband upright if he began falling while walking or standing. Edem, however, would not cook. Although Jane had managed to live separately from her husband, she also wanted to be relieved of the burden of cooking for him. Furthermore, Edem was becoming "demanding," as she put it.

Jane had told me ten months earlier that the two original care workers impressed her with their level of education and intellectual curiosity: Edem, with a master's degree in physics, and Micheline, with a master's in actuarial science. Jane described herself then as "running my own [intellectual] salon" and having "ethereal conversations" about mathematics, philosophy, and religion. She much preferred a salon to a small business. Jane once mentioned a particular mathematical formula (Poisson distribution) to Micheline, who responded by saying how wonderful it was. Jane thought "this formula is as close to God as one could get," and Micheline's recognition of its beauty thrilled her (field notes from phone conversation, May 2, 2016). As for Edem, he wanted to write a book about physics and God, in French. He had asked Jane to buy him a French textbook on quantum mechanics, which cost $250. Jane had been willing to buy him physics materials in the past, but she found the price of this textbook too steep. This morning, she told me over lunch, as she was leaving the house, she told him she could buy him a Kindle for $50 and download a mystery novel for him. Edem immediately dismissed this idea, even before she stopped talking, and she felt annoyed by his quick rejection without even considering her idea. He noticed her annoyance, she told me, and his face showed he was sorry. But Jane also felt "played" by Edem. She promised him she would get him the textbook for his birthday, which was in January, nine months away (field notes from visit, March 16, 2017, Maryland).

As we continued to eat our sandwiches, Jane described her exploration of religion. Raised and confirmed in a mainline Protestant faith, she did not currently have faith in God. However, she had been reading about religion recently, with enthusiasm. She was particularly excited by a book by Francis Collins, the director of the National Institutes of Health, who said that Christians should accept evolution (Collins 2006), which she discussed with Edem, who is also fascinated by questions of religion and science. When she said that 42 percent of Americans believe in creationism and that they are probably Trump voters, she noticed Micheline's face clouding over. She asked Micheline if she was a creationist, and Micheline responded affirmatively. Jane thought to herself, "Don't judge me." I suspect that Micheline also felt judged in this moment regarding her religious faith, which was highly important to her personally and in her care work. Micheline did not seem disrespectful, at least in Jane's portrayal of the situation to me, but Jane felt, "Here I am, paying $5,000 [a month to a care worker], and I feel judged." That her money did not buy social acceptance irritated her. She had attained a level of intimacy with her care workers: she shared her intellectual and emotional life with them, perhaps in part due to the mental and emotional absence of her husband, but they were neither her friends with common worldviews and interests nor in a position to speak their minds freely. The employer-employee relationship gave Jane more power in the discussion, to lead it in particular ways, although she wished for more power than she had. Jane expected the care workers to be servants, who attended to her interests and supported her personhood, in addition to helping her husband. But she also wished that they could be friends and book club members who could participate as intellectual interlocutors.

As Jane's situation illustrates, if the care workers' main emotional response to their work is humiliation, the main emotion of patients and their kin is irritation. The cost of care is paramount to both sides: patients do not feel their money buys enough, and care workers do not feel rewarded enough for their labor. On both sides, unhappiness with the caregiving relationship leads to the claim that they do not receive what they deserve. Annemarie Mol, Ingunn Moser, and Jeannette Pols argue that "care implies a negotiation" about how different definitions of the good "might coexist in a given, specific, local practice," which is achieved through "practical tinkering" and "attentive experimentation" (2016b 13; see also Buch 2015b). In care, important resources such as money, time, engagement, dignity, and affection are negotiated in practice between patients, their kin, and their care workers. The exchanges around these valuable resources become central to evaluating the quality of the caregiving relationship. As Viviana Zelizer puts it, "In negotiating the economic conditions of care, participants are also defining meaningful social relations" (2005, 207). This chapter examines conflicts in the care relationship due to differences in expectations about the economic and psychological reciprocities entailed by the relationship. What is appropriate? Who deserves what? These material concerns have psychic effects: feeling judged or disrespected.

The economic and the noneconomic are intertwined. Both recognition—as expressed in Jane's sense of being judged—and material benefits are forms of expected reciprocity. Although in Western discourse love is often considered separate from money, money is often entangled in issues of love, and people express love through financial gifts and exchanges (Zelizer 2005). In contrast, in Ghana, care is expressed materially quite explicitly (Coe 2011), in that gifts of clothes and money signal emotional closeness and commitment to the receiver's well-being. Drawing on Marshall Sahlins's (2012) definition of kinship as mutuality of being, I would argue that the mutuality integral to belonging requires ongoing reciprocal exchanges that support feelings of interdependence and interest in the other's well-being. Recognition is a key element being exchanged in these interpersonal relationships, and redistribution of material items is taken as symbolic of positive forms of recognition (see also Robbins 2009). Like Honneth (2003), I view redistribution as a subcategory of recognition, particularly in the interpersonal relations discussed here, although also more widely, in the sense that the distribution of Medicare and Social Security relies on the recognition of senior citizens as having particular needs. For home care workers, redistribution marks appreciation within ongoing interpersonal relationships organized around care.

Also at stake is existential reciprocity, a concept developed by Hans Lucht (2011) in a study of Ghanaian migrants in Italy. He argues that

Ghanaian migrants believe that the sacrifices they make in migrating to Italy will be reciprocated by God. The dangers of crossing the Sahara Desert and the Mediterranean Sea and the humiliations of working in the informal economy in Italy will be rewarded by future success. In this sense, accumulating suffering means accumulating good luck, and migrants thus maintain their optimism despite extraordinarily difficult conditions. Lucht describes "the challenge of coping with devastating loss . . . while retaining hope that the outside world will provide something of commensurate worth" (243). Home care workers hope that their hard work will be reciprocated. A few express faith that their current work of caring will result in others caring for them, when they too need assistance, or that God—not their employers—will reward them for their labor. They expect reciprocity from God rather than from their patients and thus claim their belonging to humanity, obviating the need to be recognized by individuals and a nation-state. However, God's reciprocity is also expected to result in material rewards and redistribution.

Exchanges at work make care workers feel humiliated despite their work of caring and result in feelings of exclusion. This sentiment also becomes an evaluation of the United States as a whole and whether they will be rewarded here for their hard work. They use their work to evaluate the promise of the American dream.

Patient Irritation at Caregivers

Care workers describe challenging relationships as those in which their dignity is assaulted by patients, as discussed in chapter 2, whereas patients are frustrated by the quality of the care. Complaints about servants have a long history in the United States (Katzman 1978), and so it should not be surprising that complaints about home health workers are also rampant. One agency staff member described the source of the conflict as "the aides are trying to meet the bills and sustain a certain level of lifestyle, and the client wants someone who walks on water but yet meets their individual needs." Focusing on the care workers, she continued, "They take a lot of abuse in an attempt to keep their job. They go above and beyond the call of duty to maintain their shifts and make sure the clients like them" (interview, April 22, 2016, Maryland). A staff member at another agency noted, "The clients only value working hard. If the caregiver is sitting there reading a book, they don't see the value in their money. But it is a safety net, like insurance [she means, the home care worker's presence prevents a patient's tumble]. So we give the families education, so they don't do demeaning things" (interview, February 17, 2016, Maryland). From the perspective of agency staff, patients expect too much, and care workers give too much because of their financial vulnerability.

Patients and their relatives did complain to me about care workers sitting around or just watching television rather than providing enough "stimulation," as discussed in the previous interlude. Jacob joked in front of Caroline that you can tell a care worker does not care when they sit down in front of the television the moment you do not need them (field notes from visit, March 23, 2016, Maryland). Marie complained that she had to ask Fatu to do the next task, such as taking out the trash, rather than Fatu undertaking the task herself. However, she also complained when Fatu initiated tasks of her own choosing, such as scrubbing out the birdbath with the wrong cleaning implement (field notes from visit, April 6, 2016, Maryland). Spouses of patients, in particular, complained because the care worker did not relieve their burden of care as they had hoped: they still cooked, could not travel, and needed to supervise the care worker.

Those happy with their care worker generally feel that she is exceptional and that other care workers are not of the same caliber. A man who was still working full-time said about his wife's care worker, Beza: "She is so entrepreneurial [by which he means: she comes up with things to do]. She cooks, she cleans, she does laundry, she never sits down" (interview, February 2, 2016, Maryland). A woman praised her husband's former care worker, Adimu: "She has a mother in Africa, but she doesn't talk on the phone when she is with someone. If the person is napping, she straightens the linen closet or cleans the refrigerator" (interview, December 4, 2015, Maryland). In particular, they appreciated care workers who were full housekeepers and who, when not needed by the patient, turned to other domestic chores rather than resting. Patients' relatives also esteemed care workers who took charge by taking patients to routine doctors' appointments, keeping the refrigerator stocked with food, and coordinating with and training any other care workers.

As noted above, for some, the irritation is about money: they feel they are paying a lot for care and are not getting enough or the right kind of care for their money. For some patients, worry about having enough money heightens their irritability about their care. It is important to keep patients' irritations in mind; however, this chapter mainly focuses on care workers' perspectives on what they deserve.

Care Workers' Perspectives on Reciprocity

Acknowledgment and Appreciation

Because most care workers have experienced degradation, even to the extent of hearing racist language, they care a lot about the respect they are given by patients and the patients' relatives. In the wake of her patient's death, Monica commented, "Don't give me food, don't give me gifts. Just give me respect" (phone interview, January 30, 2015). Some signs of respect are quite subtle. Oriane noted that her patient's husband allowed her to park her car in the garage, a sign that he considered her to be a fellow human being (interview, January 16, 2016). Care workers happily noted when they felt appreciation from the patient or patient's relatives.

For a few, respect was the major criterion in deciding whether or not to continue working in a particular case. Monica said that so long as the family appreciated her, she could help, even if the patient "was the worst person in the whole universe" (phone interview, December 23, 2014). Hope was in her late fifties and had worked in home care for fourteen years. In a loving marriage with her husband, who worked for a pharmaceutical company, she spent weeks or months away from home, working live-in in the Washington area for better pay than was available in Delaware, where she lived in a new suburban development. She cared for a woman who regularly denigrated and yelled at her. Sometimes, when the patient asked for her name, Hope would respond that her name was "Bitch." When the patient said that was not a nice name, Hope would retort, "But that is what you call me!" In the morning, when the patient was calmer, she would sometimes ask Hope, "Are you Hope?" Hope would affirm it. The patient then responded, "You are Hope from God. You are good to me." Hope tried to remember those moments throughout the day and reminded her patient of them later when the patient screamed at her. The morning's praise did not quite atone for the evening's rages, but Hope tried to make it do so (field notes from visit, July 6, 2016, Delaware). Speaking to her ambivalence about the situation, she said contradictorily, "I don't take it personally. I'm human, though." She said, "I pray to God to give me more patience. Sometimes I can't stand it. I do it quickly and not with my mind and heart. I have to tell myself, 'It is the illness' [the dementia]. I got angry and told the husband that he should find someone else to take care of his wife because she is calling me a bitch all the time. But then, later, I thought, 'Oh Lord, something is wrong [with her]. Do it from my heart.' She doesn't appreciate it, but he [the husband] does" (interview, May 2, 2016, Washington, DC). Kwadwo cared for with a man who never spoke to him. Previously, the patient had said, "Thank you" and "God bless you." But now he did not, as his dementia had increased. Because the patient's son, who lived far away in another state, was so nice and considerate, Kwadwo wanted to be able to stay in this lonely situation as long as the son needed him, and he remained until the patient died (phone interview, December 31, 2014). One agency staff member, who had recently felt demeaned by the daughter of a patient, commented, "Most of the aides, clients will get more out of them if they demonstrated gratitude. But instead, they feel, 'I'm entitled to [X].' But you can't pay me to clean poop" (interview, April 22, 2016, Maryland). This staff member seemed correct in her assessment: as noted in chapter 3, those care workers who feel appreciated go above and beyond the requirements of the job.

Care workers also appreciate patients who seem genuinely interested in their lives, illustrating the degree to which they feel invisible. Deborah told me, "Yesterday, I was chatting like friends" with her patient, with whom she had worked for seven months. "I just got my first apartment, and she asks, 'Do you have enough heat in your apartment? Do you have food?' Like she really cared" (interview, February 18, 2016, Maryland). Fatu said that during the Ebola epidemic, she worried about her family in Sierra Leone. In the nursing home where she worked, "the elderly people also have concern for you." They would ask about her family and give "encouraging words" (interview, January 15, 2016, Maryland). Linda said about a beloved patient, "She would give you advice. She would ask if you have eaten" (interview, January 11, 2016, Maryland). Small gestures, such as questions about the material and bodily well-being of care workers and of their families are taken as signs of care.

At the same time, some feel that such appreciation is false, without a deeper basis. Kwesi said about the United States in general, "Here, they don't value life. . . . They don't want to share. . . . They need you, and they pretend they like you, but they only need you for the job." He felt that patients would not insult an American care worker as they did "foreigners" (interview, February 8, 2016, Maryland, my translation from Twi). Central to his evaluation was his belief that Americans did not "want to share." I therefore turn now to the care workers' expectations that recognition should be supported through material exchanges.

"Money Is Spirit"

Nonmaterial recognition by patients and their kin of care workers' personhood and labor is welcome. At the same time, care workers do not feel materially reciprocated for their labor. Monica struggled with her sense of whether gratitude alone satisfied her. In one conversation, she told me, "I am happy with 'Thank you, Monica,' with a smile. . . . We have to live in this world, learning how to do that for everyone and not expect something in return. . . . Once in a while, you have to do things as a gift. Do things without expectation" (phone interview, July 23, 2015). Yet she found it hard to live without an expectation of a gift in return.

Some of her frustration with expecting a reward was due to her experience as a return migrant to Ghana, where people expected her to give them money for doing little things, such as picking up something from the floor that she had dropped. Like Millicent with the land guard, she felt that some of these people took advantage of migrants. She had also experienced unfair reciprocities in her romantic relationships: "The way men behave with money is alarming. They want to take all the intestines from your stomach and just leave you there [on the ground]. Money is spirit. Men are good calculators: they are always calculating how much you are [financially] worth. . . . I am doing this painful, mental depression job [of care work]. And then I go home and take care of him [her romantic partner] as my son! That love is stupid" (phone interview, July 23, 2015). When I asked her to explain why money is spirit, she talked about the effort it takes to get money: "I work hard for the little money [I get]. I am using my spirit and emotion. Otherwise, I would be dying. I lift up my emotions to do this work. I am not giving that sweat to you [her romantic partner]." She explains further, "If you have $20 in the bank, and the bank tells you that the money isn't there, you will get really upset. You will be worried. But if you hear that you have interest, you will be happy. That's your spirit. It increases your spirit. It is everything." Losing the little money she had drained her spirit, while hearing that it had increased without extra effort boosted it.

Thus, for Monica, money indicated life force and vitality. She expended her spirit to obtain money. Monica worried about wasting her life force, both on home care and on romantic relationships in which she was disrespected and her energy sapped. Such vitiation of energy was a kind of theft. Finally, the financial rewards of care work made her less able to be generous and share her life force with others. Gifts— dependent on the generosity and mood of patients—were important because of the low contractual pay and as an indicator of the patient's appreciation of her.

Gifts

Care workers and patients are in very different financial situations. Patients' ability to pay for a care worker attests to their wealth. Care workers, in contrast, often struggle financially to take care of their relatives in Ghana and the United States. They have problems with their cars, childcare, housing, and immigration applications, some of which can be resolved with additional money. These social-class disparities are obvious to care workers and become so to some patients. Care workers assess the patient's wealth using the patient's former occupation and the location, size, and décor of the patient's residence.[4] Some patients are moved to be generous with care workers, as a sign of mutuality of being, affection, and dependence. They end up sharing their resources with their care workers (see also Parreñas 2001).

Gifts between employers and their domestic workers have been noted as central to sustaining the hierarchy of relationships. In her study of domestic service in the southern United States, Susan Tucker argues, "Giving and receiving were rituals within the domestic worker-employer relationship built upon ancient traditions of interaction between people separated by class. They were also an important part of customary behavior between whites and blacks in the segregated South" (1988, 146).

Judith Rollins (1985) discusses this behavior as embodying the maternalism of female employers who give advice, cast-off clothes, and used
furniture to their domestic servants as a way of maintaining their superiority. Unequal gift giving, in which gifts only come from the employer,
"reinforces the inequality of the relationship" (193). Gifts inadequately
compensate for the low wages of domestic servants, leading many domestic servants to wonder why they were not paid better instead. At
the same time, because of their poor wages, they relied materially on
gifts from employers and do not refuse them. However, in her study
of domestic service in Los Angeles, Pierrette Hondagneu-Sotelo notes
that "maternalism, once so widely observed among female employers of
private domestic workers, is now largely absent from the occupation."
Instead,

> a new sterility prevails in employer-employee relations in paid domestic
> work. For various reasons—including the pace of life that harries women
> with both career and family responsibilities, as well as their general dis-
> comfort with domestic servitude—most employers do not act mater-
> nalistically toward their domestic workers. In fact, many of them go to
> great lengths to minimize personal interactions with their nanny/house-
> keeper and housecleaners. At the same time, the Latina immigrants who
> work for them—especially the women who look after their employers'
> children—crave personal contact. They *want* social recognition and ap-
> preciation for who they are and what they do, but they don't often get it
> from their employers. (Hondagneu-Sotelo 2001, 11)

Whereas Rollins (1985) finds that domestic workers criticize personal-
ized hierarchical relationships established through gifts from superior
to subordinate, Hondagneu-Sotelo (2001) instead finds that employers
reject contact with domestic servants seeking connection. Impersonal
relationships exacerbate the feelings of social annihilation experienced
by Latina domestic workers.

Home care agencies and nursing homes often prohibit gifts to care
workers, in part so that they can control the relationship between care
workers and patient and prevent them from establishing their own direct
employer-employee relationship (Aronson and Neysmith 1996; Buch
2014; Rodriquez 2014). Although agency staff tend to officially discour-

age gifts, in my experience they allow them when they think they are appropriate or convince the patients to offer a smaller sum. They know such gifts are important for care workers' economic survival and help mitigate the low wages and economic uncertainty of their occupation. Staff members tell care workers to report any gift to the agency, warning care workers that the patient will forget the gift and accuse them of theft. Staff members also hope to control the amount if it seems unreasonable; a gift in the hundreds of dollars is acceptable, but not one in the thousands, said one agency staff member. Patients know they skirt agency rules by giving gifts but feel a moral obligation to help the care worker because of their awareness of the care worker's need and their gratitude for the care worker's care. Gifts are thus one way of "tinkering with the good," trying to be a moral person and to act appropriately. Ohemmea told me, "Some can give you gifts, and the agency doesn't hear. I looked after one man, and he would bring me bread or bring me other things" (phone interview, February 19, 2015, my translation from Twi). Binta described "good people" who used to give her money to buy groceries: "They said that they knew the agency didn't pay well and that the agency didn't want them to give her extra money. When the woman died, I got $7,000 and everything in the woman's apartment" (interview, January 21, 2016, Maryland). Care workers do not receive gifts of used clothes and furniture on an ongoing basis, as is described in the literature on domestic service, but are offered the used clothing, furniture, and household items in the patient's residence after the patient has died.

In addition to receiving large gifts such as these (a form of practical inheritance, as discussed earlier) and help with the groceries, care workers reported receiving small amounts of money on special occasions and holidays. Millicent said that a patient had given her $500, along with some used clothes and a travel iron, when she traveled to Ghana for a visit two years prior (field notes from phone conversation, March 17, 2016). Similarly, Kwadwo had been on his way to Ghana when his patient asked how many children he had. The patient gave Kwadwo $20 for each child—a total of $100 for his four biological children and the child of a deceased sister for whom Kwadwo was responsible (field notes from visit, August 4, 2016, New Jersey). These gifts are one way: care workers never give their patients money, but they do not feel subordinate to their patients as a result. Instead, most treat these gifts as appreciation for their care and thus as reciprocal. They consider themselves entitled to these gifts. Gifts function more like payroll bonuses rather than charity. Although such gifts do not generate a hierarchical relationship in the way that charity does, they are still contingent on the generosity and financial well-being of the patient, and care workers had no right to demand them.

Patients also offer other advice and nonfinancial help in the areas of their expertise, namely schooling, money, health care, and the law. Sharon's daughter took Essenam's adolescent daughter, then a junior in high school, to visit various colleges (interview with Sharon's son, January 17, 2016, Maryland). Jane contacted one of her former coworkers, a doctor at a famous research hospital in the area when Micheline had a "health scare," so that Micheline would have the same kind of specialist care as Jane would have pursued for herself or her own kin (field notes from visit with Jane, May 21, 2016, Maryland). When Linda wrote the family reunification application to bring over her children from Ghana, her patient's two adult children—both lawyers—reviewed the letters and forms (interview with patient's daughter, May 24, 2016, Virginia). In an interview with me, the patient's son said, "It was quid pro quo," or a favor granted with the expectation of a return. Then, perhaps feeling that his phrasing was too legalistic or mercenary, he quickly amended his wording: "It was reciprocal affection" (interview, January 29, 2016, Maryland). Some gifts are material but not necessarily financial and are part of the reciprocal exchange between patients and care workers established through care.

Thus, patients, their kin, and care workers tinker with agency rules to do what they feel is right, within the moral imagination generated by care. These improvised navigations attempt to create fair exchanges in which "quid pro quo" and "reciprocal affection" mean one and the same thing.

Divine Reciprocity

Because not all patients can or want to reciprocate with financial and material gifts, care workers question whether they will be rewarded for their expenditure of life force and energy. Many sources of such rewards exist: generous, honorable and wealthy patients; American society; and

God. Although human beings can be mean spirited and inconsistent in creating fair exchanges, God is more reliable in this regard, from the perspective of my interlocutors, although the timing of the return is uncertain. "God's time is best" is a popular slogan seen on the public buses in Ghana. Unlike human reciprocity, which comes at significant times, such as on major holidays and at death, God provides in their hour of need, using human beings to reciprocate the good works of care workers.

The literature on home and nursing-home workers suggests that a religious trope is fairly common among this workforce (Ibarra 2010; Rodriquez 2014; Solari 2006; Stacey 2011). Care workers position themselves as "saints" whom a divine power will reward. Asserting a caring self provides them with dignity. Sociologists have considered this perspective as emerging from American ideologies of care, which view "true" care as selfless and unpaid (Zelizer 2005). Paid caregivers, as an oxymoron, have to position themselves as doing the job for love rather than for money. This perspective puts them at risk of working outside their contractual hours and sacrificing themselves as saints, rather than standing up for their rights as workers.

Like these care workers, many of my interlocutors discussed "bad" care workers who worked solely for money. Their greed meant that they worked too many hours, making them exhausted and impatient and at risk for health problems. This discourse seemed pervasive among care workers, even those who did not mention religious matters. Julie said that as a Christian, she was focused on the eternal life and not the money in the work (interview, May 6, 2016, Washington, DC). Janet said, "Sometimes I tell my friends, 'They pay you, but do it for God. Listen to your heart'" (phone interview, December 31, 2014). Faith said, "You shouldn't do this work because of the money. Make another person happy and encourage them. . . . At the end of the day, you have to be able to help the Lord" (phone interview, January 2, 2015). Through this lens, caregiving creates a different kind of status, in which one is doing holy and divine work. Clare Stacey (2011) has called this practice asserting a caring self.

Divine reciprocity also plays a role in accountability. Home care workers work in the privacy of someone's home, usually with an older person who lives alone and might have a dementia. The patient's kin may live out of state and only visit once or twice a year; even if they live nearby, they may only visit on the weekend. On their own and mainly unsupervised by the patient's kin, neighbors, or agency staff, some home care workers feel like they work under the watchful eye of God, who appreciates their labor and notes their moments of frailty, impatience, or lack of concern. They are not "nothing"; they are visible, and they are important because they carry out God's work of care. They feel accountable to God at the end of the day, in part because other forms of accountability from patients, their kin, or the agency seem unfair or haphazard, as Fatu's firing shows. Working in a difficult situation in which her patient insulted her a great deal, using hurtful and abusive language, Hope said that she could not sleep if she had "made a mistake" during the day, such as feeling annoyed or talking back to the patient (interview, May 2, 2016, Maryland). Yaw told me, "We [he and his wife Belinda] are doing it for God. Caregiving is good for those who fear God. Otherwise, you will do stupid things and regret it later." They then told the story of a Ghanaian nurse who cheated a widow out of her money and was arrested. They noted with approval that the American embassy seized the house she had built in Ghana (joint interview, May 14, 2016, Pennsylvania). A focus on the spiritual dimensions of the work is a way of coping with the challenges of the job (see also O'Leary 2016, 168–69). It maintains a sense of being human—and a moral human being at that—in the face of the everyday depredations and humiliations of the work itself, as well as the temptation to strike back emotionally, be impatient, or engage in negative reciprocities such as theft.

In contrast to Clare Stacey's (2011) research on home care workers, I found that only ten of my sixty-two interlocutors considered care work a calling, in which they obtained divine rewards from care work rather than being motivated by more earthly motives of pay and status. Nine of the ten in this group were Christian, and one was Muslim; nine were women, and one was a man. Both the religious and gender breakdown reflected the larger demographics of my research participants, who were overwhelmingly female and Christian.

For these care workers, the spiritual nature of the work gave immediate emotional satisfaction. Deborah said, "There is the religious part [of the work] that you know you are doing the right thing. You are able to help" (interview, February 18, 2016, Maryland). Mariatu, who worked part-time in a nursing home and otherwise cared for her disabled daughter, said, "I personally am a spiritual person. You come into someone's life. It is not easy, because they have dementia. They are calling you names while you are helping them. It is rewarding to make a difference in someone's life. It is a good feeling" (interview, May 20, 2016, Maryland). Micheline said that what she liked about care work was that it accorded with her Christian values. She said, "I feel I'm doing great work for humanity. I could do it for free, but I am getting paid" (interview, May 21, 2016, Maryland). Faith, for whom this sentiment was particularly strong, said the work "gives me a lot of joy. You can't water someone and not be watered. If you give a smile, the person will smile in response." She saw her role as being an "encourager" for people approaching the end of life, to "give them hope" (phone conversation, January 20, 2015). A few weeks later, she told me about caring for someone who seemed to be dying at the age of ninety-five: "It is a gift," she said. "God is helping me." She continued, "I feel so blessed and fulfilled that I am able to help. I feel so fulfilled at the end of the day. . . . I am happy to have the privilege of taking care of her" (phone conversation, February 12, 2015). Her sense of belonging was to humanity, in which reciprocity would come from God.

This perspective also complicates the opposition between money and love, because God's help in response should also result in physical and material well-being. Furthermore, divine reciprocity seems more reliable than—and outweighs—the financial and emotional reciprocities of recognition and redistribution possible through inconsistent patients. God will recognize the care worker's goodness and assistance in God's project and will reward the care worker financially and with good health. The immediate emotional and spiritual reward is further encouraged by the knowledge that serving an older person will generate a blessing in the future. These expressions emerged most often when I asked care workers about how their work affected their plans for their own aging. Many care workers were concerned about their own aging, given their exposure to the expense of care in the United States and to the poor conditions of even expensive institutional care facilities. However, the subset of care workers who expressed religious convictions about caregiving did not express anxiety. Hope said about care work, "God will also reward you for it. Do it with joy." When I asked her about her own aging, she said,

"If you do good to someone, someone will do good to you. When aging, someone will take care of you" (interview, May 2, 2016, Washington, DC). Mavis, who was ready to retire, said, "If you have patience and a good heart, God will bless you if you do good. When you go into a case, you see the pictures before the person was in a wheelchair or in bed, and you feel, 'What about you?' If you are bad to her, you are bad to yourself" (interview, March 17, 2016, Maryland). Valerie, in her fifties, said, "Good things follow those who do good. Someone will take care of you in the future, if you do good now" (interview, May 10, 2016, Maryland). These care workers hoped that their good deeds would result in their receiving the kind of care they had provided, as a kind of expected reciprocity, although they were not sure where exactly that care would come from. I will note that they expressed this trust in divine reciprocity vaguely, without specific individuals or plans being named. Their lack of specificity worried me, partly because of my more long-term relationships with four care workers, two of whom had retired in Ghana, but it did not seem to worry my interlocutors. As Yaw said, "Money is not the issue in life. You do good with it, and the rest will come" (interview, May 14, 2016, Pennsylvania).

I met one care worker who was critical of this perspective. Gilbert said that in Ghana, they say that "a teacher's reward is in heaven," but he did not believe it: "I have to live like an earthly person, and when I go to heaven, I will have a heavenly reward. I know the agencies make money. They need to take good care of the staff. If you read the mission statement, it is all about the client. But they need some essentials for the staff, in terms of motivational factors." He was particularly impatient with the agency's lack of affordable health care and paid leave (phone interview, February 19, 2015). Familiar with the discourse about divine reward, from both Ghana and the United States, he asked for material rewards through the agency.

My interlocutors did not say very specific things about the religious aspects of their care work, although I encouraged them to do so. Instead, they tended to rely on pronouncements and aphorisms: "Do it for God," "God will reward you," or "Good things follow those who do good." These were articles of faith, to attempt to live out in daily practice; they were also deeply felt. This discourse was shared with other care workers, to encourage them to keep their spirits up or to do the work patiently and kindly. Religion helped them to gracefully and cheerfully survive some of the obstacles that they encountered in the United States and gave them the dignity that they were sometimes denied by other human beings in the political realm. It also encouraged inward-oriented, reflective approaches to conflict resolution and emotional management—of watching one's heart, of praying to God—rather than legal challenges or political action in response to the ethical issues posed by lack of reciprocity in their work. However, as María de la Luz Ibarra argues, such a religious vision is also a way of "creating a more just world, of critiquing through deeds the inequality of globalization that makes human intimacy so difficult" (2010, 118). In this vision, justice is generated through reciprocity in a much wider sphere than the nation-state, through political belonging to humanity. Thus, care workers can transcend political belongings to the nation-state by focusing on their belonging to the kingdom of God.

Negative Reciprocity: Theft

One of the concerns that patients feel about letting someone into their life and house is that the care worker may harm them. This fear emerges among patients primarily as a discourse about theft rather than physical abuse or neglect; employer suspicion and fear of theft has a long history in domestic service (Katzman 1978). In continuing care communities, tales of theft abound. Patients circulate stories about theft within their social networks, and these stories are also reported in the local media. For example, the *Washington Post* featured a multipage story, accompanied by a large color photograph, about a wealthy couple robbed by three care workers (Bahrampour 2016). These stories have a horrific and dramatic aspect to them, emphasizing the vulnerability of the older person and the power of the care worker. Thus, an acquaintance of my mother, who lives in a continuing care community and does not have a care worker, told me a story about a care worker writing checks from a fellow resident's checkbook and double billing for her hours (field notes from phone conversation, March 29, 2016). Susan, in the same continuing care community, told a story of her grandmother being "robbed blind" by her care workers, who forged checks and stole the china (interview, April 21, 2016, Maryland). Sharon's son was told by his brother to hide his mother's jewelry when Essenam came to work in her house (interview with Sharon's son, January 17, 2016, Maryland).[5] One sign of mistrust is patients' use of security cameras to monitor care workers.

My interlocutors among home care agency staff had varying notions of the prevalence of theft. Some blamed paranoia and dementia on the loss of patients' items. Others conceded that theft happened and that they were currently prosecuting such cases with the help of the police. Others said that they wondered what had happened in cases where the patient complained to the home care agency about theft but refused to file a police report. One agency owner wondered if Africans were accused of theft because many people associated blacks with criminality (interview, May 18, 2016, Maryland). Another agency owner said that patients had become so dependent on home care that accusations of theft had declined (interview, April 12, 2016, Maryland).

Care workers are aware of this mistrust. Most are resigned to the initial lack of trust from patients, which they deal with by showing their trustworthiness over several months (see also Karner 1998). Oriane noted, "They don't trust you at first because of all they know of stealing and mistreatment" (interview, January 19, 2016, Maryland). As a result, she did not mind hidden cameras because they allowed patients to trust her more quickly. Paulina noted that the lack of trust made new cases anxiety producing: "The first time you are coming to do a job, it is hard, because they don't know if you will steal something from them or harm them. Filling in [substituting for another care worker] is hard. Even the good case is not easy at first. You are a stranger and you go to their house. It is not easy for them and not easy for us. You have to be patient and show them that you are not here to harm them" (phone interview, January 2, 2015). Care workers see mistrust as something they can overcome; however, the initial lack of trust makes them prefer to remain in a case with which they are familiar.

Others are more sensitive to accusations and terminated jobs for this reason, taking it as a sign of lack of respect or recognition. As in similar studies (Stacey 2011), accusations of theft are emotionally painful to home care workers. Seth, the son of a patient, described how his sister once noticed that the common grocery purse in their mother's kitchen drawer contained only a little money and asked the Afghan care worker, a former doctor who was now a refugee in the United States, "What happened to the $40?" The care worker was offended by the implied accusation and left the case, although Seth felt that the care worker might have been looking to leave anyway, finding home health work beneath her level of skill and education (interview, March 23, 2016, Maryland).

Julie described an incident in which she had been wounded by an accusation of theft from a patient. Noticing that the supply of toilet paper was low, she planned to buy some before she left for the day at 8 p.m., at the end of a twelve-hour shift. The patient had given her $10 to make the purchase from a grocery store on the first floor of the same building. Julie then found some toilet paper in a cabinet and decided not to go shopping, instead hurrying to empty the trash cans before she left. When the patient asked where the $10 was, Julie exploded: "I told her I was in the middle of something. She asked a second time and a third time. I said to her, 'Madame, what are you trying to tell me? Are you suggesting that I will steal? Will I jeopardize my life for a lousy $10?' I got nasty too. It was the first time I got mad and went off. I asked, 'Who do you think I am? You are treating me like a thief. I can leave you right now. I can't accept this.' But then I thought, 'If I leave now, what am I doing?'" I responded, "Yes, you could lose your license" for leaving a patient alone, but perhaps Julie was also worried about losing the job. Julie continued, "It was the first time I got so angry. I was very, very angry. I lost my temper." No doubt, the stress of the long day and the desire to leave had worn through her patience.

I asked how the patient had responded to her anger, and she said that the patient said, "I'm sorry." But an apology did not suffice. Julie responded, "'I don't need your apologies. The harm is done. I am going to report you to the agency. You won't see me anymore. You call me names.' I was very angry. The following day, I called the agency. 'You people,' I said to them. 'I am not going again. She called me a thief.' I told the whole story. They told me, 'She does it all the time. The moment anyone goes in there, they quit.' I told them, 'Well, I'm not going back'" (interview, May 6, 2016, Washington, DC). For Julie, being accused of theft was deeply insulting and legitimate grounds for leaving a particular case. The agency staff agreed, mainly because it accorded with the experience of multiple care workers. Although Julie seemed angrier at her patient than the agency, it is important to note that the agency staff had neither tried to protect Julie nor warned her ahead of time. Julie was on her own in dealing with the accusation.

Comfort described being accused of stealing water and juice from a patient's refrigerator, even though she had brought the bottles with her and placed them in the fridge for her night shift. "That is hard as a human being," she said. In this case, Comfort felt that the complaint affected her employment, as the agency did not send her to good jobs anymore but only to distant jobs that were hard to reach, and so she applied to work at another agency. She commented, "The agency always defends the client" (phone interview, January 18, 2016).

In these conflicts over stealing, the care worker focuses on issues of trust, which some observers have seen as necessary for a caring relationship (Held 2005). Patients' concerns about theft are the dark underbelly of their concern with the fairness of the legitimate exchange, in which their expectations for care are not met. The patients worry about the theft of money; the care workers, about the theft of their spirit without compensation.

Conclusion

Both care workers and patients are concerned about the reciprocities of their relationship. On the patients' side, reciprocity is framed as an issue of money: Are they receiving sufficient labor from their employees in exchange for the life savings they are spending? Are the strangers in their homes stealing from them? Patients expect to buy care, household labor, and respect with their money, and their anxieties concern the value of that money. Some patients recognize the financial straits of their care workers and are generous with them, sharing a portion of their wealth.

Care workers, on the other hand, appeal to respect, of which financial redistribution is seen as a sign. They attend to the lack of appreciation, both in terms of respect and in terms of the valuing of their life and spirit, including financial valuation. Sensitive to issues of respect, they take offense at accusations of theft. Their own sense is that the care they provide puts their patients in their permanent debt, so that gifts are their due, rather than putting them in a subordinate position. Some see care as God's work, in which they spread love and salvation, rather than giving their labor in exchange for money. God's rewards, given across the life course, will be more significant than the direct material rewards of the work, which are so few.

In these evaluations of the exchanges, care workers and patients are tinkering with the idea of the good. They establish a just universe in which they are moral people. Care workers use these exchanges to evaluate character—of patients, of Americans at large—and to create belonging, particularly in humanity at large. Thus, reciprocity is one index of belonging to a moral community. These exchanges are particularly salient at the end of life, as I explore in the next interlude.

Interlude

Intangible Gifts at the End of Life

After several generations in which death was medicalized and occurred in hospitals in the United States, more and more people are seeking to die at home, drawing on a particular image of a good death. A home death requires home care, sometimes under the management of a nurse in a hospice program. However, home deaths lead to ritual uncertainty and confusion on the part of kin about what to do and how to respond during and after the dying process (Ariès 1981). Kin often find themselves struggling to create the proper ritual space or sense of union and communion with the dead and with one another. They do not have a cultural script of what to do, which leads to greater grief. This lack of ritual around home death results from the cultural desire to avoid death for as long as possible; the expertise of medical authorities in organizing the dying process in hospitals (Kaufman 2005); and the fact that aging in general is somewhat unstructured, with relatively few rituals in comparison to the transitions of childhood and youth (Myerhoff 1984; Rosow 1974). Given the lack of structure in home death, kin are amenable to guidance from others, including from home care workers.

Home care workers, who experience many deaths through their work, become midwives of death or death doulas, directing kin members in the proper actions during home deaths. Care workers warn kin to visit when death is imminent, protect them from the more disturbing signs of death, and help them establish emotional connections to the dying patient. Care workers' actions during the dying process cement kin members' already-existing affection for the care worker and make them consider the care worker exceptional because she has created a sacred moment that honors the personhoods of participants.

Seth told me the story of his father's death after many years of physical suffering. Afterward, his father's care worker, Yaema, asked for Seth's help bathing his father's body. Seth said he could have refused, but he went into the bedroom, and "it was a gift to wash him," although he hesitated to touch his father. They struggled to close his father's jaw because they had waited too long. He remembered that Yaema washed and oiled his father's body before dressing him. Seth does not know why Yaema asked him: Was it because he was the eldest son out of four siblings? Because she needed help turning his father? "We never talked about it," he said. Preparing his father's body felt sacred to him. It was Yaema's gift to him; he would not have thought of doing it on his own (interview, March 23, 2016, Maryland).

Yaema considered that moment less poignant and instead a matter-of-fact occurrence: bathing the deceased was a familiar ritual to her. Yaema said that in Sierra Leone, "We bathe the person immediately. [Although some people are afraid of dead bodies] I have the belief: I am more afraid of the living than of the dead. I was not mean to the person [so she has nothing to fear from his spirit after death]. I wish them the best. It is the last respect I can give them." Furthermore, nursing-aide school had taught her how to prepare the body. As I also learned through my nursing-aide course, bathing the deceased is similar to the bed baths that a care worker regularly gives to a living patient, although it is more strenuous because a living patient can help and because bathing the dead requires additional steps. Yaema told me that there was no significance to asking Seth as the eldest son; it was somewhat random that she asked him, as opposed to one of his other siblings, who were all present in the house that morning (interview, May 9, 2016, Virginia).

The Wiesniewskis also had a story to tell about how important Caroline was at the moment of death. Jacob's wife died suddenly early one morning—"a terrible morning," said her daughter, Lucy. Jacob was trying to get his wife out of bed for an early morning doctor's appointment, but his wife refused to get up, yelling at him for bothering her. He called Lucy, who lived nearby, to help, and her mother died in Lucy's arms. Lucy called her mother's care worker, Caroline, who was scheduled to come an hour later, to tell her the news, and Caroline asked if she should come. Lucy responded, "Yes, please." Lucy described the rest of the morning:

> My mother spent three hours on the floor, waiting for a doctor to sign a death certificate [or she would have needed an autopsy to determine

the cause of death]. Three police officers were sitting at the table, talking about a course at [the local community college] they were taking. My father was weeping, holding my mother's hand. I was trying to make arrangements and called a former neighbor [to communicate the news]. Caroline came in and sat next to my Dad, held his hand, and told stories about my mother. She was invaluable. I couldn't have done that, but she did. . . . She just understands; she is so sensitive. (interview, May 21, 2016, Maryland)

In Lucy's eyes, Caroline was the only one who responded appropriately to her father's grief at suddenly losing his wife of sixty-five years, particularly in comparison to the police officers' profane discussion and her own busy actions of making phone calls, which insulated her from her father's grief and her own. Another woman similarly described how her husband died at home, under hospice care: "He faded away in the afternoon." She called her husband's care worker to come look at her husband, to ascertain that he had truly passed away. After her husband's death, the multiple care workers "were genuinely concerned about me," staying with her and helping her deal with the arrangements. One even came to the funeral, along with her baby (interview, January 14, 2016, Maryland).

Edem described his initial fear of death, but he became used to it through care work. Once you had seen the process several times, he said, "You can predict what time they will die and what function will be lost next." He described in detail how to care for a patient who could no longer swallow or drink and how to be careful to clean up the patient's bowel movements quickly; you needed to "be on top of that cleanup," he said, because a dead body was harder to clean and change. He also commented on the importance of bathing the deceased's body "with a lot of compassion" and care because the kin are around and emotionally volatile due to their grief (interview, May 25, 2016, Maryland).

Hope described taking care of a couple for seven years: "I was part of them. . . . I loved them. They took me as their daughter; I took them as my parents." Hope kept the wife company while she died, feeding her pureed food and propping up her head, which tended to slump. After she died, "In school, we knew what to do when it happened. I straightened her up, so she wouldn't get rigid, and covered her up to her neck" (interview, May 2, 2016, Washington, DC). Dying and death make care workers operate at the top of their skill and sensitivity, like athletes playing in a particularly important game: they monitor changes, stay near the patient, relieve fearful and distraught kin, and provide special forms of care. Agnes said, "The fact that they are dying is more a reason to give the best of me. I want to make them happy" (interview, April 23, 2016, Maryland).

Some care workers prefer not to be present during death. Although Valerie now found deaths normal, after twenty years of care work, she still cried and cried about a patient's death. It raised existential questions for her, which she would have preferred to avoid: "The human being is not there. You see death and the dead body lying there. Is this the end of the human being? You worry. Life is unpredictable. One minute can change your life" (interview, March 15, 2016, Maryland). The deaths of those in their fifties and sixties upset care workers the most; that of ninety-year-olds made one feel "sorry," said Edem, but they were ultimately "okay" (interview, May 25, 2016, Maryland). Julie prayed for death to happen during other care workers' shifts, so that she would not be present, but she made herself available to help the patient's kin mourn. Although she refused to come on the day that her patient, aged sixty with three teenaged children, died, she visited the following day. One of the daughters opened the front door for her: "She came into my arms and wept. It was very difficult. I let her weep. I knew it wouldn't take long. I told the daughter, 'Do it! Cry. Let it go. Don't resist it when you feel the urge to cry. The more you resist, the more you are harming yourself. Just cry.' Then I talked to the mother [the wife of the patient]. I told her, 'You have to be strong. Yes, cry, but you have kids. They will rely on you. You are the only one.' It's very hard. You just sympathize with them" (interview, May 6, 2016, Washington, DC). Julie found ways to protect herself from the nearness of death but made herself emotionally available in other ways.

Their familiarity with death and their knowledge of the process mean that care workers can manage a delicate moment in which official kin are inept because of their grief and inexperience. Care workers spoke to me about their experiences of death with pride in their skills and calmness. They talked about controlling their own emotions. Yaema said, "The family depends on you. You mourn later; you hold everything in" (interview, May 9, 2016, Virginia). Care workers share their knowledge about death with official kin, instructing them on what to do to connect to the dying person. Janet said, "I would call them [the kin], telling them that they have to come [because the patient is near death]. They would say that their mother wasn't listening, because her eyes were closed, but I would say, 'Hold her hand; say something sweet. She is listening'" (phone interview, December 31, 2014).

Sometimes care workers try to protect official kin from distress about the patient's dying, taking their place, in a way. Children and spouses have a responsibility to be present, as part of what Joanna Pfaff-Czarnecka calls a regime of belonging, or "institutionalized patterns insisting upon investments of time and resources, loyalty and commitment—that are the price people have to pay for belonging together" (2011, 205). Being present at death constitutes a regime of belonging for official kin, but sometimes, because of the substitution of the care workers, official kin can avoid this obligation. Mavis said that the children of one of her dying patients could not "bear to be in the room," so Mavis rubbed the patient's arm and back and prayed for her. Alone with the patient when she died, Mavis came out of the bedroom to inform the children of their mother's death. She got "a big gift" from that family (interview, March 17, 2016, Maryland).

In addition to being practical kin who substitute for official kin in accompanying the dying patient to the end, care workers also perform a sleight of hand to enable official kin to connect to the dying person. Diane said that kin stay away at the end because they do not want to see death and dying: "It's on us [the care workers]." She said she would call a kin member to visit with the patient for an hour, when the patient was alert. "I'll take the bad time," she said, so that the family would see the patient at his or her best (interview, January 8, 2016, Maryland). One agency staff member with whom I spoke about death complained that care workers would sit with the dying person, "holding her hand. And where is the family? The family is totally not involved" (interview, May 4, 2016, Maryland). Yaema described sitting with a patient and the patient's older sister while the patient died, with Yaema reading the Bible (Psalm 23) at the patient's request and the older sister holding the patient's hand and encouraging her to go to "a good place." The patient, in her late fifties, refused to have her husband called at work, protecting him from this process. After the patient's death, Yaema bathed and dressed the patient with the sister (interview, May 9, 2016, Virginia). Care workers shield official kin from the distressing aspects of dying, handle the dirty moments of making the patient comfortable and smell good, and simply accompany and sit by the patient during the slow process of dying.

Care workers also facilitate the dying process for the dying person. In general, they want their patient to live because death means the loss of a job. However, sometimes they recognize that passing away might be preferable to the patient's suffering. They ease the transition through their words and prayers.[1] Reflecting on her more than thirteen years of care work, Elizabeth remembered two good cases, each lasting more than a year, where they "treated me like part of the family." In one case,

> the old man was dying, and his son was screaming [about it]. The father would hear his son screaming and come back from dying. His soul would come back to the body. So I told the son to leave the room, and the son didn't want to leave the room. I told him, "You've done your job." He left the room, and the man died. The two children occasionally call me to take me out to dinner. Every year, they send me $200. I have used them as a reference, and they are good. They still get in touch. (interview, February 29, 2016, Maryland)

Once Elizabeth formed an interpretation of what was happening, she took charge, organizing the movement of people in space and time. From her perspective, the son's dramatic performance of love kept the father alive and attached, prolonging his agony. In her retelling of the incident, she convinced the son to leave the room by treating the son's grief as a work-related responsibility. She relieved him of his "job" of being a son—the regime of belonging—as if that role could be relieved and as if she supervised him morally. Although technically an employee, she gained control through this discourse, managing him directly, to facilitate his father's death. Apparently, her clear direction was appreciated, rather than causing distress and anger, given her report of an ongoing relationship with the children.

When I asked Micheline how she dealt with death, she told me, "My secret is that I am a Christian," and death is "an opportunity for me to bring this soul to Christ." She took charge privately with the patient, praying on behalf of the patient's soul. "I pray when the person is leaving. I hold hands. I pray for mercy, whatever faith they are." Only one of her patients refused her prayers, or rather, a patient's daughter said that it was the "will of my Mom" to refuse it. Micheline said, "I thought, 'Okay, there is nothing I can do.'" But when a patient accepted her prayer, "There is grace through this." One sixty-five-year-old patient in a nursing home called Micheline when she was dying. Micheline had memorized several verses of prayer but did not know those for a dying person. "The Holy Spirit guided me. I looked in my prayer book and found prayers for dying, and I said those prayers. She [the patient] cried and said, 'I can feel the Holy Spirit.' It was grace and a gift." Three hours later, the patient passed away. "I was happy. Everyone else was sad; the nurse was crying. I told them, 'She is an angel right now. She made it'" (interview, May 21, 2016, Maryland). Thus, Elizabeth's faith helped her ease her patient's suffering, as well as her own grief by imagining her in heaven. María de la Luz Ibarra has described how a "religiously inspired agency" among Mexicana care workers in the United States helps "to establish a clear line of action" (2010, 130). For Micheline as well, her "secret" as a Christian motivated her to offer spiritual resources to her patients and act in ways that she felt certain were moral and right.

Linda described how she had recently shepherded her patient to die. She had taken care of the patient for more than four years and was deeply attached to her, saying she was "like her own mother." Even though the patient had not spoken for two years, Linda knew her so well that she felt confident that she knew what her patient wanted. At the end of the patient's life,

> I could see she didn't want to leave us. I told her, "You have three children, three grandchildren, and [an unclear number of] great-grandchildren, with one more on the way. You have two caregivers [whom she names]. We love you. Please, please. There is someone who loves you more [that is, God]. They [your children] are not small children; they are big. You can leave us." At that stage of life, they can hear you. I said, "You know how I love you; you love me. Let me find somebody who is like you when you are gone." She opened her eyes a bit and smiled at me. (interview, January 11, 2016, Maryland)

Perhaps because her patient was a Holocaust survivor living in a Jewish continuing care community, Linda referred to God's love obliquely rather than explicitly, as Micheline tended to do. Through her prayer, Linda consoled herself, in addition to her patient, that all would be well.

Through their work in assisting the dying process, care workers feel in control and connected to their patient, in what Ibarra calls "a deep alliance" (2010, 130). Kin members can be corralled into this alliance with the patient through the regime of belonging, but if not, their presence is extraneous: what matters is that the patient has a good death. Home care workers draw on techniques from their personal experiences—namely prayer and a familiarity with bathing the body—as well as their nursing-aide training and multiple experiences of caring for dying patients, which informs them when death nears and allows them to be calm at its closeness. The end of life is a heightened moment for them, when their skills of observation, sensitivity, and physical care are used at full capacity. Therefore, despite their grief at the loss of a person, they feel proud of their competence. They take over when they see things going awry, and kin members, recognizing their expertise, let them do so. Matter-of-factly and competently, home care workers enable a good death, in their eyes, in which the patient attains salvation, does not suffer, and connects to official kin. Through their values and past experiences, care workers create a morally coherent event.

Patients' kin agree, finding home care workers helpful at the end of life. From their perspective, home care workers support a more meaningful death, including guiding patients' kin to feel belonging with the dead. Salvation does not concern them, at least in the stories that patients' kin told me, but emotional connection matters deeply. Such guidance creates belonging between the home health worker and the patient's kin through the mutual coordination of action and feeling. Just before the home care worker's care becomes unnecessary and the practical kin relationship can be dissolved, home care workers demonstrate their level of care—both their competence at care and affection for the dead—to the patients' official kin. Because of the emotional connection that binds them all together, patients' kin consider care workers' actions a gift, above and beyond the care worker's job responsibilities and highlighting the specialness of their care worker. In contrast, for the care workers, such actions are normal and anticipated, learned and practiced on the job, in which they simply ratchet up their existing skills as needed at the end of life.

Despite some patients' appreciation of their work at the end of life, in general, care workers are not well compensated for their work, with the unofficial gifts failing to reimburse the official low wages. As Valerie noted, "The job is difficult emotionally and physically. But you don't get anything for it" (phone conversation, March 7, 2016). The official compensations of home care work are the topic of the final chapter.

5

A Lack of Reciprocity

Wages, Benefits, and Contingent Employment

As discussed in the previous chapter, African care workers evaluate political belonging through the lens of reciprocity. In addition to the verbal appreciation and gifts from patients described in chapter 4, they assess reciprocity through wages and benefits, the topic of this chapter. In contrast to Claire Stacey's (2011) finding that care workers orient themselves toward spiritual and psychosocial rewards rather than pay, the material rewards of their work were foremost in my interlocutors' minds. That the material benefits of the work fell short established their lack of political belonging.

More established residents, in addition to migrants, feel a sense of belonging through their work and other benefits. Workplaces in general confer many aspects of personhood. They create pathways for focused activity and cognition; for many workers, work gives meaning and a sense of purpose. Work creates social relationships with colleagues, supervisors, and customers. Furthermore, in contemporary capitalist societies, the amount of one's wages is both a product of and produces the level of respect one receives more broadly in society; it is a sign of status, and it confers status because it allows one to care for oneself and others (see Honneth 2003, 141–42). Work in the United States becomes a major vehicle for the receipt of benefits, such as health insurance, sick and vacation leave, and retirement (Hacker 2006). Thus, the wages and benefits of work are signs of recognition.

State benefits are more directly tied to political belonging than are wages. Historically, the expansion of social-welfare programs, such as pensions, helped generate national belonging and unity in times of crisis (Thelen and Coe 2017). Furthermore, such benefits signal citizenship. Although citizenship assumes a single status, conferring the same rights and privileges to all citizens, some members of society are considered worthier than others. In Europe, pensions were first given to workers, while in the United States, Civil War veterans and widowed mothers received pensions first (Skocpol 1992), symbolizing their status and their special claim to national benefits. From these experiments with the "most deserving" citizens, benefits expanded to the populace. Thus, citizenship is not signaled solely by political rights, such as the right to vote, but also by rights to social support, such as pensions and Social Security (Marshall 1950). When the significance of national citizenship seems threatened by a world economy dominated by global trade and banking, citizenship becomes defined (perhaps solely) by rights to wages and benefits, reducing the meaning of the American dream to individual economic prosperity alone (Holston and Appadurai 1999).

Home care work does not confer much in the way of wages or benefits. As a national survey of home healthcare workers found, "The picture that emerges from this analysis is of a financially insecure workforce, with low family income, a large percentage that currently or previously received public benefits, almost one-fifth without health insurance, and more than one in 10 having at least one work-related injury in the past year" (Bercovitz et al. 2011, 8). As a historically unregulated sector, home care has tended not to provide workers with many benefits and thus has not given them full political belonging. That home care is a niche employment sector for African migrants indicates the poor conditions of labor in this occupation.

Many studies detail how migrants accept the slights of their new country because they feel that their migrant status does not guarantee them the same rights as others (Ogbu 1978; Waldinger and Lichter 2003). They tend to compare conditions in the United States with those in their home countries, through a dual frame of reference, which can make them feel fortunate and grateful in comparison to those in their country of origin. However, I did not encounter such tolerance for slights among the African home care workers whom I interviewed, despite their dual frame of reference. Instead, ten to forty years after arriving in the United States, they felt disappointed by the American dream. They had not achieved what they had hoped. Two groups of workers were the most bitter: male care workers in general and female care workers in their sixties. Male care workers tended to be more educated and to have experience in white-collar jobs in their home countries; they expected to work in offices, schools, or government employment in the United States and were disappointed to find themselves working in home care instead.[1] Women in their sixties who had worked in home care for more than a decade felt that they had not been rewarded for their effort; with exhausted bodies, they worried about what would happen to them when they could no longer work. Mariam told me that she had come to the United States as a "young woman full of life" after working as a nurse in Guinea and Sierra Leone. Now, at the age of sixty-four, after nineteen years of working in home care, her body was "broken in two" (interview, March 29, 2016, Maryland). A short woman, she walked unsteadily with a limp and listed to the right. Younger female workers felt similarly but less strongly, in part because they hoped that if they invested in their educations, they might be able to work in a more rewarding field.

Bitterness about the failure of the American dream pushes older workers to invest in their home countries, where they feel more assured of receiving care for their aging bodies and where their income, although low, may allow them to own property and a house—unlike in the expensive housing markets of the metropolitan areas of the eastern United States. Megan O'Leary (2016) finds that black migrant home care workers in the Boston area consider the United States to have a strong state system for taking care of its seniors, in comparison to the Caribbean and African countries from which they have migrated. I did not encounter such admiration for the care of older adults in the United States. Instead, my interlocutors thought of nursing homes as terrible places to age, and they knew they lacked the savings with which their wealthy patients paid for home care. Many had thus made the calculation that they could not grow old in the United States. Although the decision to leave the United States revealed their lack of political belonging, their disenchantment simultaneously indicated that they felt they had the right to make claims. However, such disgruntlement did not lead them to political engagement or labor activism, in part because they spent so many hours working. Instead, by directing their energies toward returning to their home countries, they rendered their complaints politically invisible.

Regulations in the Home Care Industry and Political Belonging

I had many conversations about home care with a friend, a second-generation Jamaican American medical doctor, who started an online service to link home care workers with multiple agencies. She called home care "the Wild West" (field notes from conversation, May 16, 2016, Maryland). Historically, she was correct. When the Fair Labor Standards Act (FLSA) was passed during the New Deal, it exempted domestic service and agriculture from national labor protections, such as minimum wage and overtime regulations. African Americans were concentrated in precisely those fields, and their exclusion won the support of southern Democrats for the FLSA (Nadasen 2010; Poole 2006). A worker was framed as a white male industrial worker, and it was this kind of worker who received the most protection. Different kinds of labor protections—and different kinds of political belonging—thus accrued to different kinds of workers. Because of the racial segregation of the workforce in the 1930s, these differences signified African Americans' lack of full citizenship, expressed also through obstacles to exercising their right to vote during the same period. Their exclusion from political participation has received more attention than their exclusion under the FLSA. As African Americans obtained wider work opportunities as a result of the civil rights movement, they increasingly moved out of domestic service and agricultural work, into a more diverse range of occupations.

Even as some African Americans left domestic service, those remaining in this occupation demanded more labor protections for domestic work, and in response, it began to be recognized by federal employment legislation. Social Security legislation included most forms of domestic labor, beginning in 1951, as did minimum wage legislation in 1974, due to organizing by African American household workers in some cities and the National Committee on Household Employment (Nadasen 2010; Rollins 1985). The expansion of the minimum wage to domestic workers in 1974 resulted in employers in Boston reducing the number of hours of employment but expecting more work during those hours (Rollins 1985). At the same time, with this change, the hourly pay rate increased substantially and the pay range contracted—from $0.60–$1.65 an hour to $1.90 an hour—as wages became less dependent on employers' personal preferences and negotiation, in which household workers carried little clout (Rollins 1985). However, two major decisions subsequently exempted domestic workers from protection under the FLSA (Hondagneu-Sotelo 2001). First, in 1975—just as demand for long-term care began to increase—the Department of Labor exempted elder-care workers and nannies from the FLSA, deciding that they provided companion care rather than household labor (Boris and Klein 2010). Second, it deemed live-in household workers exempt from overtime and minimum wage regulations.

In my interviews with home care agency owners and managers, I asked what had changed in the industry. One owner of an agency that was more than twenty years old said, "Back then, nothing was regulated" (interview, April 12, 2016, Maryland). Another owner, whose agency had opened thirty years earlier, said that she had seen the industry transform from "unregulated to regulated to regulated to death" (interview, February 4, 2016, Maryland). Another manager, who had worked in the industry for many years, said that home care used to be on the "back bench" in terms of government attention, but once home care could be paid for by Medicare, cases of fraud emerged, including several near Washington, DC, which revealed the need for more regulation. For example, a large case of fraud resulted in the arrest of more than twenty people, mainly Africans, in 2014 (USAO 2014, 2015). She continued, "It was not very regulated, not very structured, but in the last ten years, it has become the most regulated, and an increasing structure is being placed." As an example, she said, "At first, anyone could be an aide; now everyone is licensed and certified with annual updates to get what you need done" (interview, April 22, 2016, Maryland). In Maryland, Virginia, and New Jersey, home care workers have the same training and licensure as care workers working in nursing homes, a license that Washington, DC, began to require during my fieldwork (2015–16). Another change is that home care workers need to be supervised by a registered nurse. Thus, in the past ten years, home care has gradually become more regulated and similar to other kinds of health care.

One sign of comparatively weaker regulation, in comparison to other healthcare sectors, is the presence of registries in the home care market. In Maryland, Virginia, and Washington, DC, home care agencies operate either as employers of care workers or as registries of independent contractors. Most of the fifteen agencies I encountered operated as employers, because the Internal Revenue Service (IRS) understandably questioned whether independent contractors were really employees. One owner told me that her agency did not operate as a registry because of the risk of running afoul of the IRS but noted that "having employees is more expensive and more cumbersome" than hiring independent contractors (interview, February 4, 2016, Maryland). Agencies reported that patients tended to like registries because of their lower hourly rates. One agency with employees said that they struggled to compete with the registries' lower rates. Many of my interlocutors, on the other hand, were independent contractors because one very large agency with a long history and strong reputation in the area operated as two branches: one as an employer of home care workers and the other as a registry of independent contractors.

The registries take 20 percent of workers' wages, which some workers avoid paying, resulting in the registries reporting them to debt collection agencies. One registry caused an uproar among its independent contractors in the summer of 2016, when it increased the rates charged to patients (by $1 an hour) but not the wages of care workers. The justification it gave its patients for the rate increase was to create an online portal through which patients could pay their care workers and from which the agency could automatically deduct its 20 percent cut. Thus, the agency hoped to lessen the extent to which its staff cajoled and threatened its independent contractors for a substantial part of their paychecks, which the care workers were understandably unmotivated to hand over.

My interlocutors had different opinions as to whether it was better to work as an independent contractor or an employee. Some liked the benefits that accompanied being an employee; others felt that those benefits were weak or too expensive, so that being an independent contractor was better. An employee has no greater job security than an independent contractor, as work depends on the changing needs of patients. Although independent contractors earn a higher hourly wage than employees, they are responsible for paying their own Social Security contributions, and so essentially, they earn equivalent wages. Care workers warn their friends to pay their taxes, including into Social Security, or they will not be eligible for its benefits when they need them later in life.[2] Although independent contractors officially can control their own wage, in practice these wages are set by the industry and the registry. I never heard of a care worker negotiating for a wage higher than the registry's standard. Independent contractors are also exempt from overtime regulations. Thus, the presence of registries in the local private home care market and patients' preference for their lower rates tend to put pressure on agencies with employees to keep wages and benefits low.

As with domestic service, the paucity of labor regulation in home care is due to the work's location in private homes and its association with women's household labor (Boris and Klein 2010). These characteristics make the work invisible and devalued—as not real work in the public eye—unlike factory or industrial work, which is associated with men. Weaker regulation in home care has generated job insecurity and poor work conditions: short- and part-time jobs, long working hours, and cases that can end suddenly. Nursing homes, because they are reimbursed by government-funded Medicare and Medicaid, have been more subject to regulations, including for their employees. They are much more likely to provide their employees with health insurance, 401(k) plans, and sick and vacation time than home care agencies in the private care market, in which patients use their own savings or long-term care insurance to pay for services.

In the spring of 2016, home care agencies adjusted to two new regulations. One was a change in the Department of Labor's interpretation of the FLSA, by which home care became subject to overtime regulations. The second was the employer mandate, a provision of the Affordable Care Act (ACA) requiring businesses to provide health insurance plans to their employees. The first change came about through a court case brought by Evelyn Coke, a seventy-three-year-old Jamaican migrant, in 2007. Supported by the Service Employees International Union (SEIU), she sued for back pay for overtime work after working for twenty years for a Long Island home care agency (Greenhouse 2007). After years of court cases, and after Ms. Coke's death in 2010, the Department of Labor finally ruled in late 2011 that home care workers are subject to the same labor regulations concerning overtime as other occupations (Boris and Klein 2012). The regulation was subsequently extended to third-party employers, such as home health agencies, in 2013. The Department of Labor proposed that those regulations would come into force in January 2015. However, that date was delayed when home care agencies challenged the Department of Labor in court. The Supreme Court ruled in

August 2015 in favor of the Department of Labor, confirming that it had the right to change its understanding of the FLSA (Wheeler 2015). As a result of the court's decision, home care workers can now earn overtime pay, or one and a half times their regular wage, when they work more than forty hours a week. Agencies varied in whether they instituted the change early on (in response to the Department of Labor's anticipated change, as some reported doing in April 2014) or only after the legislation finally took effect in January 2016 (hoping that it would be delayed further by additional industry lobbying or court actions).

The overtime regulation had a profound effect on the care workers' lives. Workers reported working sixty to eighty hours a week prior to the change in the overtime ruling, but afterward, agencies limited them to forty hours to avoid overtime work. Although a few patients were willing and able to pay overtime in order to keep the same care worker whom they knew and trusted, most patients could or would not spend more for their care than they were already. Some agencies in Maryland applied the overtime regulation to their live-in care workers, although the New Jersey agencies I knew did not. Thus, in Maryland, live-in care workers worked three or four days a week, not seven. One agency manager told me, "The aides are not working as many hours as they want" and have seen their paychecks cut in half (interview, April 22, 2016, Maryland). Another agency manager said, "The workforce is struggling financially. They were able to count on a certain amount of money. We tried to prepare them, but they are not in a position to look ahead [in other words, they do not earn enough to save for the disruption]" (interview, January 20, 2016, Maryland). A third told me, "The agency is responsible for keeping the caregivers to under forty hours a week," on which the care workers can barely live (interview, February 17, 2016, Maryland). An agency owner commented that her employees were "stuffed down to forty hours" from twelve hours, seven days a week. On the positive side, she thought, live-in care workers were less prone to sudden breakdowns, where they would suddenly disappear from a job because they needed a break. Thus, as a result of the overtime regulation, "the care is better; the quality of care is better," she said (interview, April 12, 2016, Maryland).

The agencies also noted that the overtime regulation caused hardship for patients, who were forced to become familiar with a greater number of care workers. Before the overtime regulation took effect, a patient might have one care worker during the week and another on the weekend; after the overtime regulation, four to eight care workers replaced the previous two. One agency manager told me that having multiple care workers "is not good for dementia" patients (interview, February 3, 2016, Maryland). Another one said, "For the eighty-five-to-one-hundred-year-old clients with Alzheimer's and dementia, they feel that a hundred people are coming in and out." Also, on a twelve-hour shift, the patients used to have the same care worker from the morning when they woke up to the time they went to bed. Now, on an eight-hour shift, the patient wakes up with one care worker and goes to bed in the care of someone else. In the middle of the night, yet a third care worker arrives (interview, January 20, 2016, Maryland). I did not hear patients complain about these changes, because they did not seem to have experienced them directly. Yet care workers described patients' unpleasant reactions to having an unfamiliar person suddenly appear because of the numerous shift changes, as discussed in chapter 2. These new arrangements also affected the workload of the office staff. Because the number of care workers increased for each case, the office staff had to do more scheduling. They also said finding shifts for care workers had become harder because they had to accommodate their commuting time to other jobs. Thus, the overtime regulation has unintentionally depersonalized care, making home care more like a nursing home, which also operates in eight-hour shifts, and bringing in more care workers for a single day.

Care workers complained about the overtime regulation as much as home care agencies did, although not all knew why the change had occurred. Before the overtime regulation, home care workers had been able to earn enough on low hourly wages by working sixty to eighty hours a week. When the overtime regulations came into effect, agencies scheduled them for only forty hours. Linda said, "At first, you could do any hours that you want. But now you only do forty hours. With my two paychecks [for the month, arriving every two weeks], I can't pay rent. But this job is only forty hours" (interview, January 11, 2016, Maryland). As a result, Linda was looking for another job through another agency to supplement her current forty-hour-a-week position; overtime pay would not be calculated at the second agency because the first agency would only account for the hours she worked there. Thus, care workers still try to work sixty to eighty hours to make ends meet, but they do so by working at more than one agency or by combining nursing-home work with home care, as Fatu and many others did. Both strategies involve more careful coordination of schedules, more commuting, and a constant hustling for work, and thus most care workers do not succeed in working sixty to eighty hours a week as they did in the past. This change means that care workers feel more anxiety about finding work, and they spend more unpaid time in transportation between multiple jobs. Their experience speaks to the unintended effects of regulations. What was intended to protect workers has instead created greater instability and poverty because the agencies have responded to the regulations by reducing care workers' hours.

A second change in regulation came into effect in January 2015, with full compliance expected by January 2016, by which businesses with fifty or more full-time employees are mandated to offer health insurance to those employees who work thirty-two hours a week or more. Most of the home care agencies operating as employers had more than fifty employees, although a few of those I interviewed did not. As an effect of this provision of the ACA, home care agencies began offering health insurance to their care workers. (Office staff had already received health insurance through the agencies.)

Agencies have different mechanisms for determining eligibility for health insurance. Some offer it to care workers working thirty-two hours or more a week, with care workers having health insurance only in the weeks when they work thirty-two hours or more. Other agencies offer insurance only to those who consistently work thirty-two hours or more a week. Still others look at the employment record of each care worker and offer it only to those who have consistently worked thirty-two hours or more a week during the previous year. Thus, one agency owner said, "It is not the fact that we have to offer benefits that is the issue but that we have to track benefits. Our caregivers work full-time one week, part-time another, and then six to eight weeks full-time" (interview, February 3, 2016, Maryland). Another said she had just met with her fourth insurance broker, and she thought she had finally found an insurance company that understood the variable nature of home care employment: "We can't guarantee employment like they are office staff. So someone will be full-time for six months and for the next two months have eight hours [a week]." The insurance company that she liked recommended looking at the prior twelve months of employment and using those hours prospectively. The owner liked that idea, because "it means that with all the coming and going at the beginning for new employees," she would only offer health insurance to those who had worked for her agency for at least a year (interview, May 18, 2016, Virginia). Thus, the agency complied with the law exactly, despite the fact that the legislation made no sense given the variable nature of care work. Despite the burden of tracking care workers' eligibility, agencies prefer to limit their health insurance offerings, rather than using the health insurance mandate as an opportunity to offer health insurance to all their employees, regardless of the number of hours they work.

Even as agency staff complained about the administration of health insurance for their care workers, they told me that very few of their employees actually signed up for the agency health insurance because of its cost. For example, the director of one agency told me that only four of her hundred or so care workers signed up for the agency insurance (interview, January 20, 2016, Maryland). One agency offered it only to those who consistently worked thirty-two hours or more a week, which amounted to only 20 of its 246 employees. The manager of this agency read the health insurance premiums to me from a memo on her desk: those who covered only themselves paid $68.40 per month; themselves and a spouse, $447; themselves and a child, $402; and the whole family, $718. Of the twenty care workers to whom this health insurance was offered, only six took it, and even among this small number, four would later rescind it because they could not afford it (interview, April 22, 2016, Maryland). In this agency, the care workers received a different plan than the office staff, although some agencies offered the same health insurance plan to both office staff and home care workers.

One agency manager told me that the law stated that the premium had to be less than 9 percent of the gross wage. However, when she began investigating health insurance for care workers in 2015, "there was no decent product which met the threshold." The health insurance plans she saw had large deductibles, with a monthly premium of $125. She showed the plan to care workers, who said that they could not afford it. In 2015, two of their care workers bought health insurance on the state exchange of health insurance plans, probably subsidized by Medicaid in Maryland; the rest went without health insurance. In 2016, it became mandatory for individuals to buy health insurance; those who did not purchase health insurance would be penalized by paying a fine when they filed their tax returns. In 2016, four people signed up for the agency's health insurance plan; twelve bought a plan through the state exchange; two were covered through their spouse or another job, probably for a nursing home; and the remaining hundred or so would be penalized, said the manager (interview, January 20, 2016, Maryland).

Among my interlocutors, of the twenty-seven care workers with health insurance, only two (7 percent) were insured by an agency health plan. Both were single young women without dependents who paid less than $200 a month for the premium. Some care workers told me that, as an effect of this legislation, the agencies wanted them to work less than thirty-two hours a week so that they would not be eligible for health insurance. In general, because so few care workers purchased the agency's health insurance plan, this regulation did not affect the agencies very much, although the staff did have to research health insurance plans and figure out a new accounting system for managing eligibility. It also did not help care workers much, as they were either ineligible for or unable to afford the insurance, although most wished to be insured.

During the course of my research, two other regulations were being carefully watched by the home care industry. One was a "fair scheduling" proposal in Maryland that would require employers to give hourly employees their schedules twenty-one days in advance, proposed because of the retail industry's unpredictable shifts (Maryland House of Delegates 2016). Given that home care cases sometimes end suddenly—when the patient dies or goes to the hospital—this provision would increase the cost of home care. The Maryland-National Capital Homecare Association helped lobby against the bill in 2015, said one agency owner, and she hoped it would do so again if the bill was revived in 2016. She said, "Last year, we marched our heads off, and we killed it" (interview, February 3, 2016, Maryland). Maryland also mandated paid sick time for workers, beginning in October 2016. Those who worked forty hours a week would get ten paid sick days a year. As with overtime and health insurance legislation, employers could skirt this regulation by reducing their employees' weekly hours. At the same time, if followed and enforced, these two provisions would help increase care workers' sense of belonging by helping them feel recognized and reciprocated for their labor.

Workers' Health Insurance and Health

Of the thirty-three home care workers in Maryland and Virginia whom I interviewed and whose health insurance status I was able to determine, 82 percent had health insurance, and 18 percent did not (see table 6.1). Nationally, the uninsured rate among home care workers was slightly higher, at 26 percent (PHI 2016). Yolanda Covington-Ward (2016), in her study of thirty West African low-wage healthcare workers in Pittsburgh after the passage of the ACA, found that a third still did not have health insurance.

TABLE 5.1: Health Insurance Coverage among African Care Workers ($N = 33$)

Health insurance coverage	Number of care workers	Percentage
Does not currently have health insurance	6	18%
Currently has health insurance	27	82%
—ACA state exchange plan	16	48% of total; 59% of all those with insurance
—nursing-home employment	3	9%; 11%
—other family members	4	12%; 15%
—Medicare (over age 65)	2	6%; 7%
—agency insurance plan	2	6%; 7%

Four of the six who did not have health insurance explained that it was too expensive. Ernestina told me that the agency did not pay 401(k) and health benefits. She said that if she got sick, she paid for everything. "The Obama one is too expensive," she said (interview, December 29, 2015, Maryland). Victoire used to get subsidized health insurance through the expansion of Medicaid under the ACA, but her current job increased her income, causing the loss of the subsidy, so she had not had health insurance for the past ten months. Victoire had recently looked into purchasing health insurance again, but it cost $326 a month, which she considered unaffordable on her wages. She also had to order her previous tax returns from the IRS, which her last year's tax preparer had not kept, so she was waiting for a copy of her tax return to arrive so that she could reapply (interview, March 6, 2016, Maryland).

Millicent, in her early sixties, told a similar story. When I called her one day in March 2016 to see how she was doing, she told me that she

was on her way to the public health department "to see about Obama-
care." She had qualified for a subsidy for two years, but then she started
earning too much to qualify. Millicent told me that she had complained
to the health department on a previous occasion, explaining that she
never knew how much she would earn, because if her patient were to
die or go to the emergency room, she would lose her job or only get four
hours of work a day. Now that she had lost her patient, she was going
to see if she was eligible for a subsidy again (field notes from phone
conversation, March 29, 2016). The instability of these care workers'
employment and pay meant that they sometimes qualified for a health
insurance subsidy under the expansion of Medicaid in Maryland and
sometimes did not, rendering their health insurance unreliable.

Like other uninsured Americans, when uninsured home care workers seek medical care, they are presented with exorbitant bills. As a result, they avoid medical attention when they can. In the spring of 2015,
Kwadwo reported having chest pains—likely precipitated by a stressful
live-in case with a patient who was prone to sudden violent outbursts.
Uninsured, he went to the emergency room, staying overnight and receiving an electrocardiogram and an X-ray. After the tests showed no
sign of a heart problem, he returned to work. However, he received a
bill from the hospital for $15,722. The hospital wanted him to return for
a checkup, but he told me he was scared to do so because it would incur
another bill. I was worried about Kwadwo since he was a man in his fifties at potentially high risk of a heart attack, so I inquired closely about
his health. However, since he seemed fine, I did not press him to return
for a checkup. I spoke to a social worker I knew about his situation,
and she said he should apply for indigent status at the hospital. When I
shared this advice, Kwadwo already knew it. He planned to present the
hospital with documentation of his indigence; however, he had already
been told that his income of $400 a week made him ineligible for Med-
icaid. And yet, paying $15,000 for one emergency room visit seemed far
out of reach on his wages, particularly with his five dependent children
in Ghana (three phone conversations, December 30, 2015–January 12,
2016).

Irene articulated the lack of reciprocity of this situation, in which
care workers care for others but remain uncared for. We spoke by phone
long before the ACA, when a third of home care workers lacked health

insurance coverage (Smith and Baughman 2007, 23). She complained about her work: She had no health insurance, yet she was working hard for someone else's health. What would she do when she grew old? She said that the people who designed this system had no soul (field notes from phone conversation, June 3, 2008). Even after the passage of the ACA, Diane, working in private duty, similarly directly linked her lack of health insurance to her political belonging: "You don't feel part of society here as a result. Even at McDonald's [the archetype of low-wage work], you get benefits" (interview, January 8, 2016, Maryland). The lack of health insurance constituted an indictment of the United States and a sign of political exclusion.

Of those who had health insurance, over half (59 percent) received it through a state exchange insurance plan. Some received a subsidy through the expansion of Medicaid, but others did not. The other sources of health insurance were, all in small numbers, through full-time nursing-home employment, the health insurance plan of a spouse (or, in the case of one home care worker in her early twenties, that of a parent), Medicare in its traditional form (when a care worker was over the age of sixty-five), and an agency health insurance plan (see table 6.1).[3] Care workers reported spending between $175 and $800 a month, depending on how many people were covered: two single adults in their twenties reported paying $175 and $190 a month; one adult and two children paid $250 a month; and one adult in her sixties paid $287 a month. The highest amounts mentioned were $388 for one adult and one child (not subsidized) and $800 for a household of six (two adults, four children).

More than half of my interlocutors with health insurance had obtained it within the previous year, through the ACA. Thus, the act had a powerful effect on this group of low-wage workers, resulting in care workers having greater access to health insurance. Home care workers had been among the 40 million Americans who did not have health insurance, although their younger children had usually been covered through state health insurance programs for poor families. Home care workers were not poor enough to have qualified for Medicaid previously, and the instability of their work had prevented them from obtaining health insurance through their employer. PHI (2016) reports that the national rate of health coverage for home care workers increased by 14 percent between 2010 and 2014, when the major provisions of the

ACA were enacted. Specifically, there was a 22 percent increase in coverage through individually purchased plans, and a 27 percent increase in Medicaid coverage among home care workers. The increase in health insurance coverage among my interlocutors was thus higher than among the home care workforce as a whole. The expansion is significant given that a national survey of direct-care workers found that health insurance was a key indicator of job satisfaction: "Feeling fairly compensated for the jobs and receiving key benefits are significantly related to D.C.W (direct-care worker) satisfaction. Of all the benefits included in our study, two were significant: health insurance and a retirement/pension plan" (Ejaz et al. 2008, 67–68). On the basis of this survey, the study's authors recommend providing health insurance and retirement benefits to retain and recruit care workers.

The recent expansion of health insurance among this group of workers is particularly striking given that care work puts them at risk of high rates of injury. Citing a Bureau of Labor study, a report from the Institute of Medicine (2008) noted that the rate of nonfatal occupational injury or illness was four times higher among nursing aides, orderlies, and attendants than the average rate among all occupations and was higher than that of either construction workers or truck drivers, thus making health care a relatively dangerous occupation for workers' physical health. Fifty-six percent of injuries and illnesses among direct-care workers derived from interactions with patients, and 86 percent from overexertion. Home care workers may have a patient who needs to be regularly lifted and transferred to go to the toilet or to move from bed to wheelchair in the morning and back again at night, and such lifting can occur in cramped spaces in residential bathrooms and bedrooms requiring awkward postures and positions. In a national survey conducted in 2007, Bercovitz and her colleagues (2011) reported that 11.5 percent of home health workers had at least one injury in the previous twelve months, with most injuries coming from back injuries (44 percent) or other strain or pulled muscles (43 percent). Many care workers I talked to reported knee and back pain. I collected information about the health status of forty-three care workers currently working: Twenty-seven (62 percent) were currently in good health (aged twenty-five to sixty-three, with a median age of forty-five). Seven (16 percent) had knee problems (aged forty-one to sixty-six, with a median age of fifty-three), and another seven (16 percent) had back problems (aged twenty-three to sixty-five, with a median age of fifty-seven). Back and knee pains thus seemed to increase with age.

The care worker with the worst health among my interlocutors was Regina. She struggled with diabetes and high blood pressure. In 2008, when I first met her, she worked in home care. Aged forty-nine, she took eight different pills. Because of her diabetes, she had trouble seeing well enough to read, and she could not continue her nursing education as a result. One medication made her ill, and the doctor recommended heart surgery that cost $17,000, which she refused. Her new medication costs $90 for a three-months supply, rather than $425 a month as the last one had. She had just finished paying $25,000 in medical bills for a mild stroke she had sustained eight years earlier. She told me that she sometimes did not eat to pay for her medications (phone interview, December 30, 2008). She was able to bring her three oldest children to the United States in 2011. Her oldest son, in his midtwenties, set out on his own to try to be a college basketball star. Her two daughters, in their early twenties, stayed with her and began working as nursing assistants, mainly in long-term care facilities. By 2016, one was attending community college and studying to be a nurse.

Before Regina went to Ghana for a two-month trip in 2015, she had been working part-time at a nursing home and part-time at an institution for the mentally ill. When she returned to the United States, the nursing home wanted her to work full-time, about which she was delighted because she would then obtain health insurance benefits. When I expressed surprise that she could maintain a part-time job in addition to the full-time job, given her health condition, she told me that she had no money and that, while in Ghana, her credit card balance had increased. Also, because she shipped her car to Ghana, she needed to buy a new one. So she needed as much work as she could obtain. Plus, she liked the mental health institution because the residents were younger people who could lift themselves (although when they hit her, it hurt more). Furthermore, it had a union, which advocated for workers' wages to increase to $15 an hour (field notes from phone conversation, August 30, 2015).

Eight months later, in the spring of 2016, the full-time work that the nursing home had promised had still not been realized. Regina called the nursing-home administration "crooks" who did not want to give employees forty hours a week so that they would have to pay their health insurance. Initially, care workers were given only twelve hours a week. Then the nursing home increased the workers' schedules to sixteen hours a week because so many of their employees could not make ends meet. When Regina complained to her supervisor that she needed health insurance, her supervisor said that she did not want her to leave, as she was the "best worker." The supervisor asked Regina to give her time to figure out the schedule and guarantee Regina eight more hours. Regina was then scheduled for twenty-four hours a week and was "waiting" to receive more hours. Occasionally, she would get a text on her phone, based on her seniority, asking if she wanted eight more hours, for thirty-two hours a week. If she worked thirty-two hours for four weeks, she would receive health insurance. Because of the irregular hours, she was going on and off health insurance regularly, based on how many hours she had worked that week. Sometimes, when she went to the hospital, she would pay out of pocket; sometimes, she would be covered. So she continued working for the mental health institution part-time for extra income to cover her health bills (field notes from phone conversation, April 24, 2016). When I visited her in August 2016, she was in her late fifties, yet she moved like someone much older and seemed ready to retire. Working thirty-eight to forty-five hours a week rather than sixty, her diabetes and high blood pressure seemed more controlled. Dissatisfied with the working conditions in the northeastern United States, Regina relocated to Seattle with her youngest son, a teenager, in the fall of 2016 to work in home care again, lured by the promise of higher wages and more regular work (field notes from phone conversation, June 11, 2017).

Some care workers worry that care work makes one sick and leads to an early death. In a joint interview with spouses Yaw and Belinda, they talked about the unforeseen costs of live-in home care, which they both did. Yaw said,

> You think that the work pays a lot, you stay in one place, and your food is taken care of. But it is killing and low pay! If you are not mature minded, you will not do well. It does not give you benefits or health insurance. But they [care workers] don't look at these things; they look at the money. They have pressure back home, from children's school fees, or someone

dies [and they have to pay the funeral expenses for a relative]. After they get sick, they see why they need health insurance. Some people die in live-in [work] because they don't take off.

Belinda agreed: one care worker had died after working live-in for five years without once taking a day off. Belinda commented, "I take off once a month." She advised colleagues to do the same. Yaw continued, "Otherwise, you collapse. People don't think about it. . . . It is not good [to do this job] when you are young. You can't afford the benefits. Many people pay a doctor here and there [without insurance]" (joint interview, May 14, 2016, Pennsylvania). Instead, because of the lack of benefits, Yaw recommended that people enter home care only after they had completed a house in Ghana. And yet, to do the work when they were older and more prone to injury also seemed like erroneous advice to me. So perhaps this job was not right for anyone, at any age, at least under current conditions in the United States.

Janet also spoke in a frustrated and excited tone about the effect of the work on care workers' health:

People are dying. Last year, three people from Ghana died. One woman didn't wake up in the morning. She was too frustrated. I am not a baby anymore. I am not a baby anymore [meaning, she was no longer young enough to do this physical work]. Take her [the patient] to the bathroom, do this, do that. They will pay me, so you think it's okay. But there is a lot of tension. We don't have choice. Here, two months ago, a lady was sick. She was from the same agency [for which Janet worked]. She had a headache for three days, because she had not had any sleep. I said [when she called for advice] she had to go to the hospital, and she should call the agency. She collapsed, apparently, and people called 911. Her friend told me recently that she is still in the hospital. (phone interview, January 20, 2015)

Kwesi also worried that the frustrations of the work would result in mental health problems in retirement, such as dementia from stroke, or heart problems (interview, February 8, 2016, Maryland). Older care workers therefore felt that the work would kill them, unless they were careful.

Several of my interlocutors with back and knee injuries had left nursing-home work and entered home care because of those injuries. In a nursing home, they might have been required to take care of eight to fifteen residents during a shift, depending on colleagues' absences and whether the shift was during the day or night. In home care, the physical demands were usually less, depending on the abilities and weight of the patient. This finding is borne out by national surveys which show that home care workers tend to be older than nursing-home workers (Martin et al. 2009; Smith and Baughman 2007). Priscilla told me why she had left nursing-home work, which I summarize here:

> There was a leak in a water pipe at the nursing home, and they rushed to get the patients out of the beds because the beds were electric. The water was high, up to her knees (she shows me the height on her own leg with her hand), and Priscilla slipped, falling on her tailbone. It hurt, and she could not work for three years as a result. She was denied workers' compensation for eleven months, so she took the nursing home to court. Then, when she won, the lawyer she hired took a third of the compensation. Priscilla's daughter was studying pharmacy at the time, and because of the loss of her mother's income, her daughter switched to nursing, a shorter course of four years rather than six, and for which she had already done most of the prerequisites. Priscilla lost her car and "lost so much" during those three years. Priscilla was still in some pain, but she is careful so she does not end up back in the hospital. The compensation did not pay for all that she lost. Priscilla hoped, before the accident, to study for a licensed practical nursing license, but afterward, she realized that she could no longer do heavy lifting and gave up on this dream. (summary from interview, February 26, 2016, Maryland)

As Priscilla's story shows, the effects of injuries are broad, even affecting children's educational trajectories. Very few workers with injuries file workers' compensation claims (Qin et al. 2014); the fact that Priscilla did so was a political claim about what she deserved. Furthermore, in Maryland, one can only file a workers' compensation claim for back injuries when there is an acute onset of pain, which limits the claims of low-level back pain that result from regular strain and that represent the major source of workers' health complaints (Trinkoff et al. 2005). One could therefore consider Priscilla lucky that she could point to a specific accident that injured her tailbone.

As they age, home care workers struggle to continue working. They cut back on their hours or are more selective about the kinds of jobs they take. Some, finding Western medicine inadequate or too expensive, rely on herbal medicine from West Africa or other areas of the world. They force themselves to keep working until they are eligible to receive Social Security and Medicare at the age of sixty-five. Even home care is physically challenging, and they struggle to keep working. Comfort, aged sixty-four, said,

> You grow [older], and you are not the same person that you were. I wish tomorrow would be my retirement day! Sometimes I need a break. When you hit fifty, your knees go, and other things begin to go. But in this job, you can't avoid lifting. You are not the same as you were ten or twenty years ago. It is not at all encouraging when you are grown up [older]. If you can't lift, what job will the agency give you? You can give as a legitimate excuse that you don't want twelve hours or a particular person. If the person is too big to lift, you can say that. But if the person is a normal person [meaning a person of normal weight and size], you can't say you won't lift. They won't give you any job after that. (phone interview, January 18, 2016)

At some point, because of their physical condition, care workers decide that they can no longer work. The decision to stop working causes anxiety about how they will support themselves without working. Similar concerns about retirement affect Filipino caregivers in Los Angeles. Like the care workers I interviewed, they continue working into their sixties because they have not been able to save for retirement due to their low wages (Nazareno et al. 2014; Poo 2015).

Home care workers have been greatly affected by the recent expansion of health insurance. Important not only pragmatically in helping them obtain health care when they are working in an injury-prone field, it is also a sign that they are appreciated and that their work is reciprocated by American society. Their political belonging has been enhanced by the expansion of health insurance through the provisions of the ACA. However, they still struggle to obtain health insurance: it is expensive on their low wages, and the ACA employer mandate is not well suited for the precariousness of their employment. Like the Fair Labor Standards Act eighty years before, the ACA employer mandate posited a particular kind of full-time worker that did not reflect the conditions of home care work and other contingent labor. Although care workers maintain the health of older people, their own health is neglected, with negative consequences for their upward mobility and that of their children.

Wages

In 2005, the national median hourly earnings of direct-care workers were significantly lower than the average for all female workers. Despite working nearly full-time, about one-fifth of direct-care workers lived in poverty and half lived in low-income families, defined as less than 200 percent of the federal poverty level (Smith and Baughman 2007, 22). Among my interlocutors, hourly independent contractors and private duty care workers usually received $14–$18 an hour, before tax and Social Security withholdings. Privately hired care workers could keep what remained; independent contractors paid the agency 20 percent of their wages. Yaema, an independent contractor, was paid $18 an hour and worked forty hours a week. She broke down what that looked like: Each week, she earned $720. The agency's share was $144, and hers was $576 (interview, May 9, 2016, Virginia). Hourly (or live-out) employees of agencies generally earned $10–$13 an hour. Because agencies' rates did not vary widely differ, the care workers generally accepted cases based on the number and scheduling of hours and the location of the patient, including access to transportation, rather than the pay rate. Zainab explained why pay did not factor into her decision to take a particular job, saying, "Home health aides never expect a lot" (interview, May 27, 2016, Virginia). Ernestina said that sometimes she found it hard to figure out her actual wages when she was hired because it was unclear whether the rate was before or after tax: "When I took care of the two people [a couple] for $13 an hour, after taxes the rate was $9 an hour. It was humiliating. [And then] the agency will call you and treat you like you don't exist" (interview, December 29, 2015, Maryland). She often waited to receive her first paycheck from a case to figure out how much she would actually earn.

Live-in care workers generally earned $100–150 a day. Although they had to remain with the patient for twenty-four hours a day and were expected to assist the patient at night, this rate was based on a ten-hour working day. When I commented on this fact to Monica, she immediately elaborated on my observation, happy to have someone attuned to the injustice: she started working at 8 a.m., so ten hours later, she would expect to end her working day at 6 p.m. I noted that the patients in her continuing care community have dinner at 5 p.m. She said yes and that they came back to their apartments from the dining room at 6:30 p.m. So at 7 p.m., she gave her patient her medication, and she prepared her for bed at 8 p.m. or 9 p.m. Some patients even went to sleep at midnight or 1 a.m. "So this is a ridiculous job," she concluded (phone interview, May 15, 2015). However, the live-in care workers felt that they earned more than hourly care workers because they worked so many hours on a regular basis.

The low wages annoyed care workers. Joseph explained that he turned to live-in work because his pay of $11 an hour as an hourly worker did not cover his living expenses (interview, April 22, 2016, Washington, DC). Edem complained about his hourly rate of $10: "This way, the caregivers are frustrated, and when the clients disturb them, they are angry at them. We are human beings. . . . I have family. It frustrates me" (interview, May 25, 2016, Maryland).

In general, care workers were paid half of what patients paid the agency. For hourly workers, patients were charged $20–$25 an hour; some assisted-living and independent-living facilities were able to negotiate lower rates of $19 an hour for their residents with a specific agency. Belinda put it this way: "The office employs the caregivers and introduces you to the patient. Some offices take $300 a day from the client. We get paid $120 a day [for live-in work]" (interview, May 14, 2016, Pennsylvania). The arrangement frustrated care workers. Binta said: "I love the job, except that the agency takes 50 percent." She sent half of her salary to her mother in Guinea. "It is frustrating that this is my life," she said (interview, January 21, 2016, Maryland). Solomon complained, "We have no vacation days or sick days. We are human beings. I don't have overtime pay [because he does live-in]. . . . They [the agencies] make millions. It is like a show. They make good money" (interview, March 6, 2016, Maryland). Elizabeth said, "We bring them the money. Otherwise, they would have no office, no big building. They should give us respect, as human beings. If there is any trouble [with the patient], they say, 'We're sorry. You're on your own'" (interview, February 29, 2016, Maryland). Care workers were thus aware of the profit that agencies made from their labor.

Taking half of what patients are charged is egregious, not only because care workers struggle financially but because agencies have very low overhead. Agencies with more than a hundred care workers maintain small offices and staffs of five to seven people in suburban office parks, not expensive locations. However, the degree of turnover among care workers and patients means that the work of scheduling, recruiting patients, and hiring care workers does require lots of staff time. At the same time, although a nurse is on staff, little supervision or support of care workers occurs. When I inquired, an agency manager told me that overhead costs accounted for only 13 percent of the agency's half, leaving the remaining 37 percent as profit for the owner (interview, February 17, 2017, Maryland). The manager gave me this information because she thought the profit sufficiently high and that the owner ought to pay the care workers more, since they constituted the most important part of the business. Agencies that provide little help with difficult situations and few medical professionals to consult to improve patient outcomes are not much better than registries. Both treat workers as essentially on their own.

Independent contractors are paid more than employees, but because they have to pay their own taxes and Social Security contributions, their pay is similar to that of agency employees. Registries, which employ care workers as independent contractors, generally take less from the care workers (13–20 percent rather than 50–60 percent); however, my estimate is that they also make quite a bit of profit. One small registry was run out of the home of the owner and his wife, a nurse. This registry usually charged patients $2 more than what care workers were paid. If their one hundred care workers worked full-time (forty hours a week), my estimate is that the registry grossed $8,000 a week, or $400,000 a year, to cover the two salaries of the couple, the phone bills, office supplies such as a computer and printer, and home office space (interview, March 17, 2016, Maryland). In general, care workers' contention that the agencies make good money from their labor is correct.

Because of the differences in pay between the agencies and workers, many care workers seek a "private" job, in which they are hired directly by a patient and can take home all of their wages, after taxes. However, they also have to find a substitute among their friends and relations if they are sick or wish to visit their home country, and they may wait extensively before finding a new job after a patient's death. Hope explained, "Private pays good money, and it is all to you [it all goes to you]. But when the patient passes away, you take a long time to get work [a new job]. . . . It is just a hard time when the patient dies. Whereas the agency can fix you [with a new job] quickly. But you don't get big money. They take part of it" (interview, May 2, 2016, Washington, DC). The fact that their care labor is used to make a profit for others is quite visible to home health workers, attracting them to private duty. However, many return to agency employment because of the challenges in obtaining work in private duty in the long run.

Experienced care workers earn the same rate as new ones. As Gita told me, "Agencies don't see experience. If we come from somewhere else [another agency], they give us a starting wage. Everywhere's the same" (interview, May 26, 2016, Virginia). Some agencies do pay a higher rate to care workers who have worked with them for long time. One agency that uses independent contractors raises the rates from $14 to $18 (pre-tax) over the period of employment, but the owner told me that very few of their contractors earn $18 an hour because of the degree of turnover (interview, March 17, 2016, Maryland). Patients may also choose to pay more, but it depends on their ability to pay and their affection for the care worker, rather than seniority. Thus, Joseph earned $200 a day for live-in care because of the generosity and wealth of John, who called him his brother and soul mate. The Wiesniewskis chose to pay Caroline, whom they regarded as their "adopted daughter," $2 more an hour than the agency's standard rate (interview with Lucy, May 21, 2016, Maryland). Over the years, families may gradually increase the rate out of the kindness of their hearts, although not many do. Essenam had worked for Sharon for five years without receiving a raise; neither did Gita, who had cared for a patient for two years. Even when a care worker obtains a voluntary raise, once that generous patient passes away, the care worker returns to the same rate as other care workers at the agency. Furthermore, at a new agency, the care worker receives the starting salary no matter how many years she worked previously. Because upward mobility through home care work does not exist, to improve their status and income, care workers need to obtain further education and another kind of credential, as noted in chapter 1. A nursing assistant from Nigeria, interviewed by Yolanda Covington-Ward, said, "There's nowhere you're going unless you want to go to nursing school; there's nothing like a chief CNA [certified nursing assistant]" (2017, 713).

Because of the low wages, job insecurity, and lack of benefits in home care, home care workers struggle to make ends meet, much less attain economic mobility, particularly in the high-cost areas of metropolitan Washington, DC, and northern New Jersey. Anything left over is spent supporting others, and so care workers have little opportunity to save. Savings generally take the form of a house in their home country. Because of their low wages, care workers often have difficulty paying rent in the expensive housing markets of northern New Jersey or suburban Washington. They also cannot afford to reduce their hours in order to study to obtain another kind of educational credential that might result in financial security in the United States. In general, based on their low wages, care workers feel that the agencies care more about their profits than their workforce.

Leave and Other Benefits

During the time period of my fieldwork, home care workers received no vacation, sick days, or other benefits from agencies, whereas these benefits are generally offered by nursing homes. When they visit their home countries for a funeral or to see their children living there, care workers routinely take some savings with them and go into credit card debt. They return from their trip totally broke, eager to begin earning money again because they were not paid while they were not working. I learned of one patient in Ohio who gave her beloved live-in care worker, Sandra, a paid vacation against the recommendation of the agency. Sandra received a week's paid vacation the first year of employment; the second year, two weeks. The patient's daughter said, "We were really comfortable with each other. I had to be careful, because the agency told me, 'Don't give her time off.' I thought, 'How can it be?' I decided to give her time off" (phone interview, May 31, 2016). Furthermore, the patient's daughter gave Sandra every Sunday off. Many care workers I met longed to attend church on Sundays but could not. An agency manager also criticized home care workers' lack of break time: "In the hospital, at lunch time, you go away from your work station. You can enjoy the fresh air. But as an aide, you don't get a lunch break because you can't leave the patient. With live-ins, it used to get really bad before the aides would complain about the clients not sleeping at night or getting up three to four times in a night. This is one thing the government found, and it became important to push for the ACA and have health benefits" (interview, April 22, 2016, Maryland). The lack of benefits struck many as unfair and as leading to lower quality care.

Gilbert, who may have had higher expenses than some other care workers because his wife and children also lived in the United States, complained bitterly to me about the benefits offered by the agency. He said that he had been asking for employer health insurance since 2011 but only received it in 2015, after the passage of the ACA:

> I don't know why the office forgets about the field, and I say "forget" be-
> cause all the workers in the office can wake up in the morning, and if
> their son or daughter is sick and the worker can't come to the office, they
> can call in. Last year, when I was working for the man who passed away,
> my wife had an emergency. I called [the agency], and they told me they
> don't have anyone [to replace me]. I said that if I can't have the day off,
> perhaps I could have six hours off. They told me they don't have nobody
> [no substitute] live-in. . . . Anybody they hire at the office, whether hourly
> or salary, gets benefits and all that. We don't get that. Yet the field is bring-
> ing in the money. But we are not being assisted. We are like second-class
> workers. I am not happy.

The month before, he had wanted to take a day off to have a confer-
ence call with his three siblings, a complicated arrangement because
they lived in Ghana, Italy, and Germany, in different time zones than
the United States. They needed to plan the care of their father, who
was in the hospital in Ghana. Gilbert asked the office on Thursday to
have Saturday, Sunday, or Monday off, but the agency did not find a
live-in replacement for any of those days, instead telling him to take
off Tuesday. Fortunately, Tuesday was convenient for his other siblings,

and even more happily, his father in Ghana recovered (phone interview, February 19, 2015). Gilbert was upset that the office did not recognize his own care needs and felt like a "second-class" worker in comparison to the hourly workers and office staff employed by his agency.

Millicent complained about her agency manager: "If you say that you have an emergency or need to take time off, [the agency manager] gets mad at you. If you are ill, she tells you to come in anyway," putting the patient at risk. Millicent had told the agency manager that she needed to go to the airport to pick up her young adult daughter, who was traveling from Ghana to the United States for the first time. The manager responded that Millicent should find someone else to go to the airport in her stead. Millicent thought this response was heartless: Would the agency manager not go to the airport to pick up her own daughter? When she was ill, did she come to work? Millicent told the manager that she came to the United States to work, so if she was asking for time off, it was because she needed it (field notes from visit, January 30, 2016, Maryland).

Care workers were most aggrieved about the lack of unpaid leave when it affected their ability to care for their own kin. In general, the lack of sick and unpaid leave was another sign that the agency did not care about its workers. Job insecurity also contributed to care workers' inability to attain the American dream of middle-class status.

Job Insecurity

As noted above, job insecurity characterizes care work. The insecurity derives from the variable nature of patients' care needs and home care's association with domestic service, in which work is dependent on the personal pleasure of the individual employer. Agencies do not protect care workers, whether as employees or independent contractors, from instability. Instead, agencies fit care workers to patients' schedules and needs, which they view as the paramount good (Mol, Moser, and Pols 2010b). More and more jobs are becoming like home care, as part of "the Great Risk Shift" (Hacker 2006), in which economic risk is offloaded by companies and governments onto workers' families and households and in which more and more workers have contingent employment.

Because of both the uncertainty of employment and the low rate of pay, care workers would like as much employment as they can obtain.

Two jobs are safer than one, because if they lose one job through the death, ill health, or displeasure of the patient, they still receive income from the other job. Oriane told me, "I always have two jobs in case a client passes" (interview, January 19, 2016, Maryland). After a death, care workers can spend several months unemployed or working only substitute jobs for several shifts a week. Millicent told me about a friend who had not worked for nine months following her patient's hospitalization (field notes from visit, January 30, 2016, Maryland). Essenam, who had worked full-time for forty hours a week for five years, lost her job when Sharon died in January 2017. Two months later, in March, when I visited her, Essenam had worked only twelve hours in the past week, substituting on three different cases. During this period of employment scarcity, Essenam's daughter was making a decision about which college to attend, and Essenam recommended community college as the cheapest option. By the middle of May, five months later, Essenam was working full-time again, albeit in two separate jobs, and her daughter had convinced her to let her go to Howard University instead.

Because of the uncertainty of employment, care workers often have credit problems. Sometimes they lose their houses to foreclosure, as is highlighted in the next interlude, because mortgages, like health insurance, are based on a regular monthly income. Care workers often struggle to take advantage of these savings mechanisms or lose money because of them, due to the precarity of their jobs.

"They Don't Care"

Based on the metrics of wages, benefits, and responsiveness to the complaints of workers and patients, care workers generally feel that agencies care more about their profits than their workers. Zainab said, "In some agencies, as soon as the client calls them to complain, they tell you to leave the case" (interview, May 27, 2016, Virginia). Solomon said that as far as the agency is concerned, "the client is always right," as in a customer service approach. "If they really wanted to iron things out, they shouldn't sweep things out of [under] the carpet. Otherwise, it will catch fire or smell" (interview, March 6, 2016, Maryland). More strongly, Ernestina said, "The agency doesn't regard you as human." Nothing had ever happened to her, but she had witnessed a situation in which a patient's daughter abused a care worker, and when the care worker complained, the daughter counterclaimed and took the care worker to court. Ernestina thought that someone from the agency should have gone with her friend to court, as a sign of support. In the end, her friend was vindicated, but she was not reimbursed for the days she lost in court (interview, December 29, 2015, Maryland). Julie, in contrast, felt that the agency managed both the patient and the care worker fairly: "They [the agency staff] accept what the client says, because the client is always right, but they don't really put blame on the employee either" (interview, May 6, 2016, Washington, DC).

Agencies did not do very much to support care workers when they encounter challenges with a case. One patient, who developed a close relationship with her care worker, felt that the agency was not very helpful, with the exception of finding this wonderful care worker: "The more I had a relationship with [the care worker], the more I didn't tell them [the agency staff]. . . . They were very helpful in finding people, but otherwise they didn't do much." Initially, she said, "It [using the agency] was worth it. We did need someone. But once we found [the care worker], they were making a lot of money and doing nothing. I don't think [the care worker] had the highest opinion of them, and that seemed to be the reputation among the workers, who didn't feel it had their best interests at heart. I don't think it is that unusual" (phone interview, May 31, 2016). Her assessment—in which she gradually came to assume the perspective of the care worker with whom she worked in tandem to care for her mother—was reflected in my interviews with care workers.

Micheline said that the people who send you out from the office have never done home care work themselves: "They just take someone [a care worker] who is available and try to match the person. I don't know why they don't videotape the client. It is all about the business and money. They don't protect me." One day, Micheline was sent to a rural area where she felt that they were not "familiar with colored people." Frightened, she refused to take the case (interview, May 21, 2016, Maryland). Gilbert also felt that the office staff should have visited their workers and worked in home care for a month "to see how the field is." He complained that the training offered by the agencies was "surface" and that "they throw you into the deep. We are human beings, and the work is not an easy thing" (phone interview, February 19, 2015). Thus, the office staff's lack of experience with home care meant that they could not adequately train care workers and give them assistance; instead, care workers turned to one another for advice. Were the office to truly support and supervise its care workers, particularly through using nurses with experience as home care workers, overhead costs would increase and profits would be reduced.

Beza felt that the lack of care for her signaled that the agency also did not care for the patient: "All they want is a body there. That bothers me. Once a week, they could call to say, 'What is going on with the client? What changes do you see?' I log any changes I see at the end of the day by phone. But they have never asked me, 'Are you having a hard time?' They don't come and visit. Even when [her patient] fell, they never called back, to ask how she is doing. I am wasting my breath on the time machine [reporting what happened during the day]" (interview, May 18, 2016, Maryland). Zainab felt similarly. A feisty young woman from Sierra Leone, she had been raised in the United States since adolescence by a mother who also worked in home care. Looking younger than her twenty-three years but speaking from a much wiser vantage point, Zainab said that when she was insulted by a patient, "You write about it in the note to the agency about how the day went. But if it is constant, and going on every day for six months, you stop. The agency doesn't really do anything. That's their money. If you call them, they will just ask, 'Do you want to go to another case?' You'll say, 'No.' They say, 'The client's always right.' If they want to investigate? No one is there" (interview, May 27, 2016, Virginia). Care workers would appreciate more support from agency staff. They would like to talk about their patients and their own well-being with agency staff, given their autonomy and responsibility. The reporting systems felt like speaking into the void and were therefore considered useless.

What office staff did care about was money, both payments to the care workers and payments from the patient. Oriane complained about one office staff member who, despite being her junior in age, spoke to her in a way that she considered insulting:

> She called me and talked to me like I am a little girl, when I'm older than her. I had dropped my time sheet under the door because there was no slot [in the door]. She asked why I put the time sheet under the door? She

wasn't soft in her speech. She was loud and mad. I said, 'I'm sorry; I won't do it anymore. I can fax it to you. I forgot to clock in the first time.' She told me, 'I bet you clock out when you go.' I felt insulted, and her supervisor never called to mediate this conflict between us. (interview, January 19, 2016, Maryland)

Care workers often felt that agency staff talked to them disrespectfully, treating them as not fully human or like children.

Even some agency staff felt that they mistreated care workers and should have mistrusted the patients instead, although this concern usually involved the patient's payment to the agency rather than care issues. One agency supervisor told me that some patients' children did not want to pay the bill for their parents' care because they wanted a larger inheritance, so they would complain that the care worker had slept on the job. Sleep by a care worker was grounds for immediate termination, but sometimes the supervisor followed up with a patient regarding the complaint's accuracy. In one case, as a result of a patient's complaint about the care worker's sleeping, the agency fired the care worker. Several months later, the supervisor called the patient to ask about the care, and the patient said that the same care worker had been wonderful, making the supervisor suspicious about the previous accusation. The supervisor said, "There needs to be justice for the caregiver and client. They [the care workers] are out there on their own. It is a crazy world, and they can be killed. One caregiver called to say there were guns in the house, and they [her own agency] just told her that she should be careful" (interview, April 5, 2016, Maryland).

As a study of childcare placement agencies in Canada notes, "There are profound structural pressures on agencies to identify with the employer over the interests of the employed domestic worker. The objective class interests of the agency as a small business supported by a clientele of employing families tend to mold and alter any countervailing forces that compel identification with the domestic employee" (Bakan and Stasiulis 1995, 323). Similarly, my interlocutors did not feel cared for by their employers. The supervision of their work did not acknowledge its core: the care of another human being. Instead, through the agency's actions, their labor was devalued and they, in turn, felt like second-class employees or as nonhuman.

Political Action in the United States

Although African home care workers have many complaints about their work, they have not organized around these issues thus far. There have been many efforts to organize home care workers, dating from the mid-1970s (Boris and Klein 2010). Furthermore, many Central American migrants have been eager to unionize, in part because their extensive kinship and friendship networks enable organizing efforts (Delgado 1993; Milkman 2006). SEIU began to organize nursing-home workers in the 1980s (Lopez 2004). As we have seen, many home care workers have worked previously or simultaneously in nursing homes, and to some extent, their sense of what they are owed is based on comparing themselves to both nursing-home workers and agency office staff. Organizing efforts among home care workers began with pressing the states that have funded home care through Medicare and Medicaid to allow home care workers to unionize, as employees of the state rather than as private employees of their patients. This effort was successful in Oregon, Washington, and California (Mareschal 2007). Minnesota, Connecticut, and Vermont have also passed bills allowing the unionization of privately paid home care workers. Since 2010, the National Domestic Workers Alliance, a grassroots organization of domestic workers founded in 1990, has pressured states to adopt a domestic workers' bill of rights to bring housekeepers, nannies, and eldercare workers under existing state labor laws. So far, this effort has succeeded in Oregon, Illinois, New York, California, Hawaii, Connecticut, and Massachusetts. The fight for a minimum wage of $15 an hour, which has been occurring in many metropolitan areas, including Washington, DC, would also impact many home care workers. Organizing efforts on behalf of domestic workers have also taken place in other countries, such as Italy (Andall 2000), and internationally. In 2011, the International Labour Organization adopted the Domestic Workers Convention for the estimated 50–100 million domestic workers worldwide, many of whom cross international borders to work (Human Rights Watch 2011).

As an observer, I attended a rally for a $15 minimum wage in Washington, DC's city hall in April 2016. It was organized by SEIU, which includes many healthcare workers. Those representing the home care workforce were mainly African American women, although I did meet a male Nigerian care worker who usually worked live-in. Unfortunately, our schedules prevented us from meeting on his next day off. The other Africans present were Ethiopians who worked in the restaurants and newsstands of the Washington-area airports. Of the roughly 1,500 individuals who work in the three airports' retail shops, 60–75 percent are Ethiopian. The Ethiopian airport retail workers have become well organized and even staged a brief and small march through a terminal at National Airport on April 12, 2016. Moreover, SEIU has organized a major campaign among baggage handlers and cleaners at thirty airports nationally, which included holding a one-day strike in March 2016 (Constable 2016). The fact that Ethiopians—the African migrant group with the longest history in the United States, dating from the 1980s—have become involved in advocating for labor rights suggests that as other African migrant groups grow in number and become more settled, they too will become politically and socially organized (see Delgado 1993). However, African home care workers seemed largely unaware of these developments; I did not ask my interlocutors about them, and only one mentioned them to me. Kwesi, angry and tired of home care, said that home care workers should organize (interview, February 8, 2016, Maryland).

Aside from the complaints they voiced to me, care workers engaged in other smaller actions with a lower risk of repercussions. Caroline, a confident and forthright young woman who had lived in the United States since adolescence and who was deeply valued by her patient Jacob, said that she was willing to complain to her agency about wages. At a recent semiannual care workers' party organized by her agency, she was struck by the fact that those receiving awards for thirty years of service were paid the same wage as those hired yesterday. She said that in six months, at the agency's Christmas party, she would request a raise from the president of the agency, who by his demeanor and dress appeared to be a wealthy man. If he refused, then she would start a petition among the agency's care workers. She told me that care workers got 40 percent of what the agency charged patients. She also thought that care workers ought to receive paid sick leave and vacation days, because she knew care workers who worked while sick and made their patients vulnerable to their illnesses (interview, July 12, 2016, Maryland). Thus, like other care workers (Stacey 2011, 155), she used the cause of patients' well-being to advocate for her own.

Drawing on the work of Susan Gal (2003), Lois McNay argues that "there is a huge difference between recognizing injustice, identifying systemic domination and common interests, devising strategies for action and, finally, feeling able to act. Even when there is substantial misrecognition and subordination, resistance might not emerge if the symbolic elements with which to formulate agency are not present" (2008, 140). African home care workers certainly recognize the injustice of their working conditions. Denied reciprocities to which they feel entitled through their good care of others, they ask to be recognized as human beings deserving of care. At the same time, they have not (yet?) mobilized around their common interests or systemic discrimination, nor have they identified which discursive language and symbolic elements would allow them to act with meaning and purpose. Instead, they remain fractured, isolated in their private pain. A few sympathetic patients who feel close to their care workers have come to understand these grievances and have shifted to be in solidarity with their care workers, but most have not. Care workers' grievances are muted, shared with close associates; generally, they do not turn into political or workplace action. Instead, care workers escape from or refuse the worst situations without challenging the agency or patients directly. However, the fact that such overt political resistance has not yet happened does not mean that it will never occur.

The African home care workers' bitterness thus represents a complicated sense of belonging: they belong enough to feel entitled to certain kinds of recognition and redistribution and to feel angry at the injustice of their treatment, but not enough to organize symbolically and practically against this humiliating labor system. Many instead decide that this state of affairs confirms that they belong in their home countries rather than in the United States. It is there that they imagine they will reap the rewards of their labor and attain the human dignity denied them in the United States.

Conclusion

A key insight is that workplace conditions—which seem impersonal in that all care workers are subject to them—are taken as personal injuries and slights. Care workers feel unappreciated, both by interpersonal interactions with their patients and by agencies' immaterial and material treatment of them, in comparison to agency office staff, nursing-home workers, and fast-food preparers. Workplace conditions generate a sense of social exclusion (Aronson and Neysmith 2001). Social exclusion through work affects not only migrants but all workers who do not have benefits or a living wage. Americans' tolerance of economic inequality contradicts the political equality of citizenship in a democracy. The conditions of home care work are a major reason why African home care workers feel ambivalent about belonging and a strong sense of injustice. They refuse their recognition as not valuable or worthy of appreciation, but regardless of their attempts at self-respect, care work takes an inexorable toll on the body and mind.

Thus far, these African migrants have not advocated for themselves directly, meaning that at one level, they do not feel they belong enough to advocate for themselves. Only Caroline, who had attended high school in the United States, had a plan for confronting the agency, although I am not sure she ever did so; Priscilla went to court for workers' compensation; and Kwesi suggested home care workers should unionize. It may be that labor mobilization will occur in the second generation, among the children of these care workers, some of whom are following their parents into home care.

Thus, some modification is needed to Ogbu's point (1978) about the way that migrants respond to injustice. This research suggests that migrants do not simply accept the humiliations of their new country and feel lucky in comparison to their country of origin. Instead, African home care workers are deeply hurt and angered by workplace conditions. The lack of reciprocity for their care work indicts the political society of the United States. However, their dual frame of reference means that many put their energies into returning home rather than carving out a more just and livable space for themselves in the United States. This is particularly illustrated in the case of Elizabeth, who retired to Ghana, as illustrated in the following interlude.

Interlude

Foreclosure

I sat with Elizabeth in her small, dimly lit bedroom one evening in February 2016. We sat on two plastic chairs, facing her bed. Multiple suitcases were stacked high, almost to the ceiling, in a corner of the room. A computer sat on the desk behind us. It was the first time I had met her. Deborah, her "niece" in the United States and a thoughtful young woman who also did care work, had recommended that I talk to Elizabeth, and we had arranged to meet on one of her days off from live-in work. That day, Elizabeth had gone to the doctor and then shopping with another niece. At the end of her full day, we met at her home—a two-story, four-bedroom brick house, with a driveway, two-car garage, and yard—in a middle-class African American suburban neighborhood in Prince George's County, Maryland. The rest of the house was dark, although prayerful singing emanated from the tenant in the basement.

Elizabeth was a short woman, about five feet tall and a little fat. Her eyes were very expressive behind her glasses. About to turn sixty-six years old, she walked slowly and with difficulty, as if she were in pain. She told me that she had high blood pressure and had been diabetic for two years, which made her feel lethargic, bloated, and sleepy. She used bitter melon as an herbal medicine to help control the diabetes.

Bitterness poured out of Elizabeth when I asked her about her life and work. She had come to the United States from Ghana more than forty years earlier, in 1974. She had experienced two major betrayals in her work, among many lesser ones. The most personal was when she worked for a nursing home and hurt her back while lifting a heavy patient. After filing workers' compensation, the administration made a "plot with my coworker. They said that a patient—who couldn't talk!—said that I beat him up." Elizabeth was surprised by the accusation because the patient had cooperated when she took care of him. "I didn't understand what had happened initially, or why this accusation was made." She lost her job with the nursing home and went into home care instead. If she was very careful, her back did not hurt her. Having one patient to lift at a time, rather than eight to fifteen in the nursing home, helped. Watching her walk made me wonder how she could lift anyone at all.

The second betrayal was the imminent loss of the house in which we were sitting. Its impending foreclosure explained why the inside of the house was a bit run down, particularly the kitchen, which showed signs of smoke damage above the stove. Elizabeth had calculated she had paid half a million dollars in mortgage payments in the thirteen years since she bought the house for $320,000. Zillow, an online source of housing information, valued the house at $240,759 at the time of our interview—half of what she had spent on mortgage payments. Elizabeth had sacrificed for the sake of the house; for thirteen years she delayed visiting Ghana in order to pay the mortgage. What bothered her about the foreclosure was the money put into the house, with nothing to show for her efforts.

For most Americans, home ownership is a key symbol of the American dream. Some characteristics of personhood—such as responsibility and morality—are signaled by the possession of a house. Housing codes a person's position in the life course, as "owning a home for middle-aged Americans has been a sign that a person not only is 'making it' financially but also is 'biographically on schedule'" (Hummon 1989, 218). Thus, young adults are expected to establish their own residences separate from their parents, and older adults try to remain in their houses to thwart the symbolic implications to self that a move to a nursing home would entail (Hummon 1989; Perry 2014). Housing becomes an expression of personal identity through its decoration, form, and location and is thus subject to individuals' psychological processes (Hummon 1989). Emotions attach to a house, the materially built space. The house helps bolster a particular view of self.

For many Americans, furthermore, their home is their major asset and form of wealth. Americans expect houses will appreciate in value and provide a nest egg for retirement and other needs. Because of the centrality of home ownership to stable, middle-class adulthood in the United States, the federal government supports home ownership, particularly for whites, through publicly backed loans (nicknamed Freddie

Mac and Fannie Mae). Although home ownership may result in middle-class status, home ownership among the African care workers I knew was often a source of wealth extraction, as it was for Elizabeth.

Home ownership does not reward African Americans as it does white Americans. Although all houses lost value in 2007–8, leading to the financial crash of 2008, the housing market in general regained its vigor by 2016. But not in African American neighborhoods. A *Washington Post* analysis of the Atlanta area and a Knight Ridder analysis of the three hundred largest metropolitan areas found that housing values recovered less from the housing market crash in zip codes where African Americans were the largest group (Badger 2016). The zip code of Elizabeth's mainly middle-class African American neighborhood suffered twice as many foreclosures as the United States as a whole (6.5 foreclosures per ten thousand homes compared to 3.2, reported the real estate website Zillow). Even upper-middle-class African Americans who bought large homes in suburban neighborhoods around Atlanta saw their homes decrease in value, so that they ended up paying more on their mortgages than the worth of the houses (Badger 2016). Like Elizabeth, African Americans may feel that they ended up with nothing. Houses are a mechanism for making a self and attaining a sense of self-worth, but because inequalities of race and class are instantiated through houses, some kinds of selves are at risk of degradation and some kinds of social persons are vulnerable to downward mobility.

Why does owning a house result in wealth depletion rather than wealth creation for African Americans and African migrants who are racialized in the United States as similar? Some of the reasons reflect continued discrimination in the housing industry, with African Americans targeted for predatory lending during the housing bubble, making them more vulnerable to foreclosure and affecting the value of neighboring houses. Furthermore, African American neighborhoods are less attractive to white buyers, leading to fewer potential buyers and less price competition. These processes speak to systemic racism, which is less visible than the racial insults and deliberate humiliations discussed in chapter 2. They affect African migrants in addition to African Americans.

Finally, mortgages may make sense for those in occupations with a steady monthly income and salary increases for seniority and experience—but not for the increasingly common conditions of income volatility among American workers (Hacker 2006). In home care, as noted in chapter 5, experience and seniority do not matter. Periods of unemployment and underemployment characterize the temporal rhythm of home care, making home care workers chronically anxious about their work. Thus, Elizabeth said that she had fallen behind on mortgage payments during a period of unemployment. She was not the only care worker I met with housing troubles: For many years, foreclosure loomed over Millicent's much smaller and cheaper townhouse, estimated by Zillow to be worth $100,000 less than what she had paid for it in 2005. The foreclosure finally happened in December 2017, in the middle of a live-in job that she could not leave. For both Elizabeth and Millicent, marital conflicts compounded their financial difficulties when their husbands refused to pay their shares of the mortgage.

For Elizabeth, the loss of her house after more than a decade signaled her lack of acceptance in the United States; she could not establish a home here. Elizabeth told me that sometimes she just shut the door to her room in her patient's home and cried. When African Americans go to Ghana, she said, they are welcomed as "sisters and brothers" lost through the slave trade. But when Africans come to the United States, "we are not accepted." She sounded a little choked up saying this to me.

One sign of her exclusion was that she could not afford to live in the United States if she stopped working. Reflecting on her betrayals, Elizabeth said, "The arrangement is that when you are old, they leave you with nothing. Now that I am retiring, they are attacking your little money." Because of this "arrangement," with the rules stacked against her, she thought she would return to Ghana soon. Her Social Security based on forty years of low wages would not stretch very far in the United States; it would not cover the cost of housing and other necessities. "There is not enough money. Here you cannot make it. You would be compelled to go and work again. Your health is gone. You have broken your back, your wrist, and your shoulder." Her words made me think that what was broken was her heart or at least her sense of hope.

Elizabeth saw me out and gave me several loaves of bread that she had baked. She would be okay, she reassured me. Two "surrogate daughters," including Deborah, would help her pack up the house soon, in preparation for the upcoming foreclosure, although she wished she had more time to do so. Soon she planned to go to Ghana, to retire, where she had built a house in her hometown, the capital Accra. Her son, in his thirties, and his wife and children would stay in the United States; Elizabeth had divorced her husband for infidelity some years before.

Deborah informed me Elizabeth had returned to Ghana in September 2016, and I visited her a few months later in December 2016. Although Elizabeth continued to struggle with her diabetes and other health conditions, I was overjoyed to see her happy, relaxing and cooking under the mango tree in the large yard of her house, where she lived with her nephew, his wife, and their affectionate toddler, who was devoted to Elizabeth and on whom she doted. She compared elder care in Ghana positively to the United States: "Here [in Ghana], people take care of you," referring to her nephew and his wife. She lived on her Social Security payments and experimented with making bread for sale, distributing it for free among her congregation as advertising. As for her house in the United States, the bank's seizure was imminent. She had put half a million dollars put into it but would receive only $3,000 from its sale. Even that she struggled to wrestle from the bank. "American dream!" she said scornfully.[1] In the United States, one would end up in a nursing home. Here in Ghana, in contrast, she would grow old by enjoying the fruits of her many years of work, in the shade of her mango tree.

Conclusion

Recognition and Belonging through Care

This book has examined the complex ways in which belonging is generated and negotiated in a globalized world. Belonging comprises felt attachments, mutuality between persons, and entitlements claimed or denied. Belonging is generated through both interpersonal practices and routines across multiple contexts, in part because the nation-state is no longer a completely meaningful vehicle for social identity. New terms to claim and negotiate belonging are emerging through dependence and vulnerability (Ferguson 2013), the purchase of citizenship through capital investment (Ong 1999), and universal human rights. Another one of those contexts is work. As we have seen, for African migrants in the United States, a significant form of employment is elder-care work. Experience working in this field shapes their sense of political belonging in the United States.

Care is often considered central to the making of kin relationships and the intimate domains of family life. Yet building on the new kinship literature, I have argued that care is central to processes of belonging in general, including political belonging. Elder care structures relationships between migrants and more established residents in particular ways. A focus on elder care reveals the ways that emotions are deeply intertwined with social and political relations and the ways that relations and understandings of power shape the self. This discussion makes clear that care does not solely entail positive associations, sentimentality, or good intentions but rather involves tensions and frictions (Mol 2010). This understanding leaves room for the negative effects and experiences of care, which often involve power asymmetries (Thelen and Coe 2017). In the philosophical discussion of the ethics of care, as well as in much anthropological work on care, care is too often seen as solely positive, ignoring the kinds of hierarchies, humiliations, and power struggles that result from care. In this book, I have shown how power has profound effects on the self and emotion.

In the United States, care work is associated with domestic service, which is itself sutured to a history of racialized slavery and political exclusion. In care work, power is mediated through narratives of self and other, in which African care workers are represented as domestic servants, animals, and children. Patients employ racist, hierarchical, and gendered insults to socially exclude, discipline, and distance their African care workers. Care workers recognize themselves temporarily in these ascriptions, reject them privately while accommodating them publicly, or reject them indirectly by leaving, a form of revenge on someone who depends on their care. They affirm their dignity by investing in other social relations with coworkers and kin. They learn to laugh and attribute insulting statements to dementia, in turn making the patient less than a full human being, without agency (Taylor 2010). Despite these defenses, care workers are still affected by these assaults, which invalidate their humanity and devalue their care work. They cry momentarily before gathering support from colleagues and friends. From these experiences, they form an opinion of their political belonging in the United States.

Care also evokes and creates social intimacy and closeness, which both patients and care workers capture through the language of kinship. They use kin terms tentatively and jokingly; both patients and care workers consider their belonging to one another through kinship as temporary (for the anticipated short duration of the patient's life) and uncertain (needing to be affirmed by significant others, such as spouses, children, and others in the patient's social network). Patients tend to draw on kin relationships of affiliation through marriage or cogenerational relationships, such as siblingship, while care workers construct hierarchical relationships of parenthood based on seniority and generation. Belonging does not mean equality in the ideal sense of democratic citizenship but affection, appreciation, and service. Care workers feel appreciated by kin relations, even hierarchical and contingent ones. Practical kinship is recognized not only discursively and symbolically but also through financial assistance, advice, and participation in ritual activities for kin. Some care workers receive a significant financial gift on the death of a wealthy and affectionate patient, which is used to obtain more education, buy a house, or go on pilgrimage to Mecca, as in Binta's case. The relationships established through care thus facilitate some redistribution of wealth but not to a significant extent, as official kin inherit the bulk of wealthy patients' assets. Patients' social-class status is transmitted more regularly to their official kin than to their practical kin of care workers.

Based on this research among African home health workers in the United States, I argue that recognition is key to belonging as it is felt and performed. Recognition may not always be positive—the other person may not always be recognized as an equal other—but may instead demean or humiliate, incorporating another into the body politic in a subordinate position as a servant or excluded from it as an animal or foreigner. Furthermore, recognition is tightly connected to material forms of care. Care workers interpret material exchanges as one aspect of recognition to evaluate their worth in another's eyes. They consider reciprocity to be central to appreciation, and such material reciprocity occurs not only interpersonally, as when care workers inherit from patients, but also through the more impersonal conditions of work. such as wages, health insurance, and benefits. Care workers understand material reciprocity as indicating their status. During the period of my research, the Affordable Care Act (ACA)—particularly through its expansion of Medicaid eligibility—gave health insurance to many home care workers who had not previously had any.[1] This provision is quite significant given that care work causes chronic injuries, such as back and knee strain, and that care workers complain about the lack of health insurance as an indictment of the United States in general. In Irene's thinking, the people who designed this system have no soul. At the same time, the ACA, like other government programs before it, recognizes only a particular kind of worker—a full-time employee—which does not account for the contingent employment of home care workers and an increasing number of workers in other sectors.

Significant for the crafting of self, social relations, and social meaning (Kondo 1990; Sennett 1998; Stacey 2011), work gives people a particular social identity, both within the workplace and within society, especially in differentiated societies such as the United States, in which occupations generate prestige and pay. Care work generally does not create social mobility for African migrants. Care workers' lack of social

mobility and their inability to retain a house or to pursue further education after many years of care work leads to bitterness and tears. Thus,
their social and political exclusion is an emotional assault on the self.
This insight further shows that the private and the public are interconnected, with African care workers taking the impersonal conditions of
work as signs of their status in the United States, in which the distribution of resources indexes appreciation. Interpersonal relations with
patients, as well as wages and job security, become central to evaluating
reciprocity—whether care workers are treated fairly in the United States
and therefore belong.

It is especially important to understand the linkages between the mi-
croprocesses of work and the macroprocesses of political identification
in the current period of global aging and global migration, when both
nation-states and kin work are being reconfigured in ways that affect
how political identifications are made. Democratic notions of citizen
equality are continually being negotiated and are a source of political
conflict. For adult migrants, political subjectivity seems to be shaped
in part by the contexts of work. The state shapes such political identifications through its social-welfare provisions and labor laws but so too
do more established residents in their complex dependencies on and
interactions with migrants. Power is animated through registers of race,
geographic origin, and kinship, creating different role configurations
and emotional responses. Over time, the difference between care experiences and the registers of kinship, race, and domestic service, which
seek to imperfectly name and interpret those same experiences, may
lead to social transformations and new formulations of political identity. Care for seniors in the United States might lead to renewing political belonging based on differentiation—such as deepening second-class
citizenship for naturalized black citizens through racial constructions.
Or it might create new spaces to construct mutuality resulting in political integration and a greater redistribution of wealth across social-class
levels and globally.

This work highlights a more complex process of racialization and incorporation than is commonly posited in the literature on migration.
As we saw earlier, Ogbu (1978) contrasts narratives of opportunity for
migrants with those of caste-like or subordinate minorities in the United
States. He indicates that whereas migrants dismiss the racism and hu-

miliations they encounter as a temporary phenomenon, subordinate minorities with a longer history of discrimination in the United States consider structural racism to probably prevent their economic success. Other sociologists have posited that migrants' orientations shift as they become permanent settlers who are more willing to organize politically and in the workplace (Delgado 1993; Piore 1979). First-generation African migrant care workers attend to their socioeconomic position in the United States like nonmigrants. Through their care work, they learn of the unfairness of the United States—in which being African or black matters. They are socialized into a particular racialized identity in the United States ("we Africans" or "people of color")—one that accounts for their diminution and humiliation. This awareness leads them to an oppositional view similar to subordinate minorities, in which political and social exclusion feels pervasive and unjust.

This fact becomes particularly clear to male care workers, who are more likely to be educated and working in white-collar jobs in their home countries, and to older female migrants, who have worked in elder care for decades and now face their own retirement and aging with anxiety and uncertainty. These two groups of workers are the most bitter, and they are the ones who choose to invest their identities in their home countries, where they feel their lives are validated and their work reciprocated. Elizabeth, for example, retired to Ghana at the age of sixty-six in poor health. Tired of his low status and inability to pay for health care, Kwadwo, a former teacher and political organizer, returned to Ghana when his party won national elections in December 2016. Although African care workers feel a significant sense of entitlement to higher wages and benefits, and thus a sense of belonging to a certain extent, they do not feel secure enough to advocate for better working conditions, despite the ongoing unionization for domestic workers and highly publicized living-wage efforts, such as the Fight for $15 taking place nationally and locally.

Thus, the response to such a sense of unfairness does confirm Ogbu's theory, in that African care workers tend to respond by investing in their home countries, a transnational strategy, rather than political activism in the United States. What might become permanent settlement is thwarted by the conditions of their work, forcing some of them to become sojourners again. The exit of some workers from the United

States is both a response to material deprivation—in which home care wages do not enable retirement and certainly not the kind of care that these workers have provided their patients—and an emotional response to their outpouring of spirit across a lifetime of labor without reward. Most care workers I met intended to return to their country of origin, although whether they would actually do so remains unknown. They have learned through their work that the United States is uninhabitable for people like them.

This book has also highlighted the dysfunctions of the US healthcare system, which will come under even greater pressure with the aging of the baby boom generation. A tremendous need for care workers is anticipated. The experiences of African care workers reveal the exploitative and demeaning conditions of home care more broadly. Care workers feel that they give a lot—gradually losing their health and strength—without receiving much in return. Experience is not rewarded, skill is not recognized, and support from agency staff is inadequate. Few care workers are able to move into another profession, help their children get a better education, buy a house, or retire. These dissatisfactions make it harder to recruit and retain care workers in general, much less patient and experienced ones. Yet patients pay a lot for their care also, and the cost of care leads them to demand much from care workers. Furthermore, only a few people can afford such care and usually for a short period of time only. More broadly, the issue is how to reduce the cost of health care in the United States without impoverishing healthcare workers.

As a way forward, I can propose a few modest adjustments to the current situation to expand our "limited but real democracy" to care workers and patients alike, in enabling their recognition as full and equal members of society (Winant 2004, 209). For care workers in particular, their social mobility would be enhanced by a lattice or ladder within nursing education and the profession, such that nursing aides could advance to positions of greater seniority, skill, and authority in a stepwise fashion, with licenses for every year or six months of education, resulting in higher pay and responsibility. Mentoring should happen through formal routes, by more senior and experienced home care workers who have developed strategies for managing confused and angry patients, rather than through the current informal social networks among care workers. The mentors should be compensated for their skill and assistance of other care workers. Lower agency profits directed at raising care workers' pay and providing more support—perhaps by promoting experienced care workers to assume some supervisory roles—would improve care workers' sense of fair treatment and belonging, as well as patients' satisfaction. A lower charge to patients might also make them less demanding of care workers. An advance schedule of three weeks—as was proposed in the Maryland legislature—would reduce care workers' precarity in the face of a patient's change in health status. From the perspective of patients struggling to pay for the cost of home care, a universal long-term care insurance program, such as exists in Japan or Germany, would help (Poo 2015). Finally, for workers in general, the ACA has expanded low-wage healthcare workers' access to health insurance, but it has many flaws, including its cost and its lack of employer coverage for contingent and unpredictable work—a condition of work that may well increase. The employer mandate should be expanded to include part-time and contingent workers. Under threat from the Trump administration, the ACA should be supported to retain health coverage for low-income workers.

More radical reforms are likely to be necessary, as the above proposals may prompt only a temporary stabilization of a political problem that may grow increasingly untenable over time. As the US population ages, both care recipients and care providers should be cared for and have opportunities for dignity. Older adults and care workers are interdependent, and all of us will both need and provide care at some point in our lives. This research highlights that dignity has both material and immaterial components, in which the distribution of material resources signals appreciation and a sense of belonging—for migrant care workers and more established patients alike. Care workers and their patients are working out a politics of vulnerability—in other words, how vulnerability might be the basis of political belonging.

Despite care workers' claims for recognition of their humanity and the value of their labor, claims for recognition under liberalism historically have generally resulted in new kinds of unfreedoms, as among newly emancipated African Americans, who found themselves ensnared by debt through liberal notions of individual responsibility (Hartman 1997). Recognition of the value of certain kinds of work, such as professional nursing, has led to the devaluation of other kinds of labor and workers, such as the direct care of nursing assistants in contrast to administrative and supervisory nursing labor. Recognition of African care workers as equal partners may not be sufficient for political belonging, given that the construction of subjects as autonomous persons is itself based on a framework of property and thus inequality (Hartman 1997). Claims for particular kinds of recognition—as human—may be the basis for political mobilization in liberal democracies because of the strong levels of emotion associated with dignity and humiliation, as represented here in care workers' words about humanity. However, claims for recognition under these auspices may not be the solution. In her work on elder care, Ai-Jen Poo suggests that "we need to rethink everything—how we live, work, and play, and especially how we organize our family and community life" to "take care of each other across generations" (2015, 40). As part of this reformulation, we will also have to create a new basis by which we recognize one another as deserving of rights and resources in political systems, in order to not create new regimes of inclusion and exclusion or reproduce older ones. As the population of older adults in the United States increases and the need for care concomitantly grows this might require, following Judith Butler (2004a), reconfiguring our politics from an emphasis on individual autonomy and self-reliance to an acknowledgment of human vulnerability and interdependence.

ACKNOWLEDGMENTS

This research would not have been possible without my mother and father, with whom I stayed for eight months in the spring of 2016 to do the field research in Maryland and who inspired this project, as I attempted to grapple emotionally with their own aging. For those months, they tolerated the ups and downs of my research and mood as we learned to live together again, twenty-seven years after I had moved out for college. My mother in particular did everything in her power to introduce me to people who knew a home health worker and who were involved in aging and senior care. She was also active in organizing a "village" in the neighborhood. Villages are associations that help seniors age in place. Although we did not do the research together, as I initially hoped we would, because of her other commitments and projects, she was a consistent source of support. As an older person who was interested in organizing her community around aging in place and who had been involved in the care of her own mother and grandmother as they aged, she helped me reflect on my fieldwork. The gifts I used to reciprocate my parents' kindnesses—of cooking and yard work—fell short.

I am also deeply grateful for the home care workers, patients, and agency staff who were willing to share their stories with me and whose heartfelt plumbing of the depths of what it means to be human encouraged me to continue working on this project. I am particularly grateful to the two agencies, one in New Jersey and one in Maryland, that were curious enough about my research project to introduce me to patients and care workers. Several care workers allowed me into their lives over a longer term; they are mentioned (by pseudonyms) in the introduction.

Another source of inspiration along the way was Charlene Brown, who became a friend and intellectual interlocutor. Starting a home health company of her own after stints of working in international development as a medical doctor, she was a creative and energetic person with whom I could process what I was learning about the home care industry. Although our questions diverged, it was useful to hear what she was thinking about and learning, and we did three interviews with home care workers together.

As I began to make sense of my research, I presented at numerous fora where I received very useful comments: the Department of Anthropology at Brown University, the Program in African Studies at Princeton University, the Society for Psychological Anthropology's annual meeting in 2016, and the Workshop on Kinship and Politics at the Center for Interdisciplinary Research in Bielefeld, Germany. Comments by Jennifer Cole, Susan McKinnon, Bhrigupati Singh, and Susan Terrio were especially helpful in directing me to new sources and different approaches.

The development of my argument is deeply indebted to my working with Tatjana Thelen on a theoretical paper on "Elder Care and Political Belonging," published in *Anthropological Theory* in 2017. Erdmute Alber and her postdoctoral and graduate students at the University of Bayreuth—Jeannett Martin, Tabea Häberlein, and Nina Haberland— were influential in helping me think about kinship and belonging during a one-month fellowship with the Bayreuth Advanced Academy of African Studies in June 2016. Other people who helped me think about the overarching structure of the book were Carol Brandt, Pamela Feldman-Savelsberg, and Rachel Reynolds. My colleague Chinyere Osuji encouraged me to use my anger to write. Melissa Yates discussed with me the philosophical literature on care and recognition, challenging my perspective in several ways.

Parts of chapter 2 and interlude 3 were previously published as "Longing for a House in Ghana: Ghanaians' Responses to the Dignity Threats of Elder Care Work in the United States," *Ethos* 44, no. 3 (September 2016): 352–74. I am grateful to the American Anthropological Association for giving permission for its reuse here.

NOTES

1 All names are pseudonyms. Although patients are usually referred to by their last names, and care workers by their first names, I decided not to reproduce this social difference in the book.

2 I use the term "migrant" rather than "immigrant" in keeping with the large literature on transnationalism that reveals the ways that migrants remain connected to their country of birth. "Migrant" allows me to leave open the question of political belonging, which "immigrant" forecloses.

3 Home health workers are overwhelming women (89 percent), with a median age of forty-five years (PHI 2016).

4 I use the term "patient" to refer to the recipient of home care, as some of the care workers whom I interviewed did. Through this term, they positioned themselves as skilled healthcare providers. "Client" was an alternative term, which highlighted the employer-employee and paid care relationships. Neither term is entirely satisfactory. I considered using a term on the basis of age, but some of the patients were in their seventies and others in their nineties, and their need for care, not their age, drove them to hire a home health worker. Care recipients did not identify with either "patient" or "client" as designations.

   The term "nursing aide" can suggest an aide either to the nurse or possibly to the patient who directs care. This characterization is not entirely accurate, as sometimes the patient does not know what is happening, and an agency nurse often does not actively supervise care. As a result, I prefer to use the terms "care worker," "home care worker," or "home health worker," which I use interchangeably.

5 For a critique of this perspective, see Pierre (2004).

6 Showers (2013), in contrast, finds that West African nurses from more privileged and educated backgrounds seek to assimilate as white, a desire that did not arise among my interlocutors.

7 The book brings together literatures not commonly discussed together: the political incorporation of migrants, which is discussed widely in the sociology literature, and care, which is of burgeoning interest across the social sciences and humanities. Most discussions of care and migration have focused on global care chains, an analytic description of a common phenomenon in which women migrate from low- and middle-income countries to do care work in high-income countries so that the women they work for can enter the formal

labor market (Andall 2000; Anderson 2000; Hochschild 2001; Yeates 2009). The feminist movement of the mid- to late twentieth century in the United States brought women into the workforce, rather than revaluing women's domestic work as worthy. As women gained status and began to work outside the home, "the dirty work" that they used to do was given to other women (Palmer 1989). This phenomenon is discussed as a global care chain because migrant domestic workers are often mothers and wives who distribute their own domestic obligations to others in their countries of origin, such as their sisters, mothers, or oldest daughters. Because of migration, recent decades have seen a resurgence of domestic work in numerous high-income countries in North America, Europe, the Middle East, and Hong Kong, not only among elites but also within the middle class (Ozyegin and Hondagneu-Sotelo 2008). The migration of domestic servants illustrates the tremendous global inequalities between different countries and regions of the world (Sarti 2008). This large and significant literature on migrant domestic workers, while focusing on the ways that gender and racial ideologies affect care workers, does not focus on how care work becomes an "incorporation regime" for migrants, affecting their sense of political belonging through these gender and racial ideologies (Soysal 1994; exceptions are Ibarra 2013; Liebelt 2011).

8 "Mutual recognition is meaningful as an ideal only when it is understood as the basis for struggle and negotiation of conflict (see Pizer 1992), when its impossibility and the striving to attain it are adequately included in the concept (see Butler 1994)" (Benjamin 1995, 23).

9 In my previous work among Ghanaian transnational families, I found that some children and parents evaluated the quality of their transnational relationship through the kinds of gifts sent and received (Coe 2011, 2013).

10 For some years, beginning in the 1980s, Medicare paid for personal care, or help with dressing, cleaning, and feeding (Boris and Klein 2012). However, the services proved so popular that Medicare costs rose, and the home care program was discontinued in 1997 (Buhler-Wilkinson 2001).

11 Long-term care insurance sales have declined since 2003, just when experts expected a huge demand (Kozol 2013). Few of those who would benefit from long-term care insurance purchase it (Allaire, Brown, and Weiner 2016).

12 Economists note that it has become more common for top income earners in the United States to work for their wealth, rather than rely on inheritance or capital gains (Piketty and Saez 2003).

13 In 2010, 119,770 seniors (those over the age of sixty-five) lived in Montgomery County, with those aged sixty-five to eighty representing 9 percent of the population, and those over eighty an additional 4 percent (Montgomery County 2014). This was similar to the proportion of those aged sixty-five and older in the United States as a whole, at 14 percent of the population in 2014, with the greatest concentrations in Florida (US Census Bureau 2016). Of the seniors in Montgomery County, 71 percent were white, 12 percent black or African American, and 13 percent Asian.

14 The suburban environment caused difficulties for home care workers who relied on public transportation or who could not drive, as many patients needed someone to drive them around.

15 Showers (2013) extensively discusses Africans' entrepreneurship in starting labor brokering agencies for care work in the Washington area.

16 In their stigmatization by their own communities, African home care workers differ from African American women domestic servants in northern cities, who were respected in their communities (Clark-Lewis 1994; Dill 1994).

17 See also O'Leary (2016) on the difficulties she faced in gaining access to institutions and, when she did so, avoiding the impression that she was working for the agency or facility.

18 In 2005–15, 25 percent of the African migrant direct-care workforce were men, whereas men were only 11 percent of the workforce as a whole (Campbell 2018; PHI 2016).

19 Women are more likely to need long-term care than men (Jones, Harris-Kojetin and Valverde 2012).

20 In 2013, 31.4 percent of home care patients had a kind of dementia (CDC 2016a). Dementia patients are overly represented among my patient population.

INTERLUDE: FOOD

1 Kosher dietary rules prohibit the consumption of certain kinds of meat and fish and the mixing of meat with dairy products. Observant Jewish households keep separate utensils, cutlery, and pots for preparing dishes with meat or dairy to protect against cross-contamination.

2 In Ortner's (2003) study of her high school class from Newark, New Jersey, it was common for African American domestic servants to be given separate utensils, plates, and glasses in the mainly Jewish households of her classmates in the 1950s.

CHAPTER 1. "ANYONE WHO IS NOT AFRICAN"

1 Although the managers and owners of home care agencies I visited were usually white—but not always—the nurse supervising the home care workers and the case managers who managed relations with the patients were often African American or even African. An African American manager of a franchise talked about being perceived on the phone as white and hearing direct statements from potential patients that they would not have said had they known she was African American.

2 There is a long history of domestic service agencies favoring employers over employees (Bakan and Stasiulis 1995; Katzman 1978).

3 In 2016, 32.5 percent of employed foreign-born women worked in service occupations, compared with 19.4 percent of employed US-born women (BLS 2017b).

4 Some residents resent the presence of care workers in independent-living facilities because they want to be around healthy, vibrant older people and in a homelike, rather than institutional, environment.

5 For a higher degree of protection, I neither give her a pseudonym nor describe her.

6 In Maryland, in 2015, 48 percent of LPNs were black or African American, and 41 percent were white (Maryland Board of Nursing 2016). In comparison, in 1970, black women were 7.3 percent of registered nurses, 22 percent of practical nurses, and 25 percent of nursing assistants (Cannings and Lazonick 1975).

7 Showers discusses in greater depth the entry of "1.5 generation" and second-generation African migrants into healthcare (2013, 180).

8 I am indebted for this insight to audience members at the Workshop on Politics and Kinship at the Center for Interdisciplinary Research (ZiF) in Bielefeld, Germany, to whom I presented portions of this research in May 2017.

9 Rodriquez (2014) notes how nursing-home workers use their emotions to generate compliance, but this was the only such incident mentioned to me among my interlocutors.

10 This discourse of respect for older adults was also prominent among care workers (mainly from Haiti) in the Boston area (O'Leary 2016, 87–89).

11 I have written about the variability and uncertainty of cultural capital in another context (Coe and Shani 2015).

12 I met a few young women (1.5 or second generation) whose mothers worked in home care.

13 Similarly, an African American woman who came to Boston from the south in the 1920s said about domestic service, "I did it because I had to. There wasn't nothing else a colored woman could do then" (Rollins 1985, 108).

14 Thus, the agencies I encountered functioned more like the lower-tier nanny agencies Hondagneu-Sotelo (2001) describes in Los Angeles.

INTERLUDE: SILENCES ABOUT SERVANTS

1 In fact, one of the women interviewed by Tucker relates a story of an older white woman who refused to be cared for by a white nurse hired by her son in the 1950s, because she was used to being taken care of by African American women (1988, 101). Another black domestic in Boston in 1982 said that she thought her employer preferred a black maid to an Irish one because that way everyone could see that she had a maid and "we give them much more status" (Rollins 1985, 105).

2 The earliest senior communities opened in 1954 and 1960 in Arizona.

CHAPTER 2. STORIES OF SERVITUDE

1 Etienne Balibar (1991) rightly considers racism concerned with extermination (disbelonging) and racism concerned with oppression (belonging through subordination) to share many features and overlap.

2 Rollins also considers how subordinate-superior relations affect the employer of a domestic worker, including her view of her own society, in justifying inequality:

The presence of the "inferior" domestic, an inferiority evidenced by the performance she is encouraged to execute and her acceptance of demeaning treatment, offers the employer justification for materially exploiting the domestic, ego enhancement as an individual, and a strengthening of the employer's class and racial identities. Even more important, such a presence supports the idea of unequal human worth: it suggests that there might be categories of people (the lower classes, people of color) who are inherently inferior to others (middle and upper classes, whites). And this idea provides ideological justification for a social system that institutionalizes inequality. (Rollins 1985, 203)

3   Dinner in continuing care communities is often served in the early evening, and residents will sometimes go early in anticipation of the highlight of the day.

4   Elana Buch (2014) also provides an example of the son of a patient pressuring a home care worker to do more household labor, including cleaning the entire house, washing all the household dishes, and taking care of the family dog.

5   Technically, in most situations, the agency is the employer, but workers are aware that they will lose the job if the patient is not happy. Although they may be given a job elsewhere, they may also have to wait or go through a series of temporary or relief jobs before finding a permanent position. This is similar to other service-level work, in which customers become involved in managing workers (Fuller and Smith 1996; Leidner 1996; Lopez 1996).

6   She did not think this request was legitimate because the father could usually go to the bathroom on his own.

7   However, this is changing: in my experience in Accra, househelps are becoming older and domestic service is becoming more associated with social class and education rather than age.

8   Cold is a common complaint among African migrants. In contrast, in Chicago, home care workers found older people's apartments overheated (Buch 2013).

9   Smoking was quite offensive to most of my interlocutors, who associated it with immorality. They had also learned that a smoking patient was a reason to decline a case, which agencies considered legitimate.

10   Margaret Lock (2013) brilliantly analyzes the contestations and uncertainties among Alzheimer's researchers.

INTERLUDE: LONGING FOR A HOUSE

1   Scholars of housing in Ghana have noted that plots of land tend to be large in Ghana compared to other countries (Korboe 1992; Tipple et al. 1999).

CHAPTER 3. MAKING AND BREAKING PRACTICAL KINSHIP

1   As the Italian novelist Natalia Ginzburg writes, "Families can be awful, repressive, oppressive, or cool and uncaring and distracted, or toxic, tainted and maggoty. Very often they are like that" (quoted in Parks 2017, 33). Ginzburg's observations were not the aspects of kinship emphasized by care workers and patients.

2   In contrast, O'Leary (2016) notes patients in the Boston area who called their black migrant care workers by generational terms, such as "child" and "baby."

3 In general, a female patient with a male care worker is unusual. However, some-times a man cares for a married male patient, and when the wife becomes frail, he takes care of both members of the couple. Also, a widow may contact her husband's former care worker as someone she knows and trusts when she herself needs care. I am not sure which situation pertained in this case.

4 Since the sister lived in the house before her mother's death, she probably had the right to stay in the house after her mother's death, even if her brother owned the house jointly with her.

5 Donkor (2018, 84) similarly reports on a Ghanaian live-in care worker who was disappointed that she was not invited to the funeral.

CHAPTER 4. RECIPROCITY

1 Memory-care units are typically physically segregated and locked units of nursing homes: "All claimed to provide for the special needs of persons with demen-tia, while segregating them from a more coherent population of elders in the home. They shared no common approach, and their quality varied enormously" (McLean 2007, 61).

2 One meta-analysis of studies of Alzheimer's disease and related dementias found that about 40 percent of Alzheimer's patients (with a range of 11–63 percent across twenty-nine studies) exhibited aggression (Zhao et al. 2016).

3 Because their marriage more than twenty years earlier was a second marriage for both of them, his money was considered his own and his children's and will not be used for her own future care needs.

4 Unlike Filipina care workers in Israel who prefer wealthy and privileged employ-ers (Liebelt 2011), my interlocutors simply noted when a patient was very wealthy.

5 Solomon commented that patients get information about African care workers from their social networks. He said,

> One tells another, "My mother and father was in care." They misinform them [to mistrust Africans]. They have this misinformation with them, without knowing who you are. It becomes a problem. When they don't find out who you are, information [from their friends] is what they carry. Some stand somewhere with their eye on you [watching to see what you are doing]. Then, after a couple of months, they say, "You're different." They have got-ten information about Africans, Ghanaians, care workers. But it is not like that. So when they are trying to work with you, they do not have an open heart; they do not enter into the relationship without reservation. (interview, March 6, 2016, Maryland)

INTERLUDE: INTANGIBLE GIFTS AT THE END OF LIFE

1 Some agency staff members complained that African care workers thought that morphine given in hospice situations was killing the patient, as indeed it was, and refused to participate in the active promotion of death. My interlocutors, however, did not raise this issue with me.

CHAPTER 5. A LACK OF RECIPROCITY

1 O'Leary (2016) notes a similar finding among black healthcare workers (mainly Haitian).

2 Yaw told me, "Every three months, we [he and his wife] pay quarterly taxes. Some Ghanaians don't pay Social Security. They think, 'I have to go back; I have to finish the house.' It is a problem in this country. I try to educate them to get their Social Security" (interview, May 14, 2016, Pennsylvania).

3 In 2014, over one third of home care workers nationally were covered by Medicaid or Medicare (PHI 2016).

INTERLUDE: FORECLOSURE

1 In contrast, Showers (2013) interviewed West African nurses from more privileged and educated backgrounds. They tended to achieve the American dream, living in large houses in suburban developments and making six-figure incomes, mainly by working long hours.

CONCLUSION

1 Donkor (2018), for example, reports that none of her twenty-six Ghanaian informants, all live-in caregivers, had health insurance at the time of her research in 2009.

REFERENCES

Abrahams, Roger. 1984. "Equal-Opportunity Eating: A Structural Excursus on Things of the Mouth." In *Ethnic and Regional Foodways in the United States: The Performance of Group Identity*, edited by Linda Keller Brown and Kay Mussell, 19–36. Knoxville: University of Tennessee Press.

Agha, Asif. 2007. "Norm and Trope in Kinship Behavior." In *Language and Social Relations*, 340–85. Cambridge: Cambridge University Press.

Akresh, Ilana Redstone. 2006. "Occupational Mobility among Legal Immigrants in the United States." *International Migration Review* 40, no. 4 (Winter): 854–84.

Allaire, Benjamin T., Derek S. Brown, and Joshua M. Weiner. 2016. "Who Wants Long-Term Care Insurance? A Stated Preference Survey of Attitudes, Beliefs, and Characteristics." *Inquiry: The Journal of Health Care Organization, Provision, and Financing* 53:1–8.

Altorjai, Szilvia and Jeanne Batalova. 2017. "Immigrant Health-Care Workers in the United States." *Migration Information Source*, June 28. www.migrationpolicy.org.

Andall, Jacqueline. 2000. *Gender, Migration, and Domestic Service: The Politics of Black Women in Italy*. Aldershot, UK: Ashgate.

Anderson, Bridget. 2000. *Doing the Dirty Work? The Global Politics of Domestic Labour*. London: Zed Books.

Aranda, Kay, and Andrea Jones. 2010. "Dignity in Health-Care: A Critical Exploration Using Feminism and Theories of Recognition." *Nursing Inquiry* 17, no. 3 (September): 248–56.

Ariès, Philippe. 1981. *The Hour of Our Death*. Translated by Helen Weaver. New York: Knopf.

Aronson, Jane, and Sheila M. Neysmith. 1996. "'You're Not Just in There to Do the Work': Depersonalizing Policies and the Exploitation of Home Care Workers' Labor." *Gender and Society* 10, no. 1 (February): 59–77.

———. 2001. "Manufacturing Social Exclusion in the Home Care Market." *Canadian Public Policy/Analyse de Politiques* 27, no. 2 (June): 151–65.

Arthur, John A. 2008. *The African Diaspora in the United States and Europe: The Ghanaian Experience*. Burlington, VT: Ashgate.

Ascione, Elisa. 2012. "Intime ineguaglianze: Migrazioni e gestione del lavoro di cura nel privato sociale." *AM: Rivista della Società italiana di antropologia medica*, no. 33–34 (October): 57–94.

Badger, Emily. 2016. "The Nation's Housing Recovery Is Leaving Blacks Behind." *Washington Post*, May 2. www.washingtonpost.com.

Bahrampour, Tara. 2016. "Couple, in 90s, Allege Theft by Caregivers." *Washington Post*, May 12, B1, B4.

Bakan, Abigail B., and Daiva K. Stasiulis. 1995. "Making the Match: Domestic Placement Agencies and the Racialization of Women's Household Work." *Signs* 20, no. 2 (Winter): 303–35.

Balibar, Etienne. 1991. "Racism and Nationalism." In *Race, Nation, Class: Ambiguous Identities*, by Etienne Balibar and Immanuel Wallerstein, 37–67. London: Verso.

Barrett, Rusty. 2006. "Language Ideology and Racial Inequality: Competing Functions of Spanish in an Anglo-owned Mexican Restaurant." *Language in Society* 35, no. 2 (April): 163–204.

Benjamin, Jessica. 1995. *Like Subjects, Love Objects: Essays on Recognition and Sexual Difference*. New Haven, CT: Yale University Press.

———. 1998. *Shadow of the Other: Intersubjectivity and Gender in Psychoanalysis*. New York: Routledge.

Bercovitz, Anita, Abigail Moss, Manisha Sengupta, Eunice Y. Park-Lee, Adrienne Jones, and Lauren D. Harris-Kojetin. 2011. "An Overview of Home Health Aides: United States, 2007." *National Health Statistics Report*, no. 34 (May 19). Hyattsville, MD: National Center for Health Statistics. www.cdc.gov.

Berdes, Celia, and John M. Eckert. 2001. "Race Relations and Caregiving Relationships: A Qualitative Examination of Perspectives from Residents and Nurse's Aides in Three Nursing Homes." *Research on Aging* 23, no. 1 (January): 109–26.

———. 2007. "The Language of Caring: Nurse's Aides' Use of Family Metaphors Conveys Affective Care." *Gerontologist* 47, no. 3 (June): 340–49.

BLS (Bureau of Labor Statistics, US Department of Labor). 2009. "Health Care." BLS Spotlight on Statistics, November. www.bls.gov.

———. 2015a. "Fastest Growing Occupations." *Occupational Outlook Handbook, 2016–17 Edition*. Published December 17. www.bls.gov.

———. 2015b. "Home Health Aides." *Occupational Outlook Handbook, 2016–17 Edition*. Published December 17. www.bls.gov.

———. 2017a. "Occupational Employment and Wages, May 2016: 31–1011 Home Health Aides." Occupational Employment Statistics. Last modified March 31. www.bls.gov.

———. 2017b. "Foreign-Born Workers: Labor Force Characteristics—2016." News release no. USDL-17-0618, May 18. www.bls.gov.

Boehm, Deborah A. 2012. *Intimate Migrations: Gender, Family, and Illegality among Transnational Mexicans*. New York: New York University Press.

Boris, Eileen, and Jennifer Klein. 2010. "Making Home Care: Law and Social Policy in the U.S. Welfare State." In Boris and Parreñas 2010a, 187–203.

———. 2012. *Caring for America: Home Health Workers in the Shadow of the Welfare State*. New York: Oxford University Press.

Boris, Eileen, and Rhacel Salazar Parreñas, eds. 2010a. *Intimate Labors: Cultures, Technologies and the Politics of Care*. Stanford, CA: Stanford University Press.

———. 2010b. Introduction to Boris and Parreñas 2010a, 1–12.

Borneman, John. 1992. *Belonging in the Two Berlins: Kin, State, Nation*. New York: Cambridge University Press.

Bourdieu, Pierre. 1977. *Outline of a Theory of Practice*. Translated by Richard Nice. Cambridge: Cambridge University Press.

———. 1991. *Language and Symbolic Power*. Edited by John B. Thompson. Translated by Gino Raymond and Matthew Adamson. Cambridge, MA: Harvard University Press.

Bourdieu, Pierre, and Jean-Claude Passeron. 1990. *Reproduction in Education, Society, and Culture*. Translated by Richard Nice. 2nd ed. Newbury Park, CA: SAGE.

Brightman, Robert. 2013. "Hierarchy and Conflict in Mutual Being." *HAU: Journal of Ethnographic Theory* 3, no. 2 (Summer): 259–70.

Brown, Tamara Mose. 2011. *Raising Brooklyn: Nannies, Childcare, and Caribbeans Creating Community*. New York: New York University Press.

Buch, Elana D. 2013. "Senses of Care: Embodying Inequality and Sustaining Personhood in the Home Care of Older Adults in Chicago." *American Ethnologist* 40, no. 4 (November): 637–50.

———. 2014. "Troubling Gifts of Care: Vulnerable Persons and Threatening Exchanges in Chicago's Home Care Industry." *Medical Anthropology Quarterly* 28, no. 4 (December): 599–615.

———. 2015a. "Anthropology of Aging and Care." *Annual Review of Anthropology* 44:277–93.

———. 2015b. "Postponing Passage: Doorways, Distinctions, and the Thresholds of Personhood among Older Chicagoans." *Ethos* 43, no. 1 (March): 40–58.

———. 2017. "Beyond Independence: Older Chicagoans Living Valued Lives." In *Successful Aging as a Contemporary Obsession: Global Perspectives*, edited by Sarah Lamb, 85–97. New Brunswick, NJ: Rutgers University Press.

Budden, Jill S., Elizabeth H. Zhong, Patricia Moulton, and Jeannie P. Cimiotti. 2013. "Highlights of the National Workforce Survey of Registered Nurses." *Journal of Nursing Regulation* 4, no. 2 (July): 5–14.

Buhler-Wilkerson, Karen. 2001. *No Place Like Home: A History of Nursing and Home Care in the United States*. Baltimore: John Hopkins University Press.

Busse, Mark, and Veronica Strang. 2011. "Introduction: Ownership and Appropriation." In *Ownership and Appropriation*, edited by Veronica Strang and Mark Busse, 1–19. New York: Berg.

Butler, Judith. 1997. *Excitable Speech: A Politics of the Performative*. New York: Routledge.

———. 2004a. *Precarious Life: The Powers of Mourning and Violence*. London: Verso.

———. 2004b. *Undoing Gender*. New York: Routledge.

Cadaval, Olivia. 1991. "Making a Place Home: The Latino Festival." In *Creative Ethnicity: Symbols and Strategies of Contemporary Ethnic Life*, edited by Stephen Stern and John Allan Cicala, 204–22. Logan: Utah State University Press.

Campbell, Stephen. 2018. *Racial Disparities in the Direct Care Workforce: Spotlight on Black/African American Workers*. Research brief, February. New York: PHI.

Cannings, Kathleen, and William Lazonick. 1975. "The Development of the Nursing Labor Force in the United States: A Basic Analysis." *International Journal of Health Sciences* 5, no. 2 (April): 185–216.

Capps, Randy, Kristen McCabe, and Michael Fix. 2012. *New Streams: Black African Migration to the United States.* Washington, DC: Migration Policy Institute.

Carsten, Janet. 1997. *The Heat of the Hearth: The Process of Kinship in a Malay Fishing Community.* Oxford: Clarendon.

CDC (Centers for Disease Control and Prevention). 2016a. "FastStats: Alzheimer's Disease." National Center for Health Statistics. Last updated October 6. www.cdc.gov.

———. 2016b. "FastStats: Home Health Care." National Center for Health Statistics. Last updated July 6. www.cdc.gov.

Chen, Melvin. 2015. "Care, Narrativity, and the Nature of *Disponibilité.*" *Hypatia* 30, no. 4 (Fall): 778–93.

Christiansen, Catrine, Mats Utas, and Henrik Vigh, eds. 2006. *Navigating Youth, Generating Adulthood: Social Becoming in an African Context.* Uppsala: Nordiska Afrikainstitutet.

Clark, Gracia. 2001. "'Nursing Mother Work' in Ghana: Power and Frustration in Akan Market Women's Lives." In *Women Traders in Cross-Cultural Perspective: Mediating Identities, Marketing Wares,* edited by Linda J. Seligmann, 103–28. Stanford, CA: Stanford University Press.

Clark-Lewis, Elizabeth. 1994. *Living In, Living Out: African American Domestics in Washington, D.C., 1910–1940.* Washington, DC: Smithsonian Institution Press.

Coe, Cati. 2005. *The Dilemmas of Culture in African Schools: Nationalism, Youth, and the Transformation of Knowledge.* Chicago: University of Chicago Press.

———. 2011. "What Is Love? The Materiality of Care in Ghanaian Transnational Families." *International Migration* 49, no. 6 (December): 7–24.

———. 2013. *The Scattered Family: Parenting, African Migrants, and Global Inequality.* Chicago: University of Chicago Press.

———. 2016a. "Not a Nurse, Not Househelp: The New Occupation of Elder Carer in Urban Ghana." *Ghana Studies* 19:46–72.

———. 2016b. "Translations in Kinscripts: Child Circulation among Ghanaians Abroad." In *Affective Circuits: African Migrations to Europe and the Pursuit of Social Regeneration,* edited by Jennifer Cole and Christian Groes, 27–54. Chicago: University of Chicago Press.

———. 2016c. "Longing for a House in Ghana: Ghanaians' Responses to the Dignity Threats of Elder Care Work in the United States." *Ethos* 44, no. 3 (September): 352–74.

———. 2017. "Transnational Migration and the Commodification of Eldercare in Urban Ghana." *Identities: Global Studies in Culture and Power* 4 (5): 542–56.

———. 2018. "Imagining Institutional Care, Practicing Domestic Care: Inscriptions around Aging in Southern Ghana." *Anthropology & Aging* 39, no. 1 (Fall): 18–32.

———. 2019. "Beyond Kin Care? Institutional Facilities in the Imaginations of Elderly Presbyterians in Southern Ghana." *Africa Today* 65, no. 4.

Coe, Cati, and Serah Shani. 2015. "Cultural Capital and Transnational Parenting: The Case of Ghanaian Migrants in the United States." *Harvard Educational Review* 85, no. 4 (Winter): 562–86.

Cole, Jennifer. 2013. "On Generations and Aging: 'Fresh Contact' of a Different Sort." In *Transitions and Transformations: Cultural Perspectives on Aging and the Life Course*, edited by Caitrin Lynch and Jason Danely, 218–30. New York: Berghahn Books.

Colen, Shellee, and Roger Sanjek. 1990. "At Work in Homes I: Orientations." In *At Work in Homes: Household Workers in World Perspective*, edited by Roger Sanjek and Shellee Colen, 1–13. Washington, DC: American Anthropological Association.

Collins, Francis S. 2006. *The Language of God: A Scientist Presents Evidence for Belief.* New York: Free Press.

Collins, Randall. 1979. *The Credential Society: An Historical Sociology of Education and Stratification.* New York: Academic Press.

Commission on Long-Term Care. 2013. "Report to the Congress." September 30. www.ltccommission.org.

Constable, Nicole. 2007. *Maid to Order in Hong Kong: Stories of Migrant Workers.* Ithaca, NY: Cornell University Press.

Constable, Pamela. 2016. "Banding Together for Higher Ground." *Washington Post*, May 3, B1, B2.

CountyStat. 2016. "Montgomery County's African Community (Beta) Highlights." PowerPoint presentation, Montgomery County government.

Covington-Ward, Yolanda. 2016. "African Immigrants Experience Prejudice and Limited Mobility in Low-Wage Health-Care Jobs." *Policy Brief* 5, no. 1 (October). Davis: Center for Poverty Research, University of California, Davis. http://poverty.ucdavis.edu.

———. 2017. "African Immigrants in Low-Wage Direct Health Care: Motivations, Job Satisfaction, and Occupational Mobility." *Journal of Immigrant and Minority Health* 19, no. 3 (June): 709–15.

Crowley, John. 1999. "The Politics of Belonging: Some Theoretical Considerations." In *The Politics of Belonging: Migrants and Minorities in Contemporary Europe*, edited by Andrew Geddes and Adrian Favell, 15–41. Aldershot, UK: Ashgate.

Csikszentmihalyi, Mihalyi. 1990. *Flow: The Psychology of Optimal Experience.* New York: Harper and Row.

D'Alisera, JoAnn. 2004. *An Imagined Geography: Sierra Leonean Muslims in America.* Philadelphia: University of Pennsylvania Press.

Delgado, Héctor L. 1993. *New Immigrants, Old Unions: Organizing Undocumented Workers in Los Angeles.* Philadelphia: Temple University Press.

Deomampo, Daisy. 2016. *Transnational Reproduction: Race, Kinship, and Commercial Surrogacy in India.* New York: New York University Press.

Diamond, Timothy. 1992. *Making Gray Gold: Narratives of Nursing Home Care.* Chicago: University of Chicago Press.

Di Leonardo, Micaela. 1987. "The Female World of Cards and Holidays: Women, Families, and the Work of Kinship." *Signs* 12, no. 3 (Spring): 440–53.

Dill, Bonnie Thornton. 1994. *Across the Boundaries of Race and Class: An Exploration of Work and Family among Black Female Domestic Servants*. New York: Garland.

Dodoo, F. Nii-Amoo. 1997. "Assimilation Differences among Africans in America." *Social Forces* 76, no. 2 (December): 527–46.

Donkor, Martha. 2018. *The Experience of Ghanaian Live-In Caregivers in the United States*. Lanham, MD: Lexington Books.

Dossa, Parin, and Cati Coe, eds. 2017. *Transnational Aging and Reconfigurations of Kin Work*. New Brunswick, NJ: Rutgers University Press.

DuBois, W. E. B. (1899) 1967. *The Philadelphia Negro: A Social Study*. Reprint, New York: Schocken Books.

Ducey, Ariel. 2009. *Never Good Enough: Health Care Workers and the False Promise of Job Training*. Ithaca, NY: Cornell University Press.

Dudden, Faye E. 1983. *Serving Women: Household Service in Nineteenth-Century America*. Middletown, CT: Wesleyan University Press.

Duffy, Mignon. 2011. *Making Care Count: A Century of Gender, Race, and Paid Care Work*. New Brunswick, NJ: Rutgers University Press.

Eaton, Isabel. (1899) 1967. "Special Report on Negro Domestic Service in the Seventh Ward, Philadelphia." In *The Philadelphia Negro: A Social Study*, by W. E. B. DuBois, 427–54. Reprint, New York: Schocken Books.

Edwards, Jeannette, and Marilyn Strathern. 2000. "Including Our Own." In *Cultures of Relatedness: New Approaches to the Study of Kinship*, edited by Janet Carsten, 149–66. Cambridge: Cambridge University Press.

Ehrenreich, Barbara, and Arlie Russell Hochschild, eds. 2002. *Global Woman: Nannies, Maids, and Sex Workers in the New Economy*. New York: Metropolitan Books.

Ejaz, Farida K., Linda S. Noelker, Heather L. Menne, and Joshua G. Bagaka's. 2008. "The Impact of Stress and Support on Direct Care Workers' Job Satisfaction." In "Better Jobs Better Care: New Research on the Long-Term Care Workforce." Supplement, *Gerontologist* 48, no. S1 (July): 60–70.

Fanon, Frantz. 1967. *Black Skins, White Masks*. Translated by Charles Lam Markmann. New York: Grove.

Faubion, James D. 2001. "Toward an Anthropology of the Ethics of Kinship." In *The Ethics of Kinship: Ethnographic Inquiries*, edited by James D. Faubion, 1–28. Lanham, MD: Rowman and Littlefield.

Fausto, Carlos. 2013. "The Kinship I and the Kinship Other: *La Parenté en Question* (Again)." *HAU: Journal of Ethnographic Theory* 3, no. 2 (Summer): 293–97.

Feldman-Savelsberg, Pamela. 2016. *Mothers on the Move: Reproducing Belonging between Africa and Europe*. Chicago: University of Chicago Press.

Ferguson, James. 2013. "Declarations of Dependence: Labour, Personhood, and Welfare in Southern Africa." *Journal of the Royal Anthropological Institute* 19, no. 2 (June): 223–42.

Fikes, Kesha. 2009. *Managing African Portugal: The Citizen-Migrant Distinction*. Durham, NC: Duke University Press.

Fisher, Lucy Takesue, and Margaret I. Wallhagen. 2008. "Day-to-Day Care: The Interplay of CNAs' Views of Residents and Nursing Home Environments." *Journal of Gerontological Nursing* 34, no. 11 (November): 26–33.

Folbre, Nancy. 2001. *The Invisible Heart: Economics and Family Values.* New York: New Press.

Foner, Nancy. 1994. *The Caregiving Dilemma: Work in an American Nursing Home.* Berkeley: University of California Press.

Frank, Katherine. 2002. *G-Strings and Sympathy: Strip Club Regulars and Male Desire.* Durham, NC: Duke University Press.

Frankenberg, Ruth. 1993. *The Social Construction of Whiteness: White Women, Race Matters.* Minneapolis: University of Minnesota Press.

Fraser, Nancy. 2003. "Distorted beyond All Recognition: A Rejoinder to Axel Honneth." In Fraser and Honneth 2003, 198–236.

Fraser, Nancy, and Axel Honneth. 2003. *Redistribution or Recognition? A Political-Philosophical Exchange.* London: Verso.

Freud, Sigmund. 1977. *Introductory Lectures on Psychoanalysis.* Translated and edited by James Strachey. New York: Liveright.

Fuller, Linda, and Vicki Smith. 1996. "Consumers' Reports: Management by Customers in a Changing Economy." In Macdonald and Sirianni 1996b, 74–90.

Gal, Susan. 2003. "Movements of Feminism: The Circulation of Discourses about Women." In *Recognition Struggles and Social Movements: Contested Identities, Agencies and Power,* edited by Barbara Hobson, 93–118. Cambridge: Cambridge University Press.

Gambino, Christine P., Edward N. Trevelyan, and John Thomas Fitzwater. 2014. *The Foreign-Born Population from Africa: 2008–2012.* American Community Survey Briefs, report no. ACSBR/12-16, October. Washington, DC: United States Census Bureau.

Geddes, Andrew, and Adrian Favell, eds. 1999. *The Politics of Belonging: Migrants and Minorities in Contemporary Europe.* Aldershot, UK: Ashgate.

Gibson, Margaret A., and John U. Ogbu. 1991. *Minority Status and Schooling: A Comparative Study of Immigrant and Involuntary Minorities.* New York: Garland.

Glassman, Jonathon. 2011. *War of Words, War of Stones: Racial Thought and Violence in Colonial Zanzibar.* Bloomington: Indiana University Press.

Glenn, Evelyn Nakano. 1992. "From Servitude to Service Work: Historical Continuities in the Racial Division of Paid Reproductive Labor." *Signs* 18, no. 1 (Autumn): 1–43.

Glick Schiller, Nina. 2012. "Migration and Development without Methodological Nationalism: Towards Global Perspectives on Migration." In *Migration in the 21st Century: Political Economy and Ethnography,* edited by Pauline Gardiner Barber and Winnie Lem, 38–63. New York: Routledge.

Glymph, Thavolia. 2008. *Out of the House of Bondage: The Transformation of the Plantation Household.* New York: Cambridge University Press.

Goffman, Erving. 1956. "The Nature of Deference and Demeanor." *American Anthropologist* 58, no. 3 (June): 473–502.

———. 1961. *Asylums: Essays on the Situation of Mental Patients and Other Inmates.* Garden City, NY: Anchor Books.

Gomstyn, Alice. 2014. "Home Care Staffing Crunch in New Jersey." *Bergen (NJ) Record,* November 2.

Graham, Judith. 2017. "Home Health Aide Shortage Due to Low Pay." *Washington Post,* April 25, E1, E4.

Greenhouse, Steven. 2007. "Justices to Hear Case on Wages of Home Aides." *New York Times,* March 25, B1, B35.

Hacker, Jacob S. 2006. *The Great Risk Shift: The Assault on American Jobs, Families, Health Care, and Retirement and How You Can Fight Back.* Oxford: Oxford University Press.

Haller, William, Alejandro Portes, and Scott M. Lynch. 2011. "Dreams Fulfilled, Dreams Shattered: Determinants of Segmented Assimilation in the Second Generation." *Social Forces* 89, no. 3 (March): 733–62.

Hamberger, Klaus. 2013. "The Order of Intersubjectivity." *HAU: The Journal of Ethnographic Theory* 3, no. 2 (Summer): 305–7.

Hamington, Maurice. 2015. "Care Ethics and Engaging Intersectional Difference through the Body." *Critical Philosophy of Race* 3 (1): 79–100.

Handler, Richard. 1988. *Nationalism and the Politics of Culture in Quebec.* Madison: University of Wisconsin Press.

Harmuth, Susan. 2002. "The Direct Care Workforce Crisis in Long-Term Care." *North Carolina Medical Journal* 63, no. 2 (March/April): 87–94.

Hartling, Linda M., and Tracy Luchetta. 1999. "Humiliation: Assessing the Impact of Derision, Degradation, and Debasement." *Journal of Primary Prevention* 19, no. 4 (June): 259–78.

Hartman, Saidiya V. 1997. *Scenes of Subjection: Terror, Slavery, and Self-Making in Nineteenth-Century America.* New York: Oxford University Press.

Hashimoto, Akiko. 1996. *The Gift of Generations: Japanese and American Perspectives on Aging and the Social Contract.* New York: Cambridge University Press.

Hatch, Elvin. 1987. "The Cultural Evaluation of Wealth: An Agrarian Case Study." *Ethnology* 26, no. 1 (January): 37–50.

Held, Virginia. 2005. "The Ethics of Care." In *The Oxford Handbook of Ethical Theory,* edited by David Copp, 537–66. Oxford: Oxford University Press.

Herzfeld, Michael. 1997. *Cultural Intimacy: Social Poetics of the Nation-State.* New York: Routledge.

Hine, Darlene Clark. 1989. *Black Women in White: Racial Conflict and Cooperation in the Nursing Profession, 1890–1950.* Bloomington: Indiana University Press.

Hirschman, Albert O. 1970. *Exit, Voice, and Loyalty: Responses to Decline in Firms, Organizations, and States.* Cambridge, MA: Harvard University Press.

Hochschild, Arlie Russell. 2001. "Global Care Chains and Emotional Surplus Value." In *On the Edge: Living with Global Capitalism,* edited by Will Hutton and Anthony Giddens, 130–46. London: Vintage.

———. 2003. *The Managed Heart: Commercialization of Human Feeling*. Reprinted with a new afterword. Berkeley: University of California Press. First published 1983.

Hodson, Randy. 2001. *Dignity at Work*. Cambridge: Cambridge University Press.

Holmes, Seth. 2013. *Fresh Fruit, Broken Bodies: Migrant Farmworkers in the United States*. Berkeley: University of California Press.

Holston, James, and Arjun Appadurai. 1999. "Cities and Citizenship." In *Cities and Citizenship*, edited by James Holston, 1–18. Durham, NC: Duke University Press.

Hondagneu-Sotelo, Pierrette. 2001. *Doméstica: Immigrant Workers Cleaning and Caring in the Shadows of Affluence*. Berkeley: University of California Press.

Honneth, Axel. 2003. "Redistribution as Recognition: A Response to Nancy Fraser." In Fraser and Honneth 2003, 110–97.

Honneth, Axel, and Joel Whitebook. 2016. "Omnipotence or Fusion? A Conversation between Axel Honneth and Joel Whitebook." *Constellations* 23, no. 2 (June): 170–79.

Howell, Signe. 2006. *Kinning of Foreigners: Transnational Adoption in Global Perspective*. New York: Berghahn Books.

———. 2007. "Imagined Kin, Place, and Community: Some Paradoxes in the Transnational Movement of Children in Adoption." In *Holding Worlds Together: Ethnographies of Knowing and Belonging*, edited by Marianne Elisabeth Lien and Marit Melhuus, 17–36. New York: Berghahn Books.

Human Rights Watch. 2011. *The Domestic Workers Convention: Turning New Global Labor Standards into Change on the Ground*. Human Rights Watch. www.hrw.org.

Hummon, David M. 1989. "House, Home, and Identity in Contemporary American Culture." In *Housing, Culture, and Design: A Comparative Perspective*, edited by Setha M. Low and Erve Chambers, 207–28. Philadelphia: University of Pennsylvania Press.

Ibarra, María de la Luz. 2010. "My Reward Is Not Money: Deep Alliances and End-of-Life Care among Mexicana Workers and Their Wards." In Boris and Parreñas 2010a, 117–31.

Institute of Medicine. 2008. *Retooling for an Aging America: Building the Health Care Workforce*. Washington, DC: National Academies Press.

Jackson, Michael. 1998. *Minima Ethnographica: Intersubjectivity and the Anthropological Project*. Chicago: University of Chicago Press.

Jennings, Tezra, Tam E. Perry, and Julia Valeriani. 2014. "In the Best Interest of the (Adult) Child: Ideas about Kinship Care of Older Adults." *Journal of Family Social Work* 17 (1): 37–50.

Jervis, Lori L. 2002. "Working in and around the 'Chain of Command': Power Relations among Nursing Staff in an Urban Nursing Home." *Nursing Inquiry* 9, no. 1 (March): 12–23.

Jones, Adrienne L., Lauren Harris-Kojetin, and Roberto Valverde. 2012. "Characteristics and Use of Home Health Care by Men and Women Aged 65 and Over." *National Health Statistics Report*, no. 52 (April 18). Hyattsville, MD: National Center for Health Statistics. www.cdc.gov.

Jung, Moon-Kie. 2006. "Racialization in the Age of Empire: Japanese and Filipino Labor in Colonial Hawai'i." *Critical Sociology* 32, no. 2–3 (March): 403–24.

Karner, Tracy X. 1998. "Professional Caring: Homecare Workers as Fictive Kin." *Journal of Aging Studies* 12, no. 1 (Spring): 69–83.

Katzman, David M. 1978. *Seven Days a Week: Women and Domestic Service in Industrializing America*. New York: Oxford University Press.

Kaufman, Sharon. 2005. *And a Time to Die: How American Hospitals Shape the End of Life*. New York: Scribner.

———. 2015. *Ordinary Medicine: Extraordinary Treatments, Longer Lives, and Where to Draw the Line*. Durham, NC: Duke University Press.

Kent, Mary Mederios. 2007. "Immigration and America's Black Population." *Population Bulletin* 62, no. 4 (December). Washington, D.C.: Population Reference Bureau.

Khatutsky, Galina, Joshua M. Weiner, and Wayne L. Anderson. 2010. "Immigrant and Non-immigrant Certified Nursing Assistants in Nursing Homes: How Do They Differ?" *Journal of Aging and Social Policy* 22 (3): 267–87.

Khatutsky, Galina, Joshua Wiener, Wayne Anderson, Valentina Akhmerova, E. Andrew Jessup, and Marie R. Squillace. 2011. *Understanding Direct-Care Workers: A Snapshot of Two of America's Most Important Jobs—Certified Nursing Assistants and Home Health Aides*. Washington, DC: US Department of Health and Human Services. http://aspe.hhs.gov/.

Kondo, Dorinne. 1990. *Crafting Selves: Power, Gender, and Discourses of Identity in a Japanese Workplace*. Chicago: University of Chicago Press.

Korboe, David. 1992. "Family-Houses in Ghanaian Cities: To Be or Not to Be?" *Urban Studies* 29, no. 7 (October): 1159–72.

Kozol, George B. 2013. "The Long Term Care Conundrum." *Journal of Financial Service Professionals* 67, no. 1 (January): 30–35.

Krause, Kristine, and Katharina Schramm. 2011. "Thinking through Political Subjectivity." *African Diaspora* 4 (2): 115–34.

Lambek, Michael. 2011. "Kinship as Gift and Theft: Acts of Succession in Mayotte and Ancient Israel." *American Ethnologist* 38, no. 1 (February): 2–16.

Lamont, Michèle. 1992. *Money, Morals, and Manners: The Culture of the French and American Upper-Middle Class*. Chicago: University of Chicago Press.

Lamont, Michèle, and Annette Lareau. 1988. "Cultural Capital: Allusions, Gaps and Glissandos in Recent Theoretical Developments." *Sociological Theory* 6, no. 2 (Fall): 153–68.

Lamphere, Louise. 1992. "Introduction: The Shaping of Diversity." In *Structuring Diversity: Ethnographic Perspectives on the New Immigration*, edited by Louise Lamphere, 1–34. Chicago: University of Chicago Press.

Lamphere, Louise, Alex Stepick, and Guillermo Grenier, eds. 1994. *Newcomers in the Workplace: Immigrants and the Restructuring of the U.S. Economy*. Philadelphia: Temple University Press.

Landivar, Liana Christin. 2013. *Men in Nursing Occupations: American Community Survey Highlight Report*. US Census Bureau Working Paper, February. www.census.gov.

Leidner, Bernhard, Hammad Sheikh, and Jeremy Ginges. 2012. "Affective Dimensions of Intergroup Humiliation." *PLoS ONE* 7, no. 9 (September): e46375.

Leidner, Robin. 1996. "Rethinking Questions of Control: Lessons from McDonald's." In Macdonald and Sirianni 1996b, 29–49.

Leinaweaver, Jessaca B. 2013. *Adoptive Migration: Raising Latinos in Spain.* Durham, NC: Duke University Press.

Lerner, Rebecca. 2017. "The Ten Richest Counties in America in 2017." *Forbes*, July 13. www.forbes.com.

Leutz, Walter N. 2007. "Immigration and the Elderly: Foreign-Born Workers in Long-Term Care." *Immigration Policy in Focus* 5, no. 12 (August). Washington, DC: Immigration Policy Center.

Liebelt, Claudia. 2011. *Caring for the "Holy Land": Filipina Domestic Workers in Israel.* New York: Berghahn Books.

Livingston, Julie. 2005. *Debility and the Moral Imagination in Botswana.* Bloomington: Indiana University Press.

Lock, Margaret. 2013. *The Alzheimer Conundrum: Entanglements of Dementia and Aging.* Princeton, NJ: Princeton University Press.

Lockard, C. Brett, and Michael Wolf. 2012. "Occupational Employment Projects to 2020." *Monthly Labor Review*, January, 84–108.

Lopez, Steven H. 1996. "The Politics of Service Production: Route Sales Work in the Potato-Chip Industry." In Macdonald and Sirianni 1996b, 50–73.

———. 2004. *Reorganizing the Rust Belt: An Inside Study of the American Labor Industry.* Berkeley: University of California Press.

Lucht, Hans. 2011. *Darkness before Daybreak: African Migrants Living on the Margins in Southern Italy Today.* Berkeley: University of California Press.

Lutz, Helma, 1993. "Migrant Women, Racism and the Dutch Labour Market." In *Racism and Migration in Western Europe*, edited by John Wrench and John Solomos, 129–42. Oxford: Berg.

———, ed. 2008. *Migration and Domestic Work: A European Perspective on a Global Theme.* Aldershot, UK: Ashgate.

Macdonald, Cameron Lynne, and Carmen Sirianni. 1996a. "The Service Sector and the Changing Experience of Work." In Macdonald and Sirianni 1996b, 1–26.

———, eds. 1996b. *Working in the Service Society.* Philadelphia: Temple University Press.

Manuh, Takyiwaa. 2006. *An 11th Region of Ghana? Ghanaians Abroad.* Accra: Ghana Academy of Arts and Sciences.

Mareschal, Patrice M. 2007. "How the West Was Won: An Inside View of the SEIU's Strategies and Tactics for Organizing Home Care Workers in Oregon." *International Journal of Organization Theory and Behavior* 10, no. 3 (Fall): 387–413.

Margalit, Avishai. 1996. *The Decent Society.* Translated by Naomi Goldblum. Cambridge, MA: Harvard University Press.

Marshall, Mac. 1977. "The Nature of Nurture." *American Ethnologist* 4, no. 4 (November): 643–62.

Marshall, T. H. 1950. *Citizenship and Social Class, and Other Essays*. Cambridge: Cambridge University Press.

Martin, Susan, B. Lindsay Lowell, Elzbieta M. Gozdziak, Micah Bump, and Mary E. Breeding. 2009. *The Role of Migrant Care Workers in Aging Societies: Report on Research Findings in the United States*. Washington, DC: Institute for the Study of International Migration, Walsh School of Foreign Service, Georgetown University. http://isim.georgetown.edu.

Maryland Board of Nursing. 2016. *The 2015 National Workforce Survey: Maryland LPN Data*. June 17. http://mbon.maryland.gov.

Maryland House of Delegates. 2016. HB 1175: Fair Wages, Benefits, and Scheduling Act. http://mgaleg.maryland.gov.

McCabe, Kristen. 2011. "African Immigrants in the United States." *Migration Information Source*, July 21. www.migrationpolicy.org.

———. 2012. "Foreign-Born Health Care Workers in the United States." *Migration Information Source*, June 27. www.migrationpolicy.org.

McLean, Athena. 2007. *The Person in Dementia: A Study of Nursing Home Care in the United States*. Orchard Park, NY: Broadview.

McNay, Lois. 2008. *Against Recognition*. Malden, MA: Polity Press.

McQueen, Paddy. 2015. "Honneth, Butler and the Ambivalent Effects of Recognition." *Res Publica* 21, no. 1 (February): 41–60.

Michel, Sonya, and Gabrielle Oliveira. 2017. "The Double Lives of Transnational Mothers." In *Reassembling Motherhood: Procreation and Care in a Globalized World*, edited by Yasmine Ergas, Jane Jenson, and Sonya Michel, 223–46. New York: Columbia University Press.

Milkman, Ruth. 2006. *L.A. Story: Immigrants Workers and the Future of the U.S. Labor Movement*. New York: Russell Sage Foundation.

Miller, Daniel. 2007. "What Is a Relationship? Is Kinship Negotiated Experience?" *Ethnos* 72 (4): 535–54.

Mol, Annemarie. 2010. "Care and Its Values: Good Food in the Nursing Home." In Mol, Moser, and Pols 2010a, 215–34.

Mol, Annemarie, Ingunn Moser, and Jeannette Pols, eds. 2010a. *Care in Practice: On Tinkering in Clinics, Homes and Farms*. Bielefeld, Germany: Transcript.

———. 2010b. "Care: Putting Practice into Theory." In Mol, Moser, and Pols 2010a, 7–26.

Montgomery County. 2014. "Montgomery Count Senior Demographics." PowerPoint presentation at the Commission on Aging Legislative Breakfast, November 19. www.montgomerycountymd.gov.

———. 2016. "Home Care and Home Health Providers/Personal Care Attendants Registry." Updated December 30. www.montgomerycountymd.gov.

Myerhoff, Barbara. 1984. "Rites and Signs of Ripening: The Intertwining of Ritual, Time, and Growing Older." In *Age and Anthropological Theory*, edited by David I. Kertzer and Jennie Keith, 305–30. Ithaca, NY: Cornell University Press.

Nadasen, Premilla. 2010. "Power, Intimacy, and Contestation: Dorothy Bolden and Domestic Worker Organizing in Atlanta in the 1960s." In Boris and Parreñas 2010a, 204–16.

NCHWA (National Center for Health Workforce Analysis). 2013. *The U.S. Nursing Workforce: Trends in Supply and Education*. Health Resources and Service Administration, US Department of Health and Human Services. http://bhw.hrsa.gov.

Nazareno, Jennifer Pabelonia, Rhacel Salazar Parreñas, and Yu-Kang Fan. 2014. *Can I Ever Retire? The Plight of Migrant Filipino Elderly Caregivers in Los Angeles*. Los Angeles: Institute for Research on Labor and Employment, University of California, Los Angeles.

Nedelsky, Jennifer. 1990. *Private Property and the Limits of American Constitutionalism: The Madisonian Framework and Its Legacy*. Chicago: University of Chicago Press.

Neysmith, Sheila M., and Jane Aronson. 1996. "Home Care Workers Discuss Their Work: The Skills Required to 'Use Your Common Sense.'" *Journal of Aging Studies* 10, no. 1 (Spring): 1–14.

———. 1997. "Working Conditions in Home Care: Negotiating Race and Class Boundaries in Gendered Work." *International Journal of Health Sciences* 27 (3): 479–99.

Nielsen, Morten. 2014. "A Wedge in Time: Futures in the Present and Presents without Futures in Maputo, Mozambique." In "Doubt, Conflict, Mediation: The Anthropology of Modern Time," edited by Laura Bear. Special issue, *Journal of the Royal Anthropological Institute* 20, no. S1 (April): 166–82.

Nieswand, Boris. 2011. *Theorizing Transnational Migration: The Status Paradox of Migration*. New York: Routledge.

Ogbu, John U. 1978. *Minority Education and Caste: The American System in Cross-Cultural Perspective*. New York: Academic Press.

O'Leary, Megan Elizabeth. 2016. "Caring Here, Caring There: Boston-Based Black Immigrant Caregivers as Agents of the Globalization of Eldercare." PhD diss., Boston University.

Ong, Aihwa. 1999. *Flexible Citizenship: The Cultural Logic of Transnationality*. Durham, NC: Duke University Press.

Ortner, Sherry. 2003. *New Jersey Dreaming: Capital, Culture, and the Class of '58*. Durham, NC: Duke University Press.

Ozyegin, Gul. 2001. *Untidy Gender: Domestic Service in Turkey*. Philadelphia: Temple University Press.

Ozyegin, Gul, and Pierrette Hondagneu-Sotelo. 2008. "Conclusion: Domestic Work, Migration and the New Gender Order in Contemporary Europe." In Lutz 2008, 195–208.

Palmer, Phyllis M. 1989. *Domesticity and Dirt: Housewives and Domestic Servants in the United States, 1920–1945*. Philadelphia: Temple University Press.

Pande, Amrita. 2014. *Wombs in Labor: Transnational Commercial Surrogacy in India*. New York: Columbia University Press.

Parks, Tim. 2017. "Keep the Ball Rolling." Review of *A Family Lexicon*, by Natalia Ginzburg. *London Review of Books*, June 29, 31–33.

Parreñas, Rhacel Salazar. 2001. *Servants of Globalization: Women, Migration, and Domestic Work*. Stanford, CA: Stanford University Press.

———. 2008. "Perpetually Foreign: Filipina Migrant Workers in Rome." In Lutz 2008, 99–112.

Patterson, Orlando. 1982. *Slavery and Social Death*. Cambridge, MA: Harvard University Press.

Pauli, Julia, and Franziska Bedorf. 2018. "Retiring Home? House Construction, Age Scripts, and the Building of Belonging among Mexican Migrants and Their Families in Chicago and Rural Mexico." *Anthropology & Aging* 39, no. 1 (Fall): 48–65.

Perry, Tam Elisabeth. 2014. "The Rite of Relocation: Social and Material Transformations in the Midwestern United States." *Signs and Society* 2, no. 1 (Spring): 28–55.

Pfaff-Czarnecka, Joanna. 2011. "From 'Identity' to 'Belonging' in Social Research: Plurality, Social Boundaries, and the Politics of the Self." In *Ethnicity, Citizenship and Belonging: Practices, Theory and Spatial Dimensions*, edited by Sarah Albiez, Nelly Castro, Lara Jüssen, and Eva Youkhana, 199–219. Madrid: Iberoamericana; Frankfurt am Main: Vervuert.

PHI (Paraprofessional Healthcare Institute). 2016. *U.S. Home Care Workers: Key Facts*. Bronx, NY: PHI. https://phinational.org.

Pierre, Jemima. 2004. "Black Immigrants in the United States and the 'Cultural Narratives' of Ethnicity." *Identities: Global Studies in Culture and Power* 11 no. 2: 141–70.

Piketty, Thomas. 2014. *Capital in the Twenty-First Century*. Cambridge, MA: Harvard University Press.

Piketty, Thomas, and Emmanuel Saez. 2003. "Income Inequality in the United States, 1913–1998." *Quarterly Journal of Economics* 118, no. 1 (February): 1–41.

Piore, Michael J. 1979. *Birds of Passage: Migrant Labor and Industrial Societies*. Cambridge: Cambridge University Press.

Poo, Ai-Jen. 2015. *Age of Dignity: Caring for a Changing America*. New York: New Press.

Poole, Mary. 2006. *The Segregated Origins of Social Security: African Americans and the Welfare State*. Chapel Hill: University of North Carolina Press.

Portes, Alejandro. 1995. "Children of Immigrants: Segmented Assimilation and Its Determinants." In *The Economic Sociology of Immigration: Essays on Networks, Ethnicity, and Entrepreneurship*. New York: Russell Sage Foundation.

Qin, Jin, Alicia Kurowski, Rebecca Gore, and Laura Punnett. 2014. "The Impact of Workplace Factors on Filing of Workers' Compensation Claims among Nursing Home Workers." *BMC Musculoskeletal Disorders* 15:29 (January 29).

Reddy, William M. 2001. *The Navigation of Feeling: A Framework for the History of Emotions*. New York: Cambridge University Press.

Reverby, Susan M. 1987. *Ordered to Care: The Dilemma of American Nursing, 1850–1945*. New York: Cambridge University Press.

Reynolds, Joel Michael. 2016. "Infinite Responsibility in the Bedpan: Response Ethics, Care Ethics, and the Phenomenology of Dependency Work." *Hypatia* 31, no. 4 (Fall): 779–94.

Robbins, Joel. 2009. "Rethinking Gifts and Commodities: Reciprocity, Recognition, and the Morality of Exchange." In *Economics and Morality: Anthropological Approaches*, edited by Katherine E. Browne and B. Lynne Milgram, 43–58. Lanham, MD: Altamira.

Rodriquez, Jason. 2011. "'It's a Dignity Thing': Nursing Home Care Workers' Use of Emotions." *Sociological Forum* 26, no. 2 (June): 265–86.

———. 2014. *Labors of Love: Nursing Homes and the Structure of Caring Work*. New York: New York University Press.

Rollins, Judith. 1985. *Between Women: Domestics and Their Employers*. Philadelphia: Temple University Press.

———. 1990. "Ideology and Servitude." In *At Work in Homes: Household Workers in World Perspective*, edited by Roger Sanjek and Shellee Colen, 74–88. Washington, DC: American Anthropological Association.

Rosaldo, Renato. 1994. "Cultural Citizenship and Educational Democracy." *Cultural Anthropology* 9, no. 3 (August): 402–11.

Rose, Mike. 2004. *The Mind at Work: Valuing the Intelligence of the American Worker*. New York: Viking.

Rosow, Irving. 1974. *Socialization to Old Age*. Berkeley: University of California Press.

Rouse, Roger. 2005. "Re-working Time: The Temporal Dimensions of Transnational Migration amidst Neoliberal Restructuring." Paper presented at the Ethnohistory Program, University of Pennsylvania, Philadelphia, PA, February 10.

Rutherford, Blair. 2008. "Conditional Belonging: Farm Workers and the Cultural Politics of Recognition in Zimbabwe." *Development and Change* 39, no. 1 (January): 73–99.

Sahlins, Marshall. 2012. *What Kinship Is—and Is Not*. Chicago: University of Chicago Press.

Sarti, Raffaella. 2008. "The Globalisation of Domestic Service—An Historical Perspective." In Lutz 2008, 77–98.

Sassen, Saskia. 2014. *Expulsions: Brutality and Complexity in the Global Economy*. Cambridge, MA: Harvard University Press.

Sennett, Richard. 1998. *The Corrosion of Character: The Personal Consequences of Work in the New Capitalism*. New York: W. W. Norton.

Shah, Saubhagya. 2000. "Service or Servitude? The Domestication of Household Labor in Nepal." In *Home and Hegemony: Domestic Service and Identity Politics in South and Southeast Asia*, edited by Kathleen M. Adams and Sara Dickey, 87–118. Ann Arbor: University of Michigan Press.

Sheth, Falguni A. 2009. *Toward a Political Philosophy of Race*. Albany: State University of New York Press.

Showers, Fumilayo. 2013. "Nursing the Nation: Globalization, Gender, Race, State, and African Immigrant Women in Health Care Work in the United States of America." PhD diss., Syracuse University.

———. 2015a. "Building a Professional Identity: Boundary Work and Meaning Making among West African Immigrant Nurses." In *Caring on the Clock: The Complexities and Contradictions of Paid Care Work*, edited by Mignon Duffy, Amy Armenia, and Clare Stacey, 143–52. New Brunswick, NJ: Rutgers University Press.

———. 2015b. "Being Black, Foreign and Woman: African Immigrant Identities in the United States." *Ethnic and Racial Studies* 38 (10): 1815–30.

Shyrock, Andrew. 2013. "It's This, Not That: How Marshall Sahlins Solves Kinship." *HAU: Journal of Ethnographic Theory* 3, no. 2 (Summer): 271–79.

Skocpol, Theda. 1992. *Protecting Soldiers and Mothers: The Political Origins of Social Policy in the United States*. Cambridge, MA: Harvard University Press.

Smith, Kristin, and Reagan Baughman. 2007. "Caring for America's Aging Population: A Profile of the Direct-Care Workforce." *Monthly Labor Review*, September, 20–26.

Smith, Michael Courtney. 2006. *Mexican New York: Transnational Lives of New Immigrants*. Berkeley: University of California Press.

Solari, Cinzia. 2006. "Professionals and Saints: How Immigrant Careworkers Negotiate Gender Identities at Work." *Gender and Society* 20, no. 3 (June): 301–31.

Soysal, Yasemin Nuhoğlu. 1994. *Limits of Citizenship: Migrants and Postnational Membership in Europe*. Chicago: University of Chicago Press.

———. 2002. "Citizenship and Identity: Living in Diasporas in Postwar Europe?" In *The Postnational Self: Belonging and Identity*, edited by Ulf Hedetoft and Mette Hjort, 137–51. Minneapolis: University of Minnesota Press.

Spyrou, Spyros. 2009. "Between Intimacy and Intolerance: Greek Cypriot Children's Encounters with Asian Domestic Workers." *Childhood* 16, no. 2 (May): 155–73.

Stacey, Clare L. 2011. *The Caring Self: The Work Experiences of Home Care Aides*. Ithaca, NY: Cornell University Press.

Stasch, Rupert. 2009. *Society of Others: Kinship and Mourning in a West Papuan Village*. Berkeley: University of California Press.

Stevenson, Lisa. 2014. *Life Beside Itself: Imagining Care in the Canadian Arctic*. Berkeley: University of California Press.

Stoler, Ann Laura. 2002. *Carnal Knowledge and Imperial Power: Race and the Intimate in Colonial Rule*. Berkeley: University of California Press.

Taylor, Charles. 1992. *Multiculturalism and "The Politics of Recognition."* Princeton, NJ: Princeton University Press.

Taylor, Janelle. 2010. "On Recognition, Care, and Dementia." In Mol, Moser, and Pols 2010a, 27–56.

Thelen, Tatjana. 2015. "Care as Social Organization: Creating, Maintaining and Dissolving Significant Relations." *Anthropological Theory* 15, no. 4 (December): 497–515.

Thelen, Tatjana, and Cati Coe. 2017. "Political Belonging through Elderly Care: Temporalities, Representations, and Mutuality." *Anthropological Theory*. Prepublished December 3.

Thelen, Tatjana, Cati Coe, and Erdmute Alber. 2013. "The Anthropology of Sibling Relations: Shared Parentage, Experience, and Exchange." In *The Anthropology of Sibling Relations*, edited by Erdmute Alber, Cati Coe, and Tatjana Thelen, 1–28. New York: Palgrave Macmillan.

Theodorou, Elena. 2011. "Living (in) Class: Contexts of Immigrants' Lives and the Movements of Children with(in) Them." *Anthropology and Education Quarterly* 42, no. 1 (March): 1–19.

Theophano, Janet S. 1991. "'I Gave Him a Cake': An Interpretation of Two Italian-American Weddings." In *Creative Ethnicity: Symbols and Strategies of Contemporary Ethnic Life*, edited by Stephen Stern and John Allan Cicala, 44–54. Logan: Utah State University Press.

Tipple, Graham, David Korboe, Guy Garrod, and Ken Willis. 1999. "Housing Supply in Ghana: A Study of Accra, Kumasi, and Berekum." *Progress in Planning* 51, no. 4 (May): 253–324.

Torres, Walter J., and Raymond M. Bergner. 2010. "Humiliation: Its Nature and Consequences." *Journal of the American Academy of Psychiatry and Law* 38 (2): 195–204.

Trinkoff, Alison M., Meg Johangten, Caries Muntaner, and Rong Le. 2005. "Staffing and Worker Injury in Nursing Homes." *American Journal of Public Health* 95, no. 7 (July): 1220–25.

Tucker, Susan. 1988. *Telling Memories among Southern Women: Domestic Workers and Their Employers in the Segregated South.* Baton Rouge: Louisiana State University Press.

Tung, Charlene. 2000. "The Cost of Caring: The Social Reproductive Labor of Filipina Live-In Home Health Caregivers." *Frontiers: A Journal of Women's Studies* 21 (1/2): 60–67.

USAO (United States Attorney's Office, District of Columbia). 2014. "More than 20 People Arrested following Investigations into Widespread Health Care Fraud in D.C. Medicaid Program." Press release, February 20. www.justice.gov.

———. 2015. "Owners of Home Health Care Agency Found Guilty of Taking Part in $80 Million Medicaid Fraud." Press release, November 16. www.justice.gov.

US Census Bureau. 2016. *Facts for Features: Older Americans Month, May 2016.* Profile America Facts for Features, release no. CB16-FF.08. www.census.gov.

US DHHS (US Department of Health and Human Services). 2003. *The Future Supply of Long-Term Care Workers in Relation to the Aging Baby Boom Generation: Report to Congress.* http://aspe.hhs.gov.

———. 2011. *Personal and Home Care Aide State Training (PHCAST) Demonstration Program: Report to Congress on Initial Implementation.* www.hrsa.gov.

Vickerman, Milton. 1999. *Crosscurrents: West Indian Immigrants and Race.* Oxford: Oxford University Press.

Waldinger, Roger, and Michael I. Lichter. 2003. *How the Other Half Works: Immigration and the Social Organization of Labor.* Berkeley: University of California Press.

Wallerstein, Immanuel. 1991. "Household Structures and Labour-Force Formation in the Capitalist World-Economy." In *Race, Nation, Class: Ambiguous Identities*, by Etienne Balibar and Immanuel Wallerstein, 107–12. London: Verso.

Waters, Mary C. 1999. *Black Identities: West Indian Immigrant Dreams and American Realities.* New York: Russell Sage Foundation.

Weismantel, Mary. 1995. "Making Kin: Kinship Theory and Zumbagua Adoptions." *American Ethnologist* 22, no. 4 (November): 685–704.

Weston, Kath. 1991. *Families We Choose: Lesbians, Gays, Kinship.* New York: Columbia University Press.

Wheeler, Lydia. 2015. "Court Backs Obama on Minimum Wage, Overtime for Home Health Aides." *Hill*, August 21. http://thehill.com.

Winant, Howard. 2004. *The New Politics of Race: Globalism, Difference, Justice.* Minneapolis: University of Minnesota Press.

Yeates, Nicola. 2009. *Globalizing Care Economies and Migrant Workers: Explorations in Global Care Chains*. New York: Palgrave Macmillan.

Yngvesson, Barbara. 2003. "Going 'Home': Adoption, Loss of Bearings and the Mythology of Roots." *Social Text*, no. 74 (Spring): 7–27.

Yuval-Davis, Nira. 2011. *The Politics of Belonging: Intersectional Contestations*. Los Angeles: SAGE.

Zelizer, Viviana A. 2005. *The Purchase of Intimacy*. Princeton, NJ: Princeton University Press.

Zeng, Zhen, and Yu Xie. 2004. "Asian-Americans' Earnings Disadvantage Reexamined: The Role of Place in Education." *American Journal of Sociology* 109, no. 5 (March): 1075–108.

Zhao, Qing-Fei, Lan Tan, Hui-Fu Wang, Teng Jiang, Meng-Shan Tan, Lin Tan, Wei Xu, Jie-Qiong Li, Jun Wang, Te-Jen Lai, and Jin-Tai Yu. 2016. "The Prevalence of Neuropsychiatric Symptoms in Alzheimer's Disease: Systematic Review and Meta-Analysis." *Journal of Affective Disorders* 190 (January 15): 264–71.

INDEX

adoption: in comparison with care work, 134, 135–36, 144; kinning in, 31, 131–32

advice: about home care workers, 260n5; to other home care workers, 63, 74–78, 79, 113–14, 117

Affordable Care Act: and expansion of Medicaid, 213, 215, 217; and workers' access to health insurance, 217–18, 223, 247; employer mandate of, 212–14, 224; expense of, 215, 223–24; limitations of, 223–24, 247, 251. *See also* health insurance

aggression: and dementia, 61, 103, 172–73, 178–79, 260n2; in home care, 86–87, 99, 103–5, 112, 117–18; in self-making, 87, 90

Agha, Asif, 131, 134

aging: and healthcare, 14; as becoming invisible, 116–117; as a time for learning, 66–67; class differences in, 15–16; demographics of, 1–2, 16; rituals of, 194. *See also* seniority

animal: as register of belonging, 13–14, 92, 130, 157, 246–47; name for care worker, 77, 86, 94–95, 122–23

Aronson, Jane: on care as skillful, 60–61; on exclusion, 86–87, 238; on home care, 56, 107, 182; on meaning of good care, 61

belonging, political: and bitterness, 237, 248; through care, 30, 93, 245; in comparison to citizenship, 7–9, 93, 246; definition of, 7; through food, 33–40, 258n1; through government benefits, 12, 31, 175, 204, 216–17; through kinship, 5, 130–65; through racialization, 8, 9, 63, 67–68,

86–124; through reciprocity, 175–93, 203, 216–17, 229; registers of, 13–14, 87; religious views of, 189; through subordination, 87; and temporality, 164; through work, 3–5, 8–9, 31, 203–4, 238, 247–249

Benjamin, Jessica, 87, 91, 141, 256n8

Bercovitz, Anita, 204, 218

bitterness: and career stagnation, 59, 80, 204–5; and humiliation, 88, 91; and lack of reciprocity, 6, 90, 176, 239, 249; and political belonging, 237, 248

Boris, Eileen: on care, 56, 60; on history of home care, 83, 207, 209, 235, 256n10

Bourdieu, Pierre: on cultural capital, 43; on domination, 92; on habitus, 166; on practical kinship, 131, 134, 136, 157

Buch, Elana: on care, 11, 175; on gifts in home care, 110, 182; on home care as a liminal practice, 67; on kinning in home care, 135, 137; methods of, 27; on power relations in senior care, 35, 60, 107, 112, 259n4, 259n10; on racialization in home care, 63

Butler, Judith: on personhood, 10, 13, 88, 122; on racist speech, 90–91, 96; on vulnerability, 252

care: as expressed in material exchange, 175, 256n9; and food, 33–35, 159; and global care chains, 255n7; as labor, 11–12; negative aspects of, 31, 245–246; and political belonging, 30, 93, 245; recognition in, 11, 31, 92–93. *See also* home care; home care workers; long-term care insurance

McNay, Lois, 11, 91, 237

McQueen, Paddy, 10, 91

Medicaid: and workers' health insurance, 213, 215–18, 247, 261n3; as source of healthcare regulation, 209; in home care, 17, 235; in seniors' healthcare, 14–15

Medicare: as source of care workers' health insurance, 215, 217, 223, 261n3; as source of healthcare regulation, 209; in home care, 14–15, 207, 235, 256n10; in seniors' healthcare, 14–15

migrants: African, 18–23; in home care, 1–2, 22, 56; incorporation through work of, 42–43, 45–46, 55; in employment niches, 8, 43, 45–46; unionization among, 235–36

Miller, Daniel, 135

naming: in recognition, 96, 122; of care workers, 140–41. *See also* kinship: terms

nationalism, 7–8, 12–13, 245

neoliberalism: in senior care, 14

Neysmith, Sheila M.: on care as skillful, 60–61; on exclusion, 86–87, 238; on home care, 56, 107, 182; on meaning of good care, 61

nursing: career ladders to, 57–58, 79–80, 228; gendering of, 54–56; as goal of home care workers, 58, 78, 147, 151, 222; hierarchy in, 54–55, 251–52; history of, 54–55, 56; racialization of, 54–55, 71, 258n6

nursing homes: African migrants' view of, 24, 205, 243; and aging, 15, 152, 240; emotional labor in, 258n9; employees' side jobs in home care, 3, 50, 61, 78, 158, 212, 219–20, 235; as hard for aging care workers, 222, 239–40; home care workers in, 2, 15–16, 50; kinning in, 133, 137; patients' transition to, 41, 49, 113, 152; as potential ethnographic site,

24–25, 56–57; racial insults in, 86, 121; staff benefits in, 209, 211, 214–220, 228; staff hierarchies in, 55; staff interactions at, 65–66, 92; as training for home care workers, 56–57; unionization of, 24, 235

Ogbu, John U.: critique of theories of, 6, 80, 92, 238, 248–56; description of theories of, 6, 204

older adults. *See* aging; patients; seniority

O'Leary, Megan: on Africans' views on senior care in the US, 205; on appreciation by patients' children, 101; on emotional labor in home care, 137, 186; on ethnographic challenges, 257n17; on home care agencies, 71–72; on kin terms in home care, 259n2; on migrants' concentration in lower levels of the healthcare hierarchy, 55; on racism in home care, 105, 120; on respect for elders, 258n10

Pande, Amrita, 131, 136–37, 157

Parreñas, Rhacel Salazar: on care work, 4, 56, 60, 134, 181; on contradictory class mobility, 21, 126

patients: children of, 115–16, 134–35; description of, 2, 16–17, 27–28, 150–51; stories of racism by, 101–5; stories of reciprocity of, 172–75, 189–90; use of kin terms by, 134, 142–150

Pfaff-Czarnecka, Joanna, 7, 198

phone calls: in fieldwork, 25–26, 29, 30, 34, 52; in kinning, 159, 164; as overcoming isolation of care workers, 26, 51–52, 113, 117; restrictions on care workers' use of, 51; as source of patient irritation, 105, 177; for work advice, 63, 117; in work interactions, 41–42, 63, 68–69, 233, 257n1

Pierre, Jemima, 4–5, 87, 255n5

Piore, Michael, 6, 20, 249

ABOUT THE AUTHOR

Cati Coe is Professor of Anthropology at Rutgers University. She is the author of *The Scattered Family: Parenting, African Migrants, and Global Inequality* and the co-editor (with Parin Dossa) of *Transnational Aging and Reconfigurations of Kin-Work*.